Making It Legal

Making It Legal

A Law Primer for the Craftmaker, Visual Artist, and Writer

Marion Davidson and Martha Blue

Illustrations by Mary Ann Borkoski

McGRAW-HILL
BOOK COMPANY

*New York St. Louis San Francisco
Bogotá Düsseldorf Madrid Mexico Montreal
Panama Paris São Paulo Tokyo Toronto*

Illustrated by Mary Ann Borkoski

1234567890MUMU7832109

LIBRARY OF CONGRESS CATALOGING IN PUBLICATION DATA

Davidson, Marion

Making it legal.

Includes index.

1. Law—United States. 2. Artists—United States—Handbooks, manuals, etc. 3. Artisans—United States—Handbooks, manuals, etc. 4. Authors—United States—Handbooks, manuals, etc. I. Blue, Martha joint author. II. Title.

KF390.A7D37 343'.73'078 78-23891

ISBN 0-07-015431-7

Design by Gloria Gentile / Marsha Picker

DEDICATION

We dedicate our first book
to Martha's mother, Martha Manning,
and to the memory of
Marion's father, Robert Davidson.

■ *LEGAL ADVICE, NOT ON YOUR LIFE*

This book does not contain legal advice. It is designed to provide accurate information with regard to the subjects covered as of November 15, 1978. It is sold with the understanding that neither the authors nor the publisher are engaged in rendering legal, accounting, or other professional services. If you have a legal problem, we urge you to be sure to see an attorney, or, for a tax problem, an accountant.

ACKNOWLEDGMENTS

Without the enthusiasm, interest, and support of a large number of wonderful craftmakers, artists, and writers, this book never would have happened. We are grateful to the many, many people who shared with us their experiences and opinions and provided important interest and support for this work.

Special thanks to Estelle Zannes for finding Alice in a haystack, Marlene and Dave McGoffin for, among other things, keeping us honest, and Edgerton Nez, whose fingers are tired of the same old words. We would also like to give special thanks to Oliver W. Johnson for his encouragement and moral support and to Zoë for her patience. Library research was made easier by the staffs of the libraries of the University of New Mexico Law School and Northwestern Law School.

We are deeply appreciative of Professor Leonard and Mary Ann DuBoff for their assistance in this work as well as their pioneering efforts in the field of art law. And last but not least, we wish to thank Professor Samuel Litzler, CPA, for his generous assistance.

INTRODUCTION

In the beginning, Martha was a weaver, as well as a lawyer, and many friends were potters, illustrators, poets, sculptors, photographers, printmakers, jewelers, et cetera. They seemed to know so little of the basic legal information relevant to their work. We gave them books and pamphlets. Too hard to read, they said. So we set out to make a book that would help our friends answer some of their questions.

In an attempt to inform our friends in a way which would hold their attention as well as impart useful, basic information, we presented much of the legal information in charts, forms, cartoons, memos, and, last but not least, the allegories of Alice, the Guerrilla Craftmaiden wending her way toward law and order. When particularly relevant, we also listed the major laws and cases at the end of some chapters and listed Further Readings.

Writing about the law for a lay audience is like walking a tightrope. On one side are lawyers complaining of the lack of citations and the oversimplification of this case or that missing exception. On the other side are lay people complaining that the text is too technical and hard to understand. Still, we decided that a tour of Legal Land for the craftmaker, visual artist, and writer would be a worthwhile project. As the book progressed, we handed out chapters to our friends, who agreed that the book was useful and that they wanted to hear more about this or that.

If you are the type who is still sending $9.98 to a post-office box in Peoria for the Secret of Eternal Youth, please return this book to the store and go no farther. This book does *not* contain all the answers. It does not contain legal advice for your specific legal problems. It may well be that after reading this book you will seek out an attorney or an accountant to assist from time to time with problems that arise.

This book will present an overview of the legal information that concerns craftmakers, visual artists, and writers. It will alert you to laws that you never knew existed and outline the requirements of laws to which you closed your eyes and crossed your fingers.

Be careful. This book contains dated material. Because every individual legal problem is different and because laws change, this book cannot be relied upon to solve your legal ills. The sample forms are included as guides and should be tailored to meet the needs of your particular situation. Although federal laws and regulations govern operations in the fifty states and Puerto Rico, many of the state laws discussed vary substantially from state to state. The discussion of state laws is not meant to be exhaustive but rather to impart an overall view. So see this book as a preventative, informational reference tool. It is not a substitute for a competent lawyer, an accountant, or your own common sense.

So, gentle reader, use this book wisely and enjoy.

January, 1979
P.O. Box 463
Flagstaff, Arizona 86002

Mountain under heaven:
In what is small,
perseverance furthers.
The I Ching

Contents

Chapter 1 Legal Steps in Surfacing Your Business

CHOICE OF LEGAL STATUS

Sole Proprietor
Partnership
Incorporation

FEDERAL, STATE, AND LOCAL REQUIREMENTS

Doing Your Own Detective Work
Zoning, Building, Health, and Fire Codes
Certificate of Doing Business under a Fictitious Name
State Sales Tax Number
Federal Employer Identification Number
Business License
Employees

MISCELLANEOUS CONSIDERATIONS IN SURFACING

Studio Rental Agreements
Insurance

■ LEGAL ADVICE, NOT ON YOUR LIFE

Alice's Allegory # 1

or

The Pitfalls of the Underground Craftmaiden

Alice the Craftmaiden sat behind her table of pots at the local arts and crafts fair, warming herself in the delightful spring rays, dreaming of the summer to come.

Her mellow state was shattered by the growling of Max the State Tax Collector.

"Where is your state sales tax number?" barked Max, with the proper authoritarian sneer.

Alice smiled her sweetest I-am-totally-confused, save-me smile, hoping that Max would vanish as the Cheshire cat once did.

"Rumph, rumph, rumph," barked Max.

"But I am a guerrilla craftmaiden," said Alice.

"AH the better to eat you, my dear," leered Max.

Alice was so bummed out that she could not throw a straight pot for weeks and had to drink cups of camomile tea to restore her center to herself.

INTRODUCTION

A DIRTY BUSINESS?

How do you deal with the requirements of the business system? Many artists, craftmakers, and writers have chosen their work partially to avoid contact with the *business* world. In fact, even the word, *business*, is distasteful to many in artistic professions. What's in a word—*business*—anyway? It's none of your *business*. Cut out the monkey *business*. Let's get down to *business*. That's show *business*. Is it really a dirty *business*?

Just because you don't agree with the greedy-tycoon method of doing business doesn't mean that you have to sabotage your operation by ignoring the laws that govern businesses. It is not copping out to comply with the simple legal rules governing small businesses —it may be simple survival. We hope that this chapter will overcome some of these unpleasant feelings concerning business by presenting simple information about the requirements for starting a business. Through an understanding of these basic concepts, business requirements become more manageable, and most important, you achieve more peace of mind.

This chapter is called "Legal Steps in Surfacing Your Business" because in our opinion, most artists, craftmakers, and writers don't actually decide to start a business and then go through the required steps. Getting into business is usually a more organic process. By understanding the requirements of operating a business, the decision of "going legit" or "surfacing" your business can be made at the right time—not too early and not too late. Avoid the pitfalls of the underground craftmaiden and climb through the looking glass to join us in a tour through the legal steps involved in surfacing a small business. This chapter will discuss *legal* considerations in surfacing a business. Other equally important matters such as capital, labor, markets, and materials should also be considered before starting out.*

THREE STEPS TO SURFACING YOUR BUSINESS

The three legal steps to surfacing your business are:

- choice and implementation of one of the three basic business forms—sole proprietorship, partnership, or corporation
- meeting federal, state, and local requirements
- considerations of studio rental agreements and liability insurance for your business

Remember, each individual situation is different. So are the laws of each state. We will provide you with the general legal requirements for setting up a small business. With this basic information, you can obtain the specifics from local sources in your state as well as from the federal offices of the Internal Revenue Service and the Small Business Administration; the state corporation commission, tax department, unemployment and workers' compensation departments; and the city or county treasurer's office, zoning department, building, fire, and health departments. If you decide after reading this chapter that you will require the assistance of a lawyer in starting your business, read Chapter 8, "Obtaining Legal Assistance."

CHOICE OF LEGAL STATUS

SOLE PROPRIETOR

Alice's Allegory # 2

or

The Liability of Unlimited Liability

Having regained her decorum after the Big Max Attack, Alice sat thinking of her new life. How free and beautiful it was—so simple, no bosses, no time clocks—so close to nirvana.

Suddenly, Crafty Crank the Elderly Customer tripped over a large umbrella stand that Alice had left in front of her display at the arts and crafts fair to scare away other representatives of the law. Crafty Crank the Elderly Customer lay on the floor squeaking and rapidly swelling in the area of her ancient ankle.

Alice found herself in court one day facing Handsome Harry the Famous Whiplash Lawyer who won the case for Crafty Crank the Elderly Customer. If this was not enough, before Alice could consult her astrologer, her savings account was attached even though it contained an inheritance Alice had received from Aunt Theresa, who had recently died of smog asphyxiation.

Alice said, "I should go back to being a social worker. It's hassle-free, and at least I can pay my rent."

Most businesses in America are sole proprietorships. This business form is the simplest, cheapest, and easiest to begin, manage,

* For additional reading, see Bernard Kamoroff, *Small Time Operator*, Bell Springs Publishing, Laytonville, Calif., 1977. An excellent book on starting your own business.

DEFINITION

and end. Quite simply, a sole proprietor is one who owns and runs his or her own business. To start up a sole proprietorship, you just check the zoning laws, get a license and tax number, and you are in business.

FORMATION

MANAGEMENT

SALE

TAX

Since the law does not require the preparation and filing of articles of incorporation or a partnership agreement for a sole proprietorship, the choice of this form of business results in an initial saving of both time and money. Also, the owner of a sole proprietorship has free rein in the management of the business—no partners or board of directors to deal with. The sole proprietorship can be sold at any time. Business profits are considered part of the owner's regular income and are reported on Schedule C of the individual 1040 federal income tax return.

UNLIMITED LIABILITY

The major drawback of a sole proprietorship is the fact that the owner is personally liable for any debts that the business may incur. This means that both the business and the nonbusiness property of the owner can be taken to satisfy a court judgment entered against either the owner or the business.

EXEMPTIONS FROM EXECUTION

GARNISHMENT LIMITATIONS

When considering the problem of unlimited liability, two important legal rules should be kept in mind. First, with minor exceptions, no one can force you to give up any of your belongings, wages, et cetera, except through a court proceeding which includes your rights to notice, to answer the complaint, and a trial and final judgment.* Second, even after a final judgment in your case, some of your belongings and wages are still not eligible to be taken to pay the party who has won the case against you. Each state has its own exemptions in this area. Generally, your home, car, tools of your trade, and some personal belongings cannot be taken to satisfy a court judgment.** Further, both state and federal law limit the amount of weekly wages that can be taken (garnished) to satisfy a court judgment. No *more* than one quarter of your weekly net salary can be taken through garnishment proceedings. If you are making minimum wage, then probably even less of your salary is eligible to be garnished, because the federal law only allows garnishment of any amount over thirty times the minimum wage (for 1979: $2.90 × 30 = $87.00). In many states, the amount of weekly wages protected from garnishment is higher.

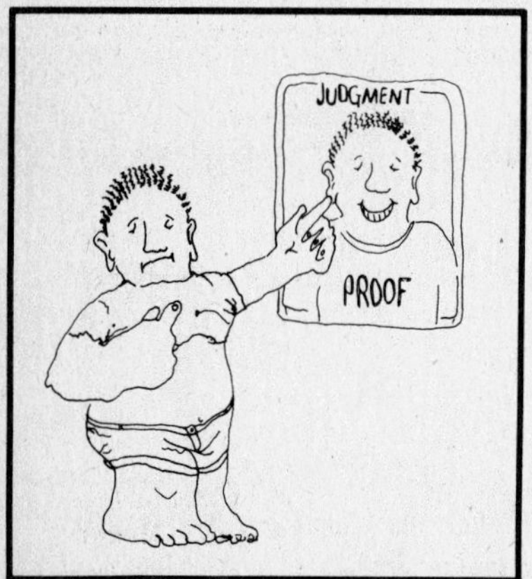

Beware: This man is judgment-proof

INSURANCE

The problem of unlimited personal liability can be dealt with to a certain extent by the purchase of business liability insurance. This insurance would protect the sole proprietor from any claims arising from a business-related injury to another person, but only to the

* Also, when considering the problem of unlimited liability, take into account any property that you own with others and, if married and living in a community-property state, any community property. The rules concerning the availability of community and joint assets for satisfaction of a court judgment obtained against an individual vary greatly. If there are common assets that could be affected, see a lawyer for more information as to your state's laws in this area.

** To get a homestead exemption, you must file documents at the county courthouse.

policy's maximum. However, the sole proprietor would still be personally liable for any business debts or loans, because liability insurance would not cover such transactions.

Alice's P.S.

For future liability problems Alice bought a year's worth of business insurance from Peter's Protection Group. She says that it is worth every one of the $150 because not only will Peter pay off the injured and the maimed but also Peter's company pays Irving the Insurance Lawyer for defending cases such as *Crafty Crank the Elderly Customer v. Alice the Guerrilla Craftmaiden.*

P.P.S. Debtor's prisons were outlawed many years ago, remember.

PARTNERSHIP

Memorandum of Law

TO: Wood Shaver File
FROM: MBD
RE: Liability for Individual and Partnership Debts

FACTS

Client Wood Shaver agreed with Smith Skiptown to rent studio space, share costs, materials, equipment, and overhead, and to produce a line of wooden bookends, each person to receive half the profits. After the studio had been rented and outfitted for the two woodworkers, materials purchased, and business cards printed, Smith Skiptown disappeared without a trace. A few months later, Carl the Car Dealer appeared at Wood Shaver's door demanding that he pay Smith's overdue car payments.

QUESTION

Who pays for:

1. The studio rent and other debts contracted by Wood Shaver and Skiptown to start the bookend production?
2. The overdue car payments?

THEORY

A partnership agreement can be either oral or written. Also, a partnership can be implied from the behavior of any one of the partners toward a third party (creditors, etc.). From the particular facts of this case it seems clear that an oral partnership agreement had been made between client Wood Shaver and Smith Skiptown.

In this state, both the assets of the partnership and the assets of the individual partners can be taken to pay the partnership debts. Also, individual indebtedness of each partner can be satisfied from that partner's share of the partnership assets.

SOLUTION

1. Wood Shaver is personally liable for all the debts contracted by him and Skiptown for the bookend venture. Of course, all the assets of the partnership are also liable for these business debts.

2. Skiptown's share of the assets of the bookend venture are available to Carl for Skiptown's car payments.
3. Wood Shaver can sue Skiptown if he ever locates him.
4. Advise Wood Shaver concerning importance of choosing the *right* partner so that he will not be burned again.
5. Offer creditors reduced settlement amount. See if they will accept Wood Shaver's work as part of compromise settlement.

CHOOSING A PARTNER

If you are going into business with a friend or group of friends, a partnership may be the business form for you. Like marriage, partnership is a very intimate relationship. Disagreements between partners account for the large number of partnership terminations, so your choice of a partner is a *very* important one. Don't choose a fox for a partner if you are a little red hen, because in a partnership, any one of the partners can bind the entire partnership in most matters, including purchase and sale of land, contracts, leases, and so on. This is true even if the partner acts without the approval or knowledge of the partnership.

DEFINITION

A partnership occurs whenever more than one person owns a business together and the business is not incorporated. A partnership is best created by the signing of a partnership agreement so that the terms of the partnership are clear to the parties.

PARTNERSHIP AGREEMENT

A partnership agreement should contain the objective of the partnership, that is, that it is an association of two or more persons for the purpose of doing business as co-owners for profit, with the profits and losses shared among the partners. Also, a partnership agreement should spell out each partner's share of the profits, losses, capital, assets, and management, and provide ways to resolve disagreements and value assets. The partnership agreement should also discuss the way that new persons can join the partnership and partners can leave. Appendix 1-1 contains a sample form for a simple partnership agreement.

FORMATION OF A PARTNERSHIP

A partnership can be formed by an oral agreement or can be found to exist by a court through an examination of the behavior of the parties to the alleged partnership (implied partnership). It is better to enter into a *written* partnership agreement when you are working with other people and sharing the profits, because most state partnership laws spell out the terms of a partnership if there is no agreement between the partners or if a partnership agreement is silent on the point in question. For example, a court will assume that the members of a partnership intended to share the profits and other interests *equally* if there is no agreement containing a different method of allocating each partner's share.

RESTRICTIONS ON DOING BUSINESS

States impose few restrictions on doing business as a partnership.

TAX

Tax on partnership profits is paid by each partner individually in proportion to his or her share of the partnership profits. The partnership itself does not pay any tax. The rate of tax is the same as that

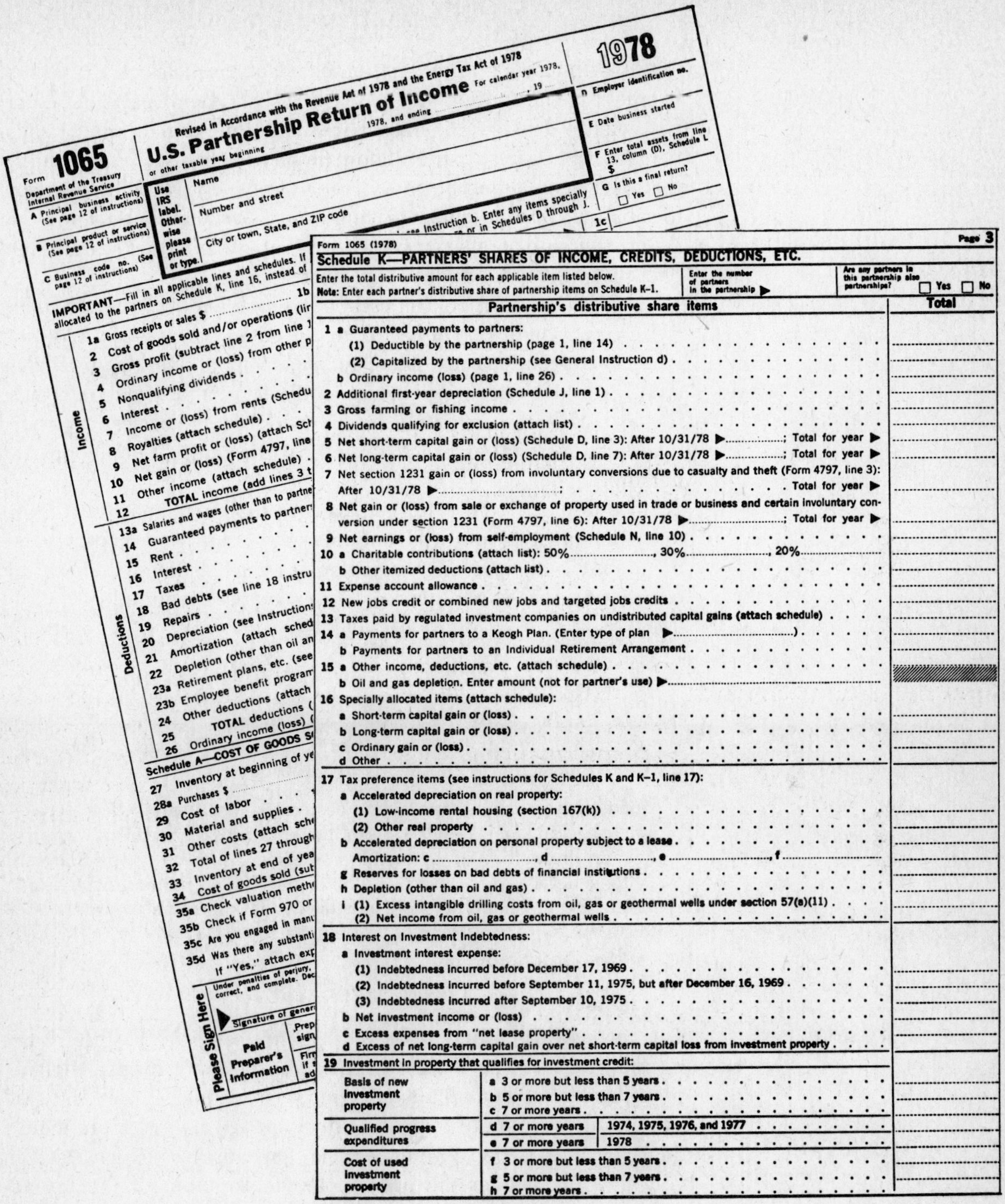

Form 1065 — Department of the Treasury, Internal Revenue Service — Revised in Accordance with the Revenue Act of 1978 and the Energy Tax Act of 1978 — U.S. Partnership Return of Income — 1978

Form 1065 (1978) Page 3

Schedule K—PARTNERS' SHARES OF INCOME, CREDITS, DEDUCTIONS, ETC.

Enter the total distributive amount for each applicable item listed below.
Note: Enter each partner's distributive share of partnership items on Schedule K–1.
Enter the number of partners in the partnership ▶
Are any partners in this partnership also partnerships? ☐ Yes ☐ No

Partnership's distributive share items	Total
1 a Guaranteed payments to partners:	
(1) Deductible by the partnership (page 1, line 14)	
(2) Capitalized by the partnership (see General Instruction d)	
b Ordinary income (loss) (page 1, line 26)	
2 Additional first-year depreciation (Schedule J, line 1)	
3 Gross farming or fishing income	
4 Dividends qualifying for exclusion (attach list)	
5 Net short-term capital gain or (loss) (Schedule D, line 3): After 10/31/78 ▶ ; Total for year ▶	
6 Net long-term capital gain or (loss) (Schedule D, line 7): After 10/31/78 ▶ ; Total for year ▶	
7 Net section 1231 gain or (loss) from involuntary conversions due to casualty and theft (Form 4797, line 3): After 10/31/78 ▶ ; Total for year ▶	
8 Net gain or (loss) from sale or exchange of property used in trade or business and certain involuntary conversion under section 1231 (Form 4797, line 6): After 10/31/78 ▶ ; Total for year ▶	
9 Net earnings or (loss) from self-employment (Schedule N, line 10)	
10 a Charitable contributions (attach list): 50% , 30% , 20%	
b Other itemized deductions (attach list)	
11 Expense account allowance	
12 New jobs credit or combined new jobs and targeted jobs credits	
13 Taxes paid by regulated investment companies on undistributed capital gains (attach schedule)	
14 a Payments for partners to a Keogh Plan. (Enter type of plan ▶)	
b Payments for partners to an Individual Retirement Arrangement	
15 a Other income, deductions, etc. (attach schedule)	
b Oil and gas depletion. Enter amount (not for partner's use) ▶	
16 Specially allocated items (attach schedule):	
a Short-term capital gain or (loss)	
b Long-term capital gain or (loss)	
c Ordinary gain or (loss)	
d Other	
17 Tax preference items (see instructions for Schedules K and K–1, line 17):	
a Accelerated depreciation on real property:	
(1) Low-income rental housing (section 167(k))	
(2) Other real property	
b Accelerated depreciation on personal property subject to a lease	
Amortization: c , d , e , f	
g Reserves for losses on bad debts of financial institutions	
h Depletion (other than oil and gas)	
i (1) Excess intangible drilling costs from oil, gas or geothermal wells under section 57(a)(11)	
(2) Net income from oil, gas or geothermal wells	
18 Interest on Investment Indebtedness:	
a Investment interest expense:	
(1) Indebtedness incurred before December 17, 1969	
(2) Indebtedness incurred before September 11, 1975, but after December 16, 1969	
(3) Indebtedness incurred after September 10, 1975	
b Net investment income or (loss)	
c Excess expenses from "net lease property"	
d Excess of net long-term capital gain over net short-term capital loss from investment property	
19 Investment in property that qualifies for investment credit:	
Basis of new investment property — a 3 or more but less than 5 years	
b 5 or more but less than 7 years	
c 7 or more years	
Qualified progress expenditures — d 7 or more years — 1974, 1975, 1976, and 1977	
e 7 or more years — 1978	
Cost of used investment property — f 3 or more but less than 5 years	
g 5 or more but less than 7 years	
h 7 or more years	

figure 1-1 Federal partnership return

for the individual, and the income is reported on an individual 1040 tax return. A partnership return (see Figure 1-1) has to be filed with the U.S. Internal Revenue Service for information purposes only. A partnership automatically dissolves upon the death, insanity, withdrawal, or bankruptcy of any partner unless the partnership agreement specifically provides for continuation after such an event.

DISSOLUTION

UNLIMITED LIABILITY

As with a sole proprietorship, the major drawback of this form of business is the unlimited liability of each general partner for *any* partnership debt and the liability of the partnership for the personal debts of a partner up to the amount of the partner's share. This means that the personal and business property of each partner is available to satisfy a court judgment arising from a partnership debt and that the partnership assets can be taken to satisfy a partner's individual debt up to the amount of that partner's share.

LIMITED PARTNER

Some of the partners can escape the problem of unlimited liability through the device of becoming a limited partner. Limited partners do not participate in the management of the business, they simply provide economic backing and receive a proportionate share of the partnership profits. Limited partners are basically passive investors. Personal assets of limited partners are not liable for partnership debts.

In order to create a limited partnership, very specific rules of formation *must* be followed, and unlike a general partnership agreement, the limited partnership agreement must be filed with a state or county office. Thus the services of a lawyer are required.

Memorandum

TO: Wood Shaver File
FROM: MBD
RE: Drafting Limited Partnership Agreement between Wood Shaver and Rich Katt

Wood Shaver has located a new partner who will provide the economic backing for the bookend production. Check Limited Partnership Act and draft a limited partnership agreement showing Wood Shaver as the general partner and Rich Katt as the limited partner. Arrange a meeting with clients to work out details of allocation of profits, et cetera.

INCORPORATION

The corporation is by far the most complicated of the three basic business forms. For these reasons, the corporate form is not appropriate for most small arts and crafts operations. However, should your business grow to the extent that you are making more money than you need to meet your personal and business expenses, then you should consider the option of incorporation for the tax advantages as well as for the benefits of limited liability and the increased ability to attract investors.* A good accountant will know the point at which it is advantageous for a business to incorporate.

TAX ADVANTAGES

Maria had an income of $40,000 after deducting her business expenses last year from her booming stitchery business. As a sole

* For an excellent discussion of the advantages of incorporation, see Judith H. McQuown, *Inc., Yourself*, Macmillan, New York, 1977.

proprietor, she would pay income tax in the amount of $12,815 for 1977:

$40,000	Net Income
−2,200	Standard Deduction Single Person
−750	Exemption
$37,050	Taxable Income

$12,815 Tax

As a corporation, Maria could reduce her tax bill for the time being by $4,816:

$20,000	Retained Corporate Earnings (profits kept by the corporation)
×20%	Corporate Tax Rate
$ 4,000	Corporate Tax
$20,000	Net Income (salary)
−2,200	Standard Deduction
−750	Exemption
$17,050	Taxable Income
$ 3,999	Personal Income Tax
$ 7,999	Total Tax

Remember, Maria will have to pay personal income tax on both the wages and dividends paid to her by the corporation. However, the corporation can delay such payments until a more opportune time by retaining earnings. Also, Maria must weigh her tax savings against the additional time and paperwork involved in maintaining a corporation.

DEFINITION

The corporation is the Cheshire cat of Legal Land because it is elusive and hard to visualize. Sometimes when searching for a corporation, all you can find is its smile. The corporate concept is a legal fiction. It is created by the law to develop business through the protection of the owners from personal liability for corporate debts.

> *"A corporation is an artificial being, invisible, intangible, and existing only in contemplation of the law."*
> —Chief Justice John Marshall

LIMITED LIABILITY

AVAILABILITY OF FINANCING

Legally, the corporation is like a separate person who can make contracts, incur debts, purchase property, sue and be sued. The individuals who make up the corporation are not personally liable for any of the corporate transactions even though their corporation may be totally bankrupt, provided the corporation operates within the law. Related to the benefit of limited liability is another advantage of the corporation—the variety of financing arrangements. In addition to contracting for loans,* the corporation can sell shares to obtain additional capital. Investors in the corporation incur no personal liability for any corporate debt and can transfer their shares of corporate stock. When a corporation reaches a certain number of actual or potential shareholders, state and federal securities laws enter the picture. State laws (Blue Sky Laws) come into play at around ten shareholders and the federal law at approximately thirty-five. Even offering shares to more than a limited number of potential investors may bring such laws into play.

TRANSFERABILITY OF SHARES

CONTINUITY

Since the corporation is separate from its shareholders, the corporation continues despite the death or withdrawal of any of the shareholders or directors. The corporation pays tax on its net profits and is liable for any other tax or licensing fee that is required in order to exist and do business in the corporate location.

COST OF FILING INCORPORATION

Among the disadvantages of the corporate form are the time and expense of incorporating. Advertised attorney's fees for a simple incorporation start in the neighborhood of $100. Fees for filing articles of incorporation with the state are usually around $50. Each year, annual reports must be filed with the state, also for a fee.

RESERVATION OF CORPORATE NAME

ARTICLES OF INCORPORATION

PUBLICATION

INITIAL CAPITALIZATION

Since the services of an attorney are pretty much necessary for incorporation, we shall only briefly cover the requirements for incorporation. In some states, the initial step of incorporation is the selection and reservation of a corporate name. Then articles of incorporation are drafted and submitted to the state corporation commission. The articles contain the details of the business of the corporation including name, purpose, location, duration, names and addresses of the initial board of directors, name and address of a designated agent for legal purposes, and information concerning the shares to be issued. Some states such as Arizona require the publication of these articles in a local newspaper for a period of time. Also, a few states require that a percentage of the value of the capital stock be deposited in a bank before the certificate of incorporation is issued by the state. These steps must be carefully followed, because a court will deny the special protection of limited liability if the corporation is not set up and managed according to the law.

DISSOLUTION

Just as starting a corporation is complicated, so is shutting it down. An attorney also will be required for this process. Dissolution requires the filing of a statement of intent to dissolve. Thereafter, steps to liquidate are taken and creditors are notified.

RESTRICTIONS ON DOING BUSINESS

Another disadvantage of the corporate form of business concerns the various restrictions on doing business within the home state of the corporation as well as outside that state. Many of the activities of the corporation are governed by state law—shareholders' and

* Most lending institutions will require the directors of small corporations to personally obligate themselves on a corporate loan.

directors' meetings, management of stock, et cetera. If a corporation wishes to do business in another state or in many states, a certificate of doing business must be filed with the state official in every foreign state where the corporation does business.

WHAT FORM OF BUSINESS ORGANIZATION?

SOLE PROPRIETORSHIP	*ADVANTAGES*	*DISADVANTAGES*
	Ease of formation	Unlimited personal liability
	Low start-up costs	Lack of continuity
	Least regulation	Difficult to raise money or get grants
	Owner control	Tax disadvantage for high profits
	All profits to owner	

PARTNERSHIP	*ADVANTAGES*	*DISADVANTAGES*
	Ease of formation	Unlimited personal liability and liability for partners' debts
	Low start-up costs	Lack of continuity
	Broader management base	Divided authority—lack of extensive control
	Shared responsibility and losses	Difficult to raise additional capital or get grants
	Limited outside regulation	Hard to find suitable partners
	No direct tax on business	Possibility of personal difficulties
	Satisfaction and benefits of working with someone	Tax disadvantages for high profits

CORPORATION	*ADVANTAGES*	*DISADVANTAGES*
	Limited liability	Closely regulated
	Possible tax advantages	Most expensive form to organize
	Continuous existence	Charter restrictions
	Legal entity	Extensive record keeping necessary
	Ownership transferable	Double taxation

VARIATIONS ON A CORPORATE THEME

Corporations come in various types. The law makes a distinction between the small (closely held) corporation and the large, public corporation. The small corporation is less strictly regulated. Some

Sole proprietorship

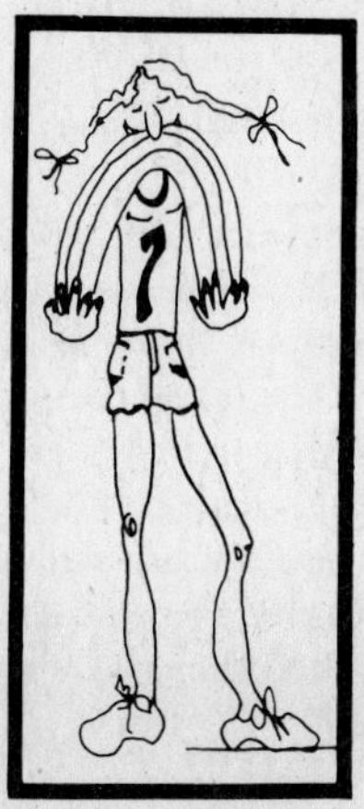

Partnership

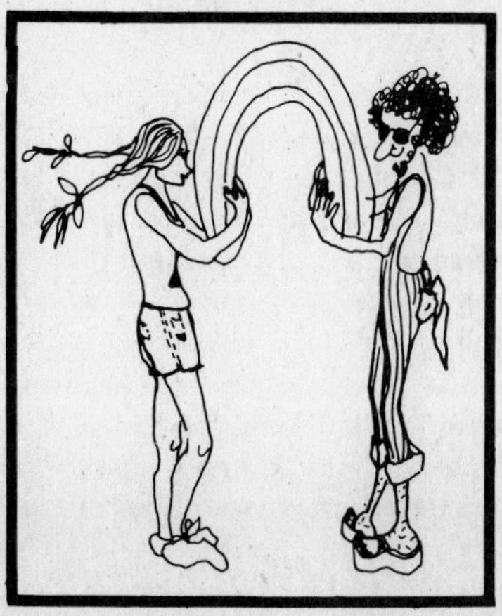

Corporation

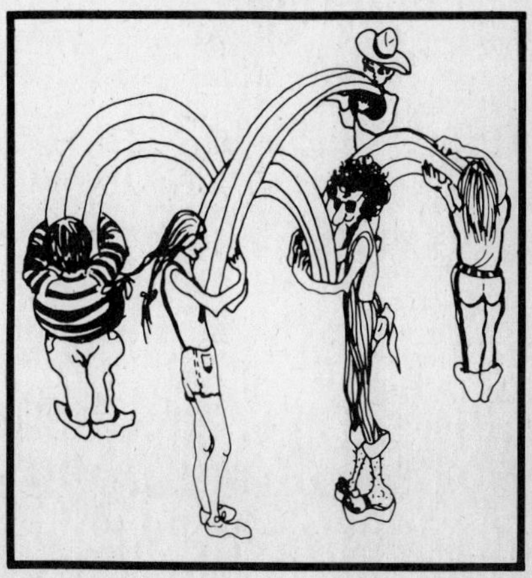

of the types of corporations that would interest artists and craftmakers are the Subchapter S corporation, the not-for-profit corporation, and the cooperative.

SUBCHAPTER S CORPORATION

The Subchapter S corporation—a hybrid business form created by the federal tax laws—is treated as a partnership for tax purposes with all the net profits allocated to individual shareholders and then taxed at the individual tax rate. For all other purposes the Subchapter S corporation is treated as a corporation, including the right to limited liability. The requirements for the formation of the special Subchapter S corporation are the same as for any corporation, but the IRS must be notified by the corporation within the first month of its existence of the intent to be taxed as a Subchapter S corporation.

NOT-FOR-PROFIT STATUS

If you are engaged in a not-for-profit operation that is set up for charitable, educational, or other worthy purposes, like a museum or an art school, you should look into obtaining special "not-for-profit" status from the Internal Revenue Service. A large portion of grants to the arts are available only to not-for-profit organizations which have been granted tax-exempt status by the IRS. An unincorporated association as well as a corporation can achieve the not-for-profit status. Once a corporation has been granted this status the corporation is not liable for sales or income tax, although the not-for-profit corporation must file an informational federal tax return.

COOPERATIVES

A cooperative is a special kind of business form usually set up under the state cooperative law.* The cooperative is in the business of providing at-cost services or goods to its members. Control of the cooperative is by its entire membership. A successful marketing cooperative I know, simply rents a small store and sells the crafts of its members. Each member works at the store a required number of hours each week.

Alice's Allegory # 3

or

To Incorporate or Not to Incorporate

Since last we have seen Alice, Romero has entered her life with hearts and flowers and a small inheritance.

Having been a lousy outlaw, Alice is trying to straighten up her business act, and so when Romero suggested a little business venture consisting of hand-glazing clay pots and distributing them to florists and nurseries on a mass basis, Alice immediately launched a full and complete inquiry into all the possible legal pitfalls, traps, Blue Sky Laws, and Green River ordinances.

To incorporate or not to incorporate, that was the question. Romero's inheritance was high on the list of problems, because without his inheritance, Romero would be a poor hippie like everyone else. The limited liability of the corporate form looked like the answer that Alice and Romero were seeking.

* A cooperative does not always require incorporation.

But the articles of incorporation, the lawyer's fee, the bylaws, the filing requirements, the corporate tax returns, the annual reports, and the annual meetings, all to protect Romero's inheritance? There must be a better way.

One day, the Fairy Godmother appeared to Alice in a dream and said, "Business insurance, my dear." Alice thought about this and realized that she already had liability insurance for her business and that simply extending the coverage would protect Romero's inheritance from all claims arising from damage or injury caused by the business.

"Hurrah," said Alice as she rushed out to find Romero who was sitting under a rainbow. Right then and there, Alice and Romero formed a partnership appropriately called the Rainbow Company, which agreement was later reduced to writing, and included a term requiring Alice and Romero to both agree to any matters involving more than $100.

FEDERAL, STATE, AND LOCAL REQUIREMENTS

In this section, we will discuss the general federal, state, and local requirements for starting a business, regardless of the legal structure of the business.* Because each location is different, the requirements for setting up a business will vary, as will the names of the licenses and taxes. However, the general requirements of obtaining a state sales tax identification number, at least one business license, and complying with health, fire, building, and zoning regulations are pretty much the same wherever the business is located.

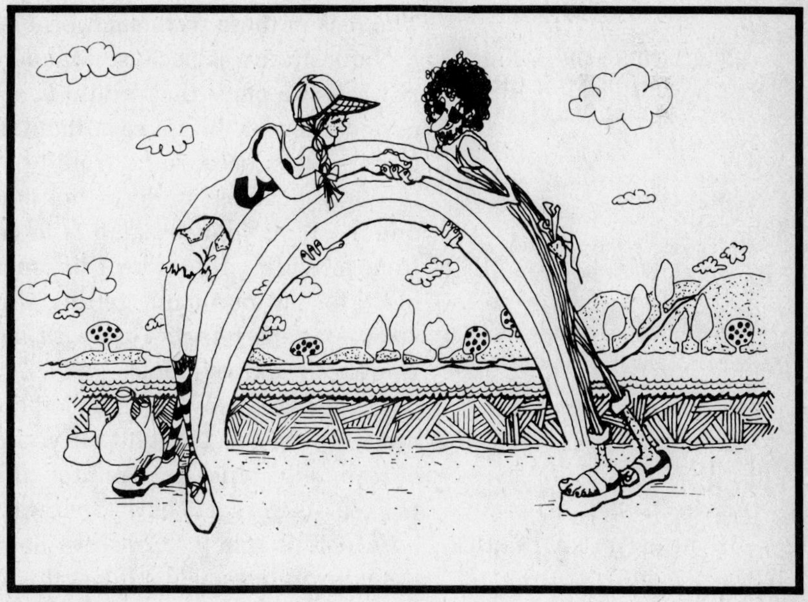

Formation of a rainbow company

* For Native American artists living and working on a reservation, the state and county requirements usually do not apply. Tribal and federal regulations would apply.

DOING YOUR OWN DETECTIVE WORK

Because each state and locality has its own requirements for starting up a business, you will have to do your own research to discover the exact requirements of starting a business in your location. Step one in your detective work is to locate the agency or office in your area equivalent to each of the agencies described in this section and to find out the exact requirements of each of these agencies. This research is not easy. If you have a friend who has already found out what to do, you are *very* lucky.

> *Dear Chatty Lawyer Syndicated Column:*
>
> HELP. I tried to find out whether my new gallery, called Manuel's Friends, is required to file a certificate of doing business under a fictitious name. I called the local chamber of commerce. They had no information but referred me to an industrial counseling service. No information either and another referral—Small Business Administration. By that time, it was 4:20 in the afternoon and I was informed that all the counselors had gone home for the day and that I should call in the morning. I doggedly pursued the directions and called back the Small Business Administration the next morning and was told that all the counselors were in a meeting and to call an organization of retired business men who volunteered their time to assist new businesses. . . . Do I need to file a certificate of doing business under a fictitious name?
>
> *Manuel*

TWO TIPS FOR DEALING WITH BUREAUCRATS

The reason there were such problems getting an answer to the gallery question was because Manuel called the wrong offices. He did not call the office that would *benefit* from providing him with the correct answer. In his case that office would have been the county clerk's office, because he would pay them a filing fee if a certificate of doing business under a fictitious name were required. So, rule one in doing your research is to contact the agency which *benefits* from providing the correct information. Don't call the city mayor's office to find out about getting a state sales tax certificate, call the state tax department. They will have the information because they want your tax payments.

Rule two is to ask as specific a question as possible, using as much of the local lingo that you can pick up. It is hard for some bureaucratic types to comprehend the fact that an "occupational license" is the same as a "business permit." Remember, the average bureaucrat's rule is "Conserve Energy—Don't Think." If after using these techniques, you still get the royal runaround, consult someone in a similar business in your location.

BUREAUCRAT'S RULE

It is also wise to untangle the various tax, licensing, and zoning requirements so that you understand which are city or county, which are state, and which are federal. Write down all the requirements. Use the following checklist as a guide.

CHECKLIST—ALL BUSINESSES
(adapt to your location)

_____ Check city zoning office or county zoning office for restrictions on use of your location for a business.

_____ Check building, health and fire codes for requirements for special equipment or construction.

_____ If required, file a certificate of doing business under a fictitious name.

_____ Apply for a state sales tax number at the state revenue department.

_____ Apply for state, city, or county business license(s).

WITH EMPLOYEES

_____ File application for Federal Employer's Identification Number.

_____ Obtain necessary forms and information from the Internal Revenue Service for federal withholding, Social Security, and unemployment taxes.

_____ Obtain necessary information and forms from the state tax department for withholding.

_____ Obtain necessary information and forms for state unemployment tax.

_____ Obtain information and forms for workers' compensation.

ZONING, BUILDING, HEALTH, AND FIRE CODES

ZONING LAWS

The first step in setting up your business is to make sure that you can legally work at the location you have selected. Usually, artists' studios are legal in residential zones. However, most zoning laws do not allow businesses with direct sales or employees to be located in a residential area, although occasional "visitors" to a studio are tolerated, provided the neighbors do not object. In most locations, zoning-office approval is required for the address stated on an application for a business license before the license is granted, so check with the zoning office before you apply for a city license. For zoning information, contact the city or county government offices, depending upon where your business is located.

VARIANCE

If you discover that the proposed location for your business is in violation of the zoning laws, you may be able to get a "variance." A variance is an exception to the zoning laws. Depending on the complexity and size of the locality, the process of obtaining a variance usually entails some cost and time besides notification of the neighbors, and a hearing will be required.

BUILDING CODES

If your business requires special equipment or construction, like a kiln, rewiring, or new plumbing, you had better check with the city or county building inspector before having the work done to make sure that the work will comply with the building-code requirements as well as the health and fire regulations. A potter we knew ran a new gas pipe to her kiln only to discover when the inspector arrived that the pipe was six inches too low and had to be raised before she could get the gas hooked up.

CERTIFICATE OF DOING BUSINESS UNDER A FICTITIOUS NAME

FICTITIOUS NAME CERTIFICATE

If you are going to do business under a name other than your own, you may be required to file a certificate of doing business under a fictitious name.* Most states require filing at the county clerk's office of the county where you do business. Some require in addition the publication of the certificate in a local newspaper. Also, some states require that this license be renewed every few years. You will have to pay a minimal filing fee. The purpose of this document is to enable a member of the public to locate the person(s) behind the fictitious business name. Incorporated businesses do not have to file these certificates because the state corporation commission has all the information necessary to locate the principals of any corporation located in the state. To find out if this certificate is required, contact the county clerk's office in your county or the state corporation commission.

STATE SALES TAX NUMBER

Alice's Allegory # 4

or

Getting It Together

After the Big Max attack, Alice was so frightened that she even got the VW's muffler fixed so that she wouldn't be stopped and thrown in jail for failure to have a state sales tax number. (Little did she know that the fear was just a figment of her imagination.)

One full moon day, Alice decided to get it together and do the tax-number thing. She put on her most powerful clothes and wore an Indian headband for protection. She and Romero got into their VW and drove down to the Bureau of Revenue's office.

Since the Bureau of Revenue was on the eleventh floor, Alice was a bit light-headed when she arrived, so she had to look twice to make sure that she saw a handsome young man behind the desk asking if she needed help. Feeling reassured, Alice told the revenue officer that she wanted to register for a state tax number. "Just fill out this form and you will receive your Registration Certificate in the mail." "That's all there is to it?" stammered Alice. The handsome young man nodded his head.

Most states that levy sales tax require that anyone in business have a state tax number.** The tax or resale number is used on the form you will complete when paying state sales tax collected on sales made within your state and when you purchase materials for use in your business.***

STATE TAX NUMBER

Sometimes a cash deposit is required to obtain a state tax number. The deposit is credited against the state sales tax due. The

* See figure 1-2: California Fictitious Business Name Statement.

**Alaska, Delaware, Montana, Oregon, and New Hampshire do not assess sales tax at the time of this writing.

*** See figure 1-3 for a sample application form.

Mail to______________________________

COUNTY CLERK'S FILING STAMP

Fictitious Business Name Statement

The following person (persons) is (are) doing business as:

____
FICTITIOUS BUSINESS NAME

at (*) ______________________________
BUSINESS ADDRESS

1 (**) ______________________________
FULL NAME—TYPE/PRINT
____
RESIDENCE ADDRESS
____
CITY

2 ______________________________
FULL NAME—TYPE/PRINT
____
RESIDENCE ADDRESS
____
CITY

3 ______________________________
FULL NAME—TYPE/PRINT
____
RESIDENCE ADDRESS
____
CITY

4 ______________________________
FULL NAME—TYPE/PRINT
____
RESIDENCE ADDRESS
____
CITY

(* * *) This business is conducted by______________________________
INDIVIDUAL, CO-PARTNERS, CORPORATION, LIMITED PARTNERSHIP, BUSINESS TRUST, ETC.

Signed______________________________ Type or print signature______________________________

This statement was filed with the County Clerk of the City and County of San Francisco, California, on the date indicated by file stamp above.

Certification

I hereby certify that the foregoing is a correct copy of the original on file in my office.

By______________________________
COUNTY CLERK

____
DEPUTY

File No.______________
Statutory Filing Fee — $10.00
Submit Original and all 3 Copies

TO BE PUBLISHED IN

SAN FRANCISCO
BANNER

SEE REVERSE SIDE FOR INSTRUCTIONS

Statement expires 5 years from December 31 of year in which filed and must be Renewed then with a new Statement.

figure 1-2 California fictitious business name statement amount of deposit required in some states is so large that many artists and craftmakers cannot afford a tax number and therefore do not make any direct sales.* Theoretically, the deposit amount is based upon the estimated sales tax liability for the business. In some states, once the state has your number, you will receive state sales tax forms on a regular basis.

SALES TAX EXEMPTION ON MATERIALS

The tax number also is used whenever you purchase materials that will be used in the making of your craft, (silver, wood, wool, clay, etc.) so that you do not have to pay sales tax on these materials when you purchase them. The reason for this exemption from sales tax is so that, for example, a mug will not be taxed twice—once when the clay is purchased from the distributor and again when the clay is sold to the customer in finished form. This sales tax exemption also applies to the cost of services purchased for use in the final product in some states. Information concerning state sales tax as well as state income tax is available from the state revenue office.** Figure 1-4 will help decipher the taxes that you must collect and pay.

FEDERAL EMPLOYER IDENTIFICATION NUMBER

A federal identification number is required for *all* corporations and partnerships and for any business with employees. The section of this chapter on employees will further discuss setting up for employees and obtaining a federal identification number.

BUSINESS LICENSE

You will also need at least one business license. If your business is located within a city limit, you should call the city for more information. If the business is located in a county, then call the county clerk's office.

PEDDLER'S LICENSE

If you make street sales or otherwise use public property, you might need a special peddler, vendor, or huckster's license or permit in addition to your regular business license. Because street sales have been cutting into more established businesses' clientele in the past few years, some cities now closely regulate street sales. The street sellers successfully challenged these restrictive regulations in some cities.

STATE LICENSE

For some peculiar reason, many states require that photographers obtain special licenses. Some of these licensing laws have been found invalid by the courts. For information on these and other state license requirements, contact the state consumer protection office.

* If you sell your work through a gallery or other outlet, they will collect the sales tax for you.

** Also see Chapter 6, "Other Taxes."

Dept. Of Taxation & Revenue
RP - 31
RPB
March, 1978

STATE OF NEW MEXICO

REVENUE DIVISION

APPLICATION FOR REGISTRATION

This application is to be used for registration for the following tax programs: Combined Reporting Systems (CRS), (Gross Receipts Tax, Compensating Tax, County Tax, Municipal Tax, Withholding Tax), Gasoline Sales Registration, Cigarette Sales Registration, Severance Tax and Resources Excise Tax Registration.

Taxpayer registration is required by New Mexico statutes under Section 72-13-29, N.M.S.A. 1953. Supplemental information and general instructions concerning reporting will be mailed to you along with the Registration Certificate. Please complete the application in full and questions which do not apply should be marked "N/A" (Not Applicable). "Date Business Activity Started in New Mexico" means that date you initially made a sale of, or derived receipts from performing services in New Mexico, selling property in New Mexico or leasing property employed in New Mexico; or the tentative date you anticipate deriving such receipts.

DEPT. USE ONLY
ID
01- -00-
Date Issued:
CX-2000 CX-2010
X-Ref Card
SIC:
☐ 6-Mo. Request

1. Business Name: Telephone No.

Principal Business Location (Street Number or general Description of Location)

City State Zip Code

2. Date Business Activity Started or is anticipated to start in N.M.:

3. Type of Ownership: ☐ Proprietorship/Sole owner ☐ Partner/Assoc/Joint Ven. ☐ Corporation ☐ Coop. Assoc. ☐ Syndicate ☐ Federal Agency ☐ State agency ☐ Munic. or county ☐ Fiduciary ☐ Indian Tribe or Pueblo ☐ Other (Please specity)

4. If partnership, list general partners. If Assoc/Joint Venture, list members. If close held corporation, list principal stockholders.

OWNER'S NAME	HOME ADDRESS	SOCIAL SECURITY NO.

5. Federal Identification Number (If any):

6. County where principal office in N.M. is located:

7. Date began paying wages in N.M.:

8. Method of Reporting: ☐ Cash ☐ Accrual

9. Mailing Address (If different from Business Location):

Street City - State Zip Code

10. Business Locations other than the one listed in Block 1 (If more space is required, attach a separate sheet):

11. Address where accounting records may be examined (If different from Business Location):

12. Primary type of business in New Mexico: ☐ Manufacturing ☐ Wholesale ☐ Retail ☐ Service ☐ Franchisor ☐ Leasing ☐ Other (Please specify)

13. Description of primary goods or services sold by your New Mexico operations:

14. Select from the table on the reverse side the Standard Industrial Classification Code which most closely describes the nature of your primary business in New Mexico.

15. If this is not a new business, give former owner's business name and address:

16. Former owner's CRS ID number:

17. Are you currently operating onother business in N.M.? ☐ YES ☐ NO

18. If yes, give CRS ID number and state whether you wish to use the CRS ID number which you have for all business locations: ID No. ☐ YES ☐ NO

19. Have you operated a business in New Mexico in the past? ☐ YES ☐ NO If yes, give name and CRS ID number

GASOLINE SALES REGISTRATION:

20. Will business sell gasoline? ☐ YES ☐ NO If yes, what type of business? ☐ Wholesale ☐ Retail ☐ Distributor

CIGARETTE SALES REGISTRATION:

21. Will business sell cigarettes? ☐ YES ☐ NO If yes, what type of business? ☐ Manufacture ☐ Distributor ☐ Wholesale ☐ Retail

SEVERANCE TAX AND RESOURCES EXCISE TAX REGISTRATION: Type(s) of Resource

22. Will the business be engaged in severing natural resources? ☐ YES ☐ NO

23. Will the business be engaged in processing natural resources? ☐ YES ☐ NO

DEPT. USE ONLY
GTX—
LUX—
SEV
RES

Under penalty of perjury, I swear or affirm that the information reported in this form and any attached supplements is true and correct as to every material matter.

This application is to be signed by the owner, if the taxpayer is a proprietorship; by a partner, if the taxpayer is a partnership; and by one of the officers, if the taxpayer is a corporation; or by a person authorized to sign.

By: Date:

Title:

Send Original to Revenue Division, P.O. Box 630, Santa Fe, New Mexico 87503. Taxpayer retain green copy.

figure 1-3 Sample application for state sales tax number

BUSINESS TAX OBLIGATIONS

Kind of Tax

FEDERAL TAXES

Employee Income Tax and Social Security Tax

Owner-Manager's and/or corporation's income tax

Unemployment Tax

STATE TAXES

Unemployment Taxes

Income Taxes

Sales Taxes

Franchise Tax

LOCAL TAXES

Sales Tax

Real Estate Tax

Personal Property Tax

Licenses (retail, vending machine, etc.)

figure 1-4 Business tax obligations (Adapted From "Steps in Meeting Your Tax Obligation," Small Business Administration Small Marketers Aids No. 142)

EMPLOYEES

INDEPENDENT CONTRACTOR

Hiring employees raises your red-tape quotient by 1,000 percent. One way to avoid these additional requirements is to use independent contractors rather than hiring employees, if this is possible. Normally, an independent contractor is paid by the job or piece and not by the hour. An independent operator who is responsible for providing any equipment required by the job generally has control over the project and performs a specialized service.

Wood Shaver needed his bookends sanded and oiled, so he contracted with a cabinetmaker in town to do this work. This way, Wood Shaver would not be required to set up the procedures necessary for businesses with employees. Before Wood Shaver made the decision to take on Leander the Sander as an independent contractor, he thought long and hard because he did not want Uncle Sam breathing down his neck for back withholding, Social Security, and unemployment taxes for Leander. Wood Shaver was so concerned with this problem that he obtained a memorandum on the question of setting up and maintaining an independent contractor relationship with Leander the Sander from his extended family lawyer.

Memorandum

TO: Wood Shaver
FROM: MBD
RE: Independent Contractor: Yes or No

THE IMPORTANCE OF BEING EARNEST
ABOUT THE SUBJECT

I am glad that you have requested this memorandum on the question of independent contractors. It is an important subject, because should a court or the government decide that your independent contractor is an employee, the consequences may be serious—for example, liability for the damage caused by an employee while on the job as well as payment of back federal and state payroll and withholding taxes.

WHAT IS AN INDEPENDENT CONTRACTOR?

There is no set answer to the question of what is an independent contractor. Each situation is different. There are many tests that can be applied to the relationship between you and your worker to see if he or she is an independent contractor. The following list of principles should be helpful in establishing an independent-contractor relationship between yourself and Leander the Sander:

1. Independent Contractors set their own hours. You just agree on the completion date.
2. Independent Contractors should keep a regular set of business books and be in business for themselves with a realistic opportunity for profit or loss.
3. Independent Contractors have the power to choose their own workers.
4. Independent Contractors should provide their own equipment and tools.

5. Independent Contractors are paid by the piece or by the job, not by the hour.
6. Independent Contractors usually work at their own place of business.
7. Independent Contractors should maintain all required business licenses, permits, et cetera, and pay all other job-related expenses.
8. Independent Contractors should not be covered by your liability and health insurance, nor any bonus, vacation, sick-pay program, or training programs that you may have.
9. Independent Contractors should not be fired if they perform according to your agreement with them.
10. Independent Contractors should perform the entire job, including cleaning up without supervision.
11. Since Independent Contractors are in business for themselves, they should not provide their services only to your company but instead make their services available to the general public.

DOCUMENT THE INDEPENDENT CONTRACTOR STATUS

It is best to write down your agreement with Leander the Sander covering as many of the points listed above as are relevant to your contract. You certainly do not have to include every item on the list—a court looks at the overall situation to determine if independent contractor status exists. Also, clip any of Leander's promotional literature or advertising to the contract. Take a picture of Leander's van showing the business name and address. Attach that to the contract.

Finally, get used to calling Leander the Sander Leander the Independent Contractor, for that is who he is.

Before you hire anyone, remember that the secret to success in the area of employee requirements is to understand the federal and state regulations regarding employees. An accountant would be of great assistance here. On the federal level, all employers must have a federal employer's identification number, which is obtained by filing an application with the Internal Revenue Service.* You will be required to withhold federal income taxes from the wages of all your employees unless your employees file Form W-4, Exemption from Withholding. You will also have to pay Social Security taxes.** Finally, you will have to pay federal unemployment tax. You will get credit for any state unemployment tax paid in this federal tax assessment.

FEDERAL EMPLOYER'S IDENTIFICATION NUMBER

WITHHOLDING

FEDERAL SOCIAL SECURITY TAX

FEDERAL UNEMPLOYMENT TAX

Since each of the above taxes require setting up of special records, filing returns, and making payments, a business about to hire employees should obtain the assistance of the local office of the Internal Revenue Service. Publication 15 of the Internal Revenue Service, *Employer's Tax Guide,* discusses withholding, Social Security, and unemployment taxes. *Your Business Tax Kit,* also available from

* See figure 1-5: Application for Employer Identification Number.

** Employers and employees each pay half of the tax on wages, which was 6.13 percent for each in 1979.

Form **SS–4** (Rev. 8–76)
Department of the Treasury
Internal Revenue Service

Application for Employer Identification Number

(For use by employers and others as explained in the Instructions)

1 Name (True name as distinguished from trade name. If partnership, see Instructions on page 4)

2 Trade name, if any (Enter name under which business is operated, if different from item 1)

3 Social security number, if sole proprietor

4 Address of principal place of business (Number and street)

5 Ending month of accounting year

6 City and State

7 ZIP code

8 County of business location

9 Type of organization ☐ Individual ☐ Partnership ☐ Other (specify) ☐ Governmental (See Instr. on page 4) ☐ Nonprofit organization (See Instr. on page 4) ☐ Corporation

10 Date you acquired or started this business (Mo., day, year)

11 Reason for applying ☐ Started new business ☐ Purchased going business ☐ Other (specify)

12 First date you paid or will pay wages for this business (Mo., day, year)

13 Nature of business (See Instructions on page 4)

14 Do you operate more than one place of business? ☐ Yes ☐ No

15 Peak number of employees expected in next 12 months (If none, enter "0") ▶	Nonagricultural	Agricultural	Household

16 If nature of business is manufacturing, state principal product and raw material used

17 To whom do you sell most of your products or services? ☐ Business establishments ☐ General public ☐ Other (specify)

18 Have you ever applied for an identification number for this or any other business? ☐ **Yes** ☐ **No**

If "Yes," enter name and trade name (if any). Also enter the approximate date, city, and State where you first applied and previous number if known. ▶

Date	Signature and title	Telephone number

Please leave blank ▶	Geo.	Ind.	Class	Size	Reas. for appl.	**Part I**

Form **SS–4** (Rev. 8–76)
Department of the Treasury
Internal Revenue Service

Application for Employer Identification Number

(For use by employers and others as explained in the Instructions)

1 Name (True name as distinguished from trade name. If partnership, see Instructions on page 4)

2 Trade name, if any (Enter name under which business is operated, if different from item 1)

3 Social security number, if sole proprietor

4 Address of principal place of business (Number and street)

5 Ending month of accounting year

6 City and State

7 ZIP code

8 County of business location

9 Type of organization ☐ Individual ☐ Partnership ☐ Other (specify) ☐ Governmental (See Instr. on page 4) ☐ Nonprofit organization (See Instr. on page 4) ☐ Corporation

10 Date you acquired or started this business (Mo., day, year)

11 Reason for applying ☐ Started new business ☐ Purchased going business ☐ Other (specify)

12 First date you paid or will pay wages for this business (Mo., day, year)

13 Nature of business (See Instructions on page 4)

14 Do you operate more than one place of business? ☐ Yes ☐ No

15 Peak number of employees expected in next 12 months (If none, enter "0") ▶	Nonagricultural	Agricultural	Household

16 If nature of business is manufacturing, state principal product and raw material used

17 To whom do you sell most of your products or services? ☐ Business establishments ☐ General public ☐ Other (specify)

18 Have you ever applied for an identification number for this or any other business? ☐ **Yes** ☐ **No**

If "Yes," enter name and trade name (if any). Also enter the approximate date, city, and State where you first applied and previous number if known. ▶

Date	Signature and title	Telephone number

Please leave blank ▶	Geo.	Ind.	Class	Size	Reas. for appl.	**Part II**

figure 1-5 Application for employer identification number

the Internal Revenue Service, contains most of the forms that are required by an employer to file and pay these taxes. If you have any questions, the taxpayer's service of the Internal Revenue Service will provide assistance. Other federal laws governing employees are the Minimum Wage Law (Fair Labor Standards Act) and the Civil Rights Act as amended (be especially aware of equal-employment-opportunity provisions).

STATE WITHHOLDING TAX

The state employees tax scheme somewhat parallels the federal system. Withholding of state income tax is required by most states. A few cities like New York City have withholding requirements. To obtain the necessary forms and information concerning state withholding tax, call the state tax department.

STATE UNEMPLOYMENT TAX

In most states, the law requires that employers pay an unemployment tax. Each state has its own rule on when an employer must provide unemployment compensation coverage. This requirement usually is based on the number of employees and employee hours per year for the business. A special state agency normally handles questions about unemployment insurance.

STATE WORKERS' COMPENSATION

Also required by state law is some form of workers' compensation insurance to cover any employee injury on the job. Again, the requirement is related to the number of employees. States vary in the manner in which workers' compensation is provided. The state office administering this program should be contacted for further information.

MISCELLANEOUS CONSIDERATIONS IN SURFACING

STUDIO RENTAL AGREEMENTS

GENERAL LEASE PROVISIONS

Any lease agreement should be checked for the following provisions: amount of rent, term of the lease, renewal provisions, right of the tenant to sublet, any restrictions on the tenant's use of the property imposed by the lease, including the tenant's right to hang out a sign or make alterations.

FIXTURES

In addition to the above considerations, the artist and craftmaker should especially check the lease agreement for a clause concerning fixtures. If you pay for the installation of special rooms, cabinets, shelving, windows, or other valuable fixtures that cannot be removed when you leave, the lease agreement should contain both a provision concerning the tenant's ownership of these improvements and a procedure for the tenant's selling of these improvements at the end of the rental period, if possible. Without this agreement, any improvements which are permanently attached to the walls, floors, et cetera of the rented premises become the property of the landlord and cannot be removed or sold without the landlord's permission.

FIRE, HEALTH, ZONING, AND BUILDING CODES

Prior to signing a lease, check the local zoning ordinances, building codes, health, and fire laws. It would be an expensive mistake to sign a lease and find a notice of zoning violation nailed on your door the next week. If there is not enough time to check with these agencies, the lease should contain a clause allowing you to break the lease if you cannot use the rented space for the intended purpose because of city zoning, fire, health, or building-code restrictions.*

INSURANCE

Business insurance is an important consideration in starting, especially if your business involves an initial investment of time and money. For most artists and craftmakers, a major loss early in their business life would spell the end to their business. For some craftmakers, like jewelers, the cost of most business insurance is prohibitive. For other artists and craftmakers, however, insurance is many times both desirable and reasonably priced.

COMPARISON SHOP

INSURANCE BROKER

The first step in obtaining business insurance is to find a good insurance broker. Get estimates from several brokers. Your broker should understand your particular business and personal needs so that he or she can develop an insurance package tailored to suit your particular situation, and generally assist in all insurance matters. Also, look for insurance from a mutual insurance company which pays profits back to the owner/customers in the form of reduced premiums. You should also make sure that your broker sells a variety of insurance so that the package can include coverage from several companies.

TYPES OF COVERAGE

When buying insurance, make sure you know what types of coverage you are getting for your money. If you look long enough, you could find insurance to protect you from most types of losses. The major types of insurance coverage are for fire, theft, extended coverage (vandalism, malicious mischief, damage caused by aircraft or vehicles, etc.), and liability. Many times, the policy only pays the fair market value of the item destroyed, not the replacement value. So if you want to get enough money from your insurance company to replace the loom that blew away when the explosion rocked your town, consider paying a little extra for a rider to the policy that contracts to pay you the *replacement* value of lost items.

As discussed in Chapter 2, "Legal Restrictions on Content and Materials," craftmakers should inquire concerning product liability coverage in addition to regular liability insurance. Product liability coverage would insure you against any loss caused by your sale of a defective item. Suits for personal injuries caused by defective products can be very costly, and depending on the nature of your product, this insurance may be prohibitive in cost, or simply unavailable.

* If you are buying business property, be sure to condition the final sale on the approval of the premises for the intended purpose by the proper authorities.

Other types of insurance available to business include business interruption and unpaid accounts receivable. Your broker should also have information about employee benefit insurance—health, life, and disability, workers' compensation, and unemployment compensation.

Since purchase of an insurance "package" can result in reduced rates for coverage, all your insurance needs should be examined when purchasing business insurance to ensure the greatest coverage for the least premiums.

Members of the American Crafts Council are eligible for health, life, and studio insurance coverage available through the ACC (122 West Fifty-fifth Street, New York, NY 10019). Both Artists Equity (3726 Albemarle Street, N.W., Washington, D.C. 20016) and the Foundation for the Community of Artists (280 Broadway, New York, NY 10007) have health and life insurance programs available to their members.

Dear Gentle Reader:

Between the guerrilla craftmaiden and the corporate executive lies vast possibilities of business forms, sizes, styles, and requirements. As with everything else in life, most businesses fall somewhere in the great gray middle between the two extremes.

My advice to you is to place a premium on keeping your business simple, manageable, and comprehensible. Simplicity means a sole proprietorship, no employees, a minimal bookkeeping system, and working out of your home.

As you become comfortable with the requirements of a business of this size and stature, all too soon your simple business will burgeon and you will take on more requirements and responsibilities.

Remember the old Chinese proverb: A journey of a thousand miles begins with a single step.

From,
Chatty Lawyer
Syndicated Column

Chapter 2
Legal Restrictions on Content and Materials

INTRODUCTION

In this chapter you will find an odd assortment of topics—rules of negligence, lawsuits for invasion of privacy, the Wool Products Labeling Act of 1939, obscenity decisions, the Consumer Product Safety Commission, the Migratory Bird Treaty Act, and so forth—all relating to legal restrictions on the content and materials used in art, craft, and writing. The information provided in this chapter cannot possibly cover every legal restriction in this area—the laws are too many, and one never can tell what might show up on the wall of an art museum. This chapter will cover only the major areas of restrictions. These are divided into two categories: limitations on content (obscenity, flag laws, invasion of privacy, and defamation); and limitations on materials that make up the work (textile labeling and flammable fabrics acts, laws governing use of bones, feathers, and other parts of wildlife and plants, the rules of negligence and product liability, laws regulating the stamping of gold and silver, and some pertinent consumer protection statutes).

JUST THE FACTS, MA'AM

As will soon be clear, this chapter covers areas of law that currently bulge with controversy—obscenity, feather laws, flag burnings, libel, and so on. Great care has been taken simply to state the law concerning each of the restrictions discussed. The speeches and solutions concerning the big picture and the long balance we leave to the politicians and philosopher kings.

RESTRICTIONS ON CONTENT

OBSCENITY

Not every "erotic" work is legally obscene. This section will attempt to provide a yardstick against which to measure works that could fall within the category of "obscene."

STATE AND LOCAL OBSCENITY LAWS

A variety of laws regulate the sale, display, and transportation of "obscene" materials in the United States. Many obscenity busts occur on the state or local level. For instance, Larry Flynt of *Hustler* magazine was prosecuted under a state law. Whereas some states like New York prohibit obscene materials from being either publicly displayed *or* sold to minors, others prohibit only the sale of such materials to minors. Many cities have their own anti-obscenity laws, some of which prohibit *any* commercial dealings in pornography. If you are curious about the anti-obscenity laws that govern your area, ask a lawyer or the local chapter of the American Civil Liberties Union.

UNITED STATES SUPREME COURT OBSCENITY RULINGS

Because obscenity laws are an exception to the citizen's essential right of free expression, the United States Supreme Court has ruled these laws must be clear and specific in their language. An old New York State law which prohibited the showing of "sacrilegious" films was deemed too vague a yardstick with which to restrict free expression.

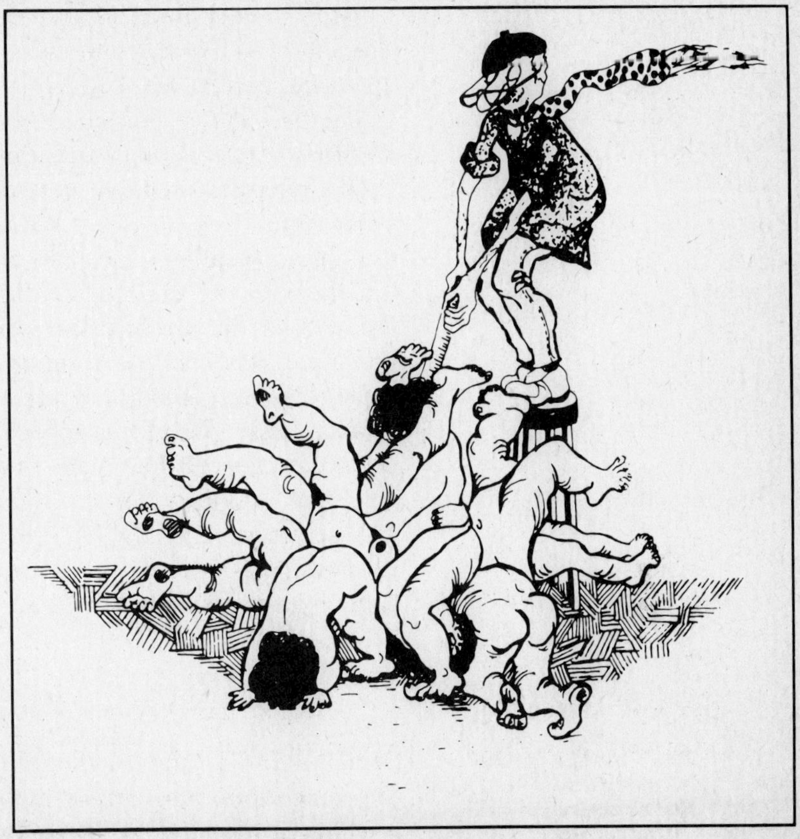

Obscenity yardstick

OBSCENITY IS . . .

MINORS

UNCONSENTING PUBLIC

". . . THE LEER OF THE SENSUALIST IN ADVERTISING . . ."

IN THE PRIVACY OF YOUR HOME

The Supreme Court currently defines obscenity as being material that expresses sexual conduct in a patently offensive way and, taken as a whole, appeals to the prurient interest in sex (applying contemporary community standards) and does not have a serious literary, artistic, political, or scientific value. The Supreme Court also has ruled that material must be truly "obscene" in order to legally send the distributor to jail. The film *Carnal Knowledge* was held *not* obscene under the test described above. Where borderline "obscene" materials are sold to minors, publicly displayed so that minors and members of the public cannot avoid them, or peddled with an emphasis on the prurient aspects of the work (like *Eros* magazine), the Supreme Court may deal more harshly with the distributor and use a looser interpretation of *obscene*. Ralph Ginsburg discovered this as he was sentenced to five years for publication and sale of *Eros*.

Possession of "obscene" material in the privacy of your home is your business, but transporting it across a state line or national border even for personal use is forbidden by federal law. It is a crime to send "obscene" material through the U.S. mail, punishable by up to five years in jail. An entry in the 1976 New York Film Festival

FEDERAL ANTI-OBSCENITY LAWS

titled *In the Realm of the Senses* was held up by U.S. Customs and did not appear in the film festival. It later was released.

Since only local, state, and federal governments and their representatives are prohibited from violating the citizens' First Amendment right to free expression, a privately sponsored art show can legally refuse to hang any works showing bare skin, et cetera. On the other hand, Straitown City Museum probably cannot legally refuse to hang a so-called obscene work until *after* a hearing determines that the work violates the local anti-obscenity law. No agency of government can legally prohibit a showing prior to such a hearing. For the city to do otherwise would violate the artist's First Amendment rights. The Supreme Court ruled that a theater leased by the City of Chattanooga violated free-speech rights by flatly refusing its use for the production of the musical *Hair* because of the play's allegedly "obscene" content. For those adventuresome souls who still find themselves running afoul of the authorities for violating the obscenity laws, the National Coalition Against Censorship in New York City or your local branch of the American Civil Liberties Union may provide assistance.

NATIONAL COALITION AGAINST CENSORSHIP

FLAGS AND PROTEST ART

"CONGRESS SHALL MAKE NO LAW . . . ABRIDGING FREEDOM OF SPEECH. . . ." FIRST AMENDMENT TO THE CONSTITUTION

Some general principles should be kept in mind when considering the content of protest art. First, the important constitutional right of freedom of speech governs works of visual expression as well as the spoken and written word, and physical behavior. So important is the right of this freedom that the courts have ruled that the laws restricting the right to freedom of expression—obscenity, flag desecration, and so forth—must be very clear and specifically describe the prohibited activity. Usually, the courts require a hearing before a judge prior to seizure by the police. The reason for this is that no governmental body is supposed to place a restraint on speech or expression without a judicial hearing.

LAWS RESTRICTING FREE SPEECH MUST BE CLEAR AND SPECIFIC

HEARING PRIOR TO SEIZURE

Most of the cases in the area of protest art involve the use of flags. Many of these have occurred in times of political controversy. Many states have two kinds of laws that apply to the use of flags—desecration statutes and misuse statutes. The desecration statutes prohibit behavior that would heap contempt on the flag. Misuse statutes sound like: "No person shall . . . affix . . . to any flag . . . any inscription, design, symbol, name, advertisement. . . ." The New Hampshire Supreme Court voided the flag misuse law quoted above because its language was too broad for a law that restricted important freedoms of speech and expression. Courts examining several of the flag desecration and misuse laws have found them to be in conflict with the First Amendment to the Constitution.

FLAG LAWS

Recently, the Supreme Court has established a two-part test in flag cases to see if the flag creation is protected by the free-speech

TEST FOR PROTECTION

guarantees of the Constitution. First the Court will determine if the flag-related conduct is within the protection of the First Amendment, that is, whether the work was intended to convey a particular and comprehensible message. If the Court finds this to be so, then the Court will look to see if there is some state interest so important that the constitutional right of free expression can be restricted. For example, this overriding governmental interest was more important than the free-expression rights of a sixties draft-card burner.

A WORD TO THE WISE . . .

If you are using a flag motif in your work, check to see what sort of laws your state has concerning the use of the flag. Then remember, the clearer your message, the more likely it is that a court will rule that your work is protected from the application of the flag laws by the First Amendment right of free speech. So the conviction of an owner of a gallery displaying flag sculptures to express anti–Vietnam War sentiment was reversed after a seven-year court battle. But convictions of persons using a flag motif in advertising generally have been upheld by the courts. You also should remember that the written or spoken word is better protected than a purely visual work, so mixing media may help keep your work before the public view and you out of jail.

INVASION OF PRIVACY

Alice's Allegory # 5

or

Lessons from City Park

With all the messages from the human potential movement (hpm) bombarding his peaceful hillside home, Romero realized that he had to humanize his art. Porcelain portrait hangings would do it—from each plaque a shining human face, full of expression and love!

Romero gathered up Alice, his trusty camera, and chugged off one windy day in search of portraits. City Park at lunch time seemed a good place to begin.

Sitting on the bench surrounded by pigeons was a luscious portrait complete with horn-rimmed glasses and a three-piece, gray suit. Just before Romero snapped the shot, the portrait spoke: "Tsk, Tsk, my friend, you might be invading my privacy, so please do not proceed. Do let me introduce myself, Cautious Caldwell attorney-at-law, at your service."

Romero knew that he had finally found the lawyer of his dreams and stuck Cautious Caldwell's card in his hatband.

DEFINITION

Invasion of privacy is what Ron Galella did to Jackie Kennedy Onassis when he poked his camera lens too closely into her life. State law spells out the areas protected from invasion by private parties. Most living persons have a right to privacy. It is basically the right (with many qualifications) to be let alone. If invasion of privacy could be a problem in your work, see Chapter 8, "Obtaining Legal Assistance," for information on getting good legal advice concerning the privacy rules of your state.

CHECK IT OUT

APPLICATION

A state privacy law usually prohibits commercial exploitation of the name or portrait of a living person without consent. It does not apply to the commercial use of photographs of animals, buildings, and so forth, although other restrictions (copyrights, ownership rights) could prohibit the commercial use of these.

What about your sneak street shot of that gorgeous tuba player in last year's Independence Day Parade? Don't sell it to a tuba company for their next big advertising campaign. Without a release (written permission) you might get sued for invasion of the tuba player's privacy. But the local gazette could print the photograph of the tuba player alongside an article on the Independence Day festivities with no problem because the photograph was not used for commercial purposes but rather as part of a news story.

FREE SPEECH AND FREE PRESS: EXCEPTION TO PRIVACY LAWS

Many of the cases in this area focus on whether the use of the plaintiff's name et cetera is for commercial and trade purposes or for news purposes. The line dividing the public's right to know and the individual's right to privacy is a fine one. The recent court decisions on this issue seem to be leaning in the direction of favoring the public's right to know over the individual's right of privacy. A participant in a St. Patrick's Day Parade lost his invasion-of-privacy case against *New York* magazine. The court ruled that printing the marcher's photograph on the front of the magazine to illustrate an article called "The Last of the Irish Immigrants" was published "in connection with the presentation of a matter of legitimate public interest to readers" and therefore no recovery for invasion of privacy was available. Since anyone thrust willingly or unwillingly into the public eye is considered a "public figure," he or she, as such, is fair game for comment. A "public figure" will have a hard time winning an invasion-of-privacy suit unless a clear commercial purpose can be demonstrated.

RELEASE

COMMERCIAL PURPOSE

You should give a dollar and obtain a release from any subject of a portrait or photograph you may use for advertising or other commercial purposes. Figure 2-1 contains a sample release form, which should be tailored to your specific needs. When photographing identifiable human subjects, it is a good idea to get a release whenever possible. You never know what you might do with the photograph or drawing. You do not need a release to publish or distribute a photograph of someone involved in a truly newsworthy event. But because of the great gray area between the clearly newsworthy and the clearly commercial, when in doubt, get a release.

DEFAMATION

Defamation laws are as old as Moses and are designed to protect a person's reputation (including artistic reputation) from the taint of falsehood. Under defamation laws, private citizens can sue to recover money damages for the harm caused by any oral or written

RELEASE

For the sum of $1.00 [or more], receipt of which is hereby acknowledged, I hereby grant to ______________ ______________, and
(photographer)

to anyone whom he or she may appoint or assign, the right to make any use of the photographs taken of me on ______________ at
(date)

______________.
(location)

I do/do not waive the right to inspect the finished photograph.

____
(signature)

____
(address)

____
(date)

figure 2-1

SLANDER misrepresentation of their name, personality, or behavior. So don't depict your worst enemy with an unnatural or obscene deformity. When the defamatory statement is oral, it is called *slander;* when it

LIBEL is written it is called *libel.*

The defamatory material can be a drawing, photograph, et cetera, as well as the printed or spoken word. A business organization can be defamed as well as an individual. California's libel law, enacted in 1872, looks like this:

> Libel, what. Libel is a false and unprivileged publication by writing, printing, picture, effigy, or other fixed representation to the eye, which exposes any person to hatred, contempt, ridicule, or obloquy, or which causes him to be shunned or avoided, or which has a tendency to injure him in his occupation.

The person making a defamatory statement is liable to the defamed person. So is anyone else who participates in its distribution—publisher, newspaper editor, gallery owner.

In order to win a defamation suit, the defamed person must prove that the defamatory statement was *communicated* to others; that the statement clearly *identified* the plaintiff (the person bringing the suit); that the plaintiff suffered *injury* because of the statement; and most important, that the maker of the statement was somehow at *fault* with regard to the statement. Because each state has its own definition of defamation, these requirements will vary.

COMMUNICATION · IDENTIFICATION · INJURY

A notorious falsehood whispered to a friendly tree would not be defamation, nor would a statement calling the mystery man a thief and a philanderer. You can defame a person without using his or her name—"All the kids from Juniper Grove are swindlers." The requirement of showing *injury* is slightly complicated by the fact that if the defamer *knew* that the statement was false or at least entertained serious doubts as to its truth, then no actual injury has to be shown in order to win a defamation case.

FAULT · PUBLIC FIGURES

It is the requirement of proving fault in a defamation suit that has made headlines for the last few years. In order to strengthen the constitutional right of free speech, the Supreme Court has adopted two standards of fault—one which applies to public officials and figures and another which governs private persons. A public figure must prove that the defaming statement was made either with knowledge of its falsity or with reckless disregard for the truth. Barry Goldwater recovered $50,000 from *Fact* magazine and $25,000 from its editor, who ran a story portraying Goldwater as a latent homosexual, a "cruel" practical joker, a paranoid, and so on. But a deputy sheriff who had been falsely accused of bribery, lost his defamation suit for lack of proof that the defamer acted with reckless disregard for the truth.

PRIVATE PERSONS

Private persons only have to show that the defamer acted negligently in failing to check the truthfulness of the statement. So a lawyer accused of framing a Chicago policeman and of being a "communist fronter" by the John Birch Society magazine won his libel case. Because he was not a public figure, he only had to prove that the magazine was negligent in not checking out the statements made about him. Mrs. Firestone, a Palm Beach socialite, also recovered a $100,000 libel judgment from Time, Inc., for defamatory remarks concerning her divorce. The Supreme Court refused to throw out the judgment saying that Mrs. Firestone's divorce case was not of sufficient *legitimate* public interest to apply the test for public figures.

TRUTH IS A DEFENSE · RETRACTION

Usually truth is a defense to a lawsuit for libel. However, the truth is sometimes hard to prove, especially in controversial areas in which libel suits usually occur. Retraction of the libelous statement is not a defense to libel but can serve to reduce the amount of damages recovered.

Fiction writers are not immune from libel actions. As fact becomes stranger than fiction, and fiction writers become "faction" (fact plus fiction equals faction) writers, this area raises a whole list of new questions concerning libel which have not yet been considered by the courts.

To avoid lawsuits for defamation, follow these rules. Research factual material very carefully. Any potentially defamatory statements should be confirmed and verified and the notes of this research retained. In fiction, carefully disguise beyond recognition any real-life persons that are used as a model for a character. Obtain a release if possible.

RESTRICTIONS ON MATERIALS

INTRODUCTION

To discuss every material that is somehow regulated by state or federal law and that an artist or craftmaker might use in his or her work would take more pages than this book has room for. So this section concerning the legal restrictions on materials will cover only the major federal laws governing materials ordinarily used by artists and craftmakers and the rules of product liability and negligence. Because health hazards to artists and craftmakers arising from materials used in their work are beyond the scope of this work, we do not discuss this important area. For more information, contact Art Hazards Project, Center for Occupational Hazards, Inc., 5 Beekman, New York, NY 10038.

STATE LAWS

Because there is so much variation in the state laws in the area and because the major areas are covered by the federal laws, state laws concerning the use of certain materials are not discussed here. Those craftmakers selling stuffed things—quilts, pillows, and so forth—should get information on their state's "bedding laws"—the law that requires those threatening tags that are attached to most pillows and comforters indicating the fiber content of the filling. Your state consumer protection office should be able to give you information on your state's law. A special state license may also be required under these laws. Figure 2-2 has a sample of a bedding law label.

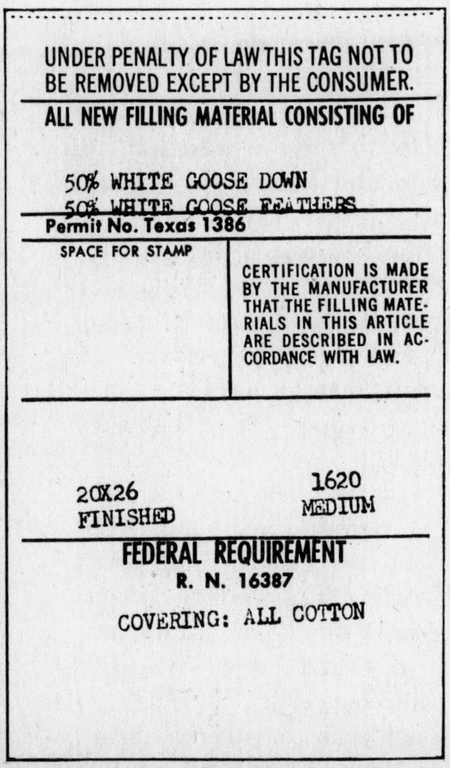
UNDER PENALTY OF LAW THIS TAG NOT TO BE REMOVED EXCEPT BY THE CONSUMER.

ALL NEW FILLING MATERIAL CONSISTING OF

50% WHITE GOOSE DOWN

50% WHITE GOOSE FEATHERS

Permit No. Texas 1386

SPACE FOR STAMP

CERTIFICATION IS MADE BY THE MANUFACTURER THAT THE FILLING MATERIALS IN THIS ARTICLE ARE DESCRIBED IN ACCORDANCE WITH LAW.

20X26 FINISHED

1620 MEDIUM

FEDERAL REQUIREMENT

R. N. 16387

COVERING: ALL COTTON

figure 2-2 State bedding law tag

In this section there will be many references to the laws covering sales of products that have crossed state lines. This is because under the commerce clause of the Constitution, the federal government is allowed to regulate commerce between states (interstate commerce) but not commerce within a state. As the power of the federal government grows, the necessary contact with another state may be very slim. Ollie's Barbecue, a family-owned restaurant in Birmingham, Alabama, discovered this when the Supreme Court ruled that the federal anti-discrimination-in-public-accommodations laws applied to their restaurant, through the commerce clause.

NEGLIGENCE AND PRODUCT LIABILITY

Alice's Allegory # 6

or

The Mexican Connection

Alice and Romero spiffed up Viola the VW, bought some Mexican auto insurance, and headed off for a few lost weeks on the coast of Mexico. The pineapples and the papayas were delicious and the sun was warm and wonderful.

Alice, in her new tan, was checking out the *mercado* in town when she came across clay glazes for sale. Since Romero was the Spanish-speaker of the group, Alice dragged him away from his third fruit-juice treat of the day to negotiate the sale of the glazes.

No way could Romero remember the word for *lead* in Spanish. So Alice bought a small jar full of glaze to bring home and have tested before she purchased enough glaze to do a whole line entitled Lost Mexico Reverie.

Although there is no law on the books which says "No one shall sell ceramics with poisonous glazes for home use," a potter could be successfully sued for selling a clay platter with a glaze which caused the purchaser to become ill, after eating food served on it. There are a growing number of consumer suits for defective products or service and they can be brought against artists and craftmakers, just as against doctors, car manufacturers, and airlines. Recently, a potter was engaged in a very long lawsuit brought by a customer when his flameware skillet exploded. You could be liable if your macrame plant hanger collapses into the mouth of a silly customer who hung it full of a passionflower vine over his bed. Who wants a plaster wall hanging to come crashing down on top of a good patron's prize Lhasa Apso? Especially hazardous areas where great care must be taken to protect the consumer from injury are neon and kinetic sculptures and children's items. But all craftmakers and artists should be concerned about injuries to their customers arising from the sale of a defective product.

YOU COULD BE LIABLE

WHY CONSUMER VICTORY?

The legal doctrine of product liability tips the scales in favor of consumer victory. It is the theory of many that this concern for consumer injury grows from a mass-production economy which unavoidably produces defective products, and that manufacturers and retailers are better equipped to bear the loss caused by defective products than injured Charlie Consumer.

RULE OF PRODUCT LIABILITY

The legal rule amounts to: defective product plus injury arising from customary or foreseen use equals maker or seller pays. It is no defense that the customer should have known to cover the transformer box to your Flash Jordan neon sculpture—you are liable for the frizzled ball of fur that used to be a kitten.

AN OUNCE OF PREVENTION

Several steps can be taken to guard against customer injury and consequent liability of the seller. First, exercise some quality control—make sure you are not selling items with defects that could harm a customer, such as chipped goblet rims, fragile-handled mugs, and so on. Second, "idiot-proof" your work—figure out all the possible mishaps that could be caused by your work and guard against them by changing the design, perhaps adding a guard rail, a heavier gauge hook, et cetera. If you cannot design away the potential harm, then warn the public of this harm. Include instructions on use of your work to avoid the possible harm. Also, write the name and

WARNINGS

address of each customer on your carbon copy of the sales receipt, so you have that information in the event of a recall. The Ford Pinto is not the only item recalled these days. Take any consumer complaint quite seriously and do not delay in beginning settlement negotiations, if called for. Finally, look into the possibility of purchasing product liability insurance coverage for your business, if it is available.

FIBERS, FUR, AND TEXTILES

If you are selling fiber or fur products like wool hangings, tie-dyed scarves, handwoven pillows, batik shirts, quilts, fur jackets, wool hats, and so on, the federal laws governing the labeling of textiles concern you. Although individual artists and craftmakers seldom are prosecuted for violation of these laws, some of your works could well be covered by the labeling requirements contained in these laws.

At first reading, these labeling requirements look like a lot of trouble. But federal requirements aside, many in the fiber field routinely do inform their customers concerning the fiber content as an integral part of the creation and sale of handmade fiberwork. In addition to notifying your customers of exactly what they are getting, the fiber-content information also helps with the care of the textile.

The major federal laws and regulations in the textile area are the Wool Products Labeling Act of 1939, the Fur Products Labeling Act, the Textile Fiber Products Identification Act, the Flammable Fabrics Act, and the Care Labeling of Textile Wearing Apparel. There is also a Trade Practice Rule on shrinkage of woven cotton yard goods. These laws pretty much cover most people who sell textile, wool, and fur creations and require that these products be labeled with certain information. This section will amplify who and what is covered by these laws and the labeling requirements for each law.

WOOL PRODUCTS LABELING ACT OF 1939

The Wool Products Labeling Act (WPLA) of 1939 was the first of the textile labeling acts passed and covers any wool product sold in the United States, except wool rugs and upholstery fabric. Wool rugs are covered by the Textile Fiber Product Identification Act. The purpose of the law is to protect the unsuspecting consumer and processor from buying wool goods that are supplemented with undisclosed nonwool fibers or used wool.

COVERAGE

If you are selling wool products, you probably are covered by the requirements of WPLA of 1939. Technically the wool product must cross a state line in the course of its sale or distribution for the federal law to apply. If you sell a shawl woven from the wool of your own sheep to a well-known gallery that sells it to a tourist from out of state, the WPLA would apply and you are required to label it.

LABELING REQUIREMENTS

A label for a handwoven wool jacket might look like this (William places his copyright notice on the same label).

The law requires the name of the maker or seller, the percentages of new wool, "reprocessed" wool (wool which was made into a product and then respun or woven into new fibers), and "reused" wool (wool which was respun or woven after use by the consumer). The law also requires that any other fibers that constitute 5 percent or more of the fibers present in the product be disclosed on the label. Nonwool fibers present in individual portions of less than 5 percent must be disclosed together as "other fibers."

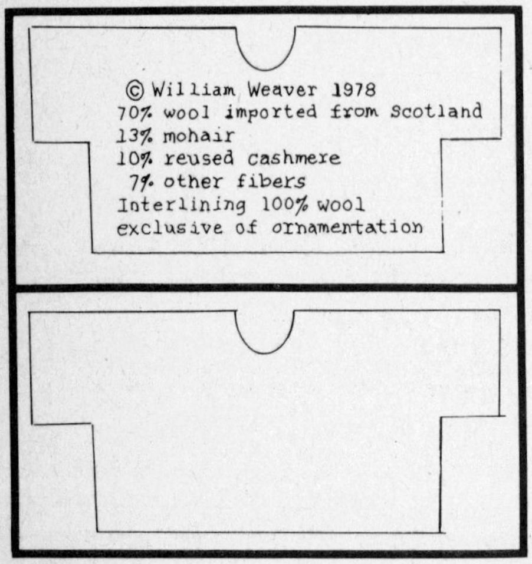

There is no need to disclose the fiber content of any ornamentation, if it is 5 percent or less of the entire product, provided you state on the label that the fiber content information is "exclusive of ornamentation."

Disclose the fiber content of lining, padding, stiffening, trimming, and facing that:

- contains wool
- is included for warmth
- is customarily disclosed
- or if wool product is *not* wearing apparel

ORNAMENTATION

Interlinings *must* be labeled separately, as William Weaver did on his handwoven-jacket label. A quiltmaker using miscellaneous wool and other cloth scraps can state: "Made of miscellaneous cloth scraps, composed chiefly of cotton, minimum of 40 percent reused wool," on the quilt label. The percentage of any nonfibrous filling material must also be disclosed.

RECORDS REQUIRED

The WPLA of 1939 requires that records substantiating the information on the label be kept for at least three years. These records must show the date and item(s) involved in any purchase or sale, the fiber contents of the item sold, and the source of the raw materials in the sold item, including source, quantity, fiber content, and the date of purchase of these materials.

A simple way to do this is to use the job work cards reproduced and discussed in Chapter 5, "Federal Income Tax." This card should show among other things the percentage by weight of each fiber contained in each piece of work and the date of sale, if any. Additionally, a fiber card with a snip of the fiber, fiber name, description, source, and receipt date (or attached receipt) would give you a cross-reference between raw materials used and final products sold.

SELLER'S GUARANTEE

If you are concerned that the label of some wool you are buying is incorrect, you should get the seller to write on your invoice, "We guarantee that the wool indicated on this receipt is not misbranded under the Wool Products Labeling Act." This guarantee would protect you if it later turned out that the wool was indeed misbranded.

Since the law is geared for large commercial manufacturers of wool items, their labels usually comply with the law. So if you have any questions about how to label a piece, check your local department store for labels on similar products.

FUR PRODUCTS LABELING ACT

Unlike the Wool Products Labeling Act of 1939, the Fur Products Labeling Act (FPLA) requires disclosures on invoices and advertising as well as on a label attached to most fur wearing apparel sold in this country. The exceptions to coverage by the FPLA are even more complicated than those of the WPLA of 1939, so it would seem simplest to label all wearing apparel containing fur.

The following information must appear on the fur product label and on any invoice or advertising:

LABELING REQUIREMENTS

- name of animal that produced the fur
- name of maker
- if the fur is used using the words "second-hand used fur"
- if the fur is colored or bleached in any way
- if the product contains waste furs (ears and throat) or paws, tail, or belly fur
- if imported, the country of origin
- number assigned to each item*

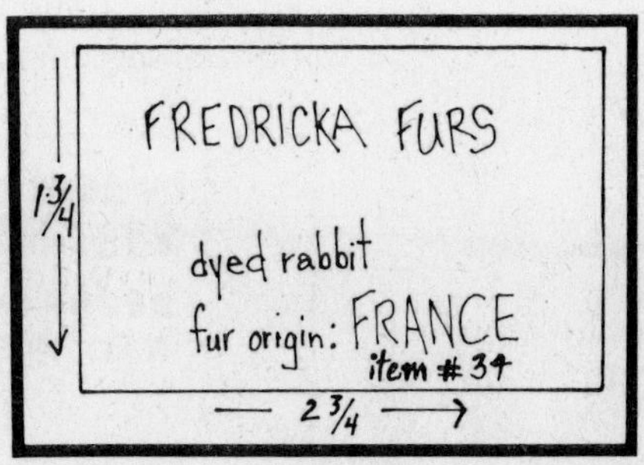

The label is required to be no smaller than Fredricka's label (1¾ by 2¾ inches) and can contain hand printing but no handwriting. The print on the label must be at least twelve-point type—the size of pica typewriter type.

RECORDS REQUIRED

As with the WPLA of 1939, the Fur Products Labeling Act has extensive record-keeping requirements, which include retaining any documents regarding the purchase or sale of the furs. Essentially you must maintain all records necessary to prove the information disclosed on the label for three years and also keep the purchase and sale documents and the number you are required to give each finished fur piece. See the above discussion on record keeping for the Wool Products Labeling Act for more information. You also have to keep a record showing that any processing (bleaching, dyeing, pointing, etc.) of the fur was done according to the regulations concerning the processing of furs. Appendix 2-1 reproduces the processing rule.

* Not required to appear on invoice or advertising.

Read it very slowly and at least ten times and it will become comprehensible.

Also, if you purchase a mislabeled fur for your next fur jacket creation and pass along the misinformation concerning the fur to your customer, you are responsible under the FPLA for the mislabeling unless you get a guarantee from the seller of the fur stating: "We guarantee that the fur products listed on this receipt are not misbranded under the provisions of the Fur Products Labeling Act."*

SELLER'S GUARANTEE

TEXTILE FIBER PRODUCTS IDENTIFICATION ACT

COVERAGE

The Textile Fiber Products Identification Act (otherwise known as TFPIA) generally applies to those folks who are selling or advertising household creations made of nonwool fibers, but also includes wool rugs.** The textile products covered by this labeling law include clothes, bedding, pillows, curtains, quilts, tablecloths and napkins, rugs, towels—generally articles normally used at home. Wall hangings, hats, handbags, and luggage are not covered.

LABELING REQUIREMENTS

This law requires first that the label contain the name of the maker or processor of a textile. William Weaver is fine for the label on his handwoven bedspread. The labels must state the names of each fiber contained in the work in a quantity of 5 percent or more and the percentage of each such fiber.***

bedspread
bedspread
bedspread
handwoven by William Weaver
50% Linen
22% Cotton
10% Thai Silk
8% Other Fibers
(Exclusive of Decoration)

"Other fibers" is used to designate other fibers present in the material in individual quantities of less than 5 percent. William Weaver used 4 percent acrylic and 4 percent acetate in his bedspread and disclosed these fibers under "8 percent other fibers." You need not disclose the fiber content of decorative trim if you state on your label "exclusive of decoration" and the trim does not exceed 15 percent of the product's fiber content. Those selling quilts and anyone else selling warmies with interlinings, fillings, or padding included for warmth should label these separately. The stuffing contents may

QUEEN'S QUILTS
100% COTTON
FILLING 100% COTTON

* Not required to appear on invoice or advertising.

** Handwoven Navajo rugs which are labeled with a certificate of genuineness of the Indian Arts and Crafts Board of the U.S. Department of Interior are exempt from the disclosure requirements of the Act.

*** Commissioned handwoven drapery or upholstery fabrics do not need to have the percentages of each fiber stated if the order is under 100 yards.

require a label under the state bedding law or the federal down product guide. The TFPIA requires that *reused* stuffing be labeled.

RECORDS

Under the TFPIA, records must be kept concerning the fiber content of a textile product for at least three years from the date of manufacture. For information on the specific content of the required records see the discussion of record keeping under the Wool Products Labeling Act earlier in the chapter. If you substitute your own tag for the one on the shirt you bought to tie-dye, then you need to keep the information concerning the old tag and where you purchased the shirt as well as all the other required information.

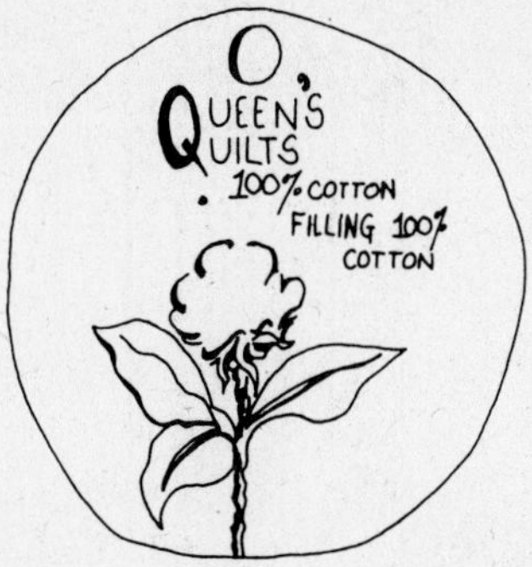

PENALTIES

Enforcement of the Wool Products Labeling Act, the Fur Products Labeling Act, and the Textile Fiber Products Identification Act is in the hands of the Federal Trade Commission, which can seize the mislabeled or unlabeled wool, fur, and textile products, obtain cease and desist orders, and finally prosecute offenders for willful violation of the law. Free pamphlets on these labeling acts are available from the FTC, Washington, D.C. 20580.

FLAMMABLE FABRICS ACT

The Flammable Fabrics Act basically prohibits the sale across a state line, or the in-state sale of materials obtained from out of state, of any product which fails to conform to the federal flammability standards. The law applies to clothing, children's sleepwear, fiber rugs, mattresses, and mattress pads.

FLAMMABILITY STANDARDS

The concern of the legislators who passed this law was for special fabrics that were highly flammable, like synthetic fabrics that melt when heated, cotton and rayon which burn faster than wool, and fuzzy fabrics that go up in a flash. The standard for clothing prohibits the interstate sale of any highly flammable wearing apparel. The standard for the remaining items covered by the law—children's sleepwear, fiber rugs, mattresses, and mattress pads—is higher. These products must be "flame retardant," which usually requires either using a natural fiber that does not burn readily or chemically treating the fabric. For more information on the individual standards set forth by the Flammable Fabrics Act, see Figure 2-3.*

The U.S. Consumer Product Safety Commission in Washington, D.C., oversees the enforcement of the law and will provide interested parties with additional information concerning the Flammable Fabrics Act. At the time of this writing, the Consumer Product Safety Commission has a toll-free number: 800/638-8326 (800/492-8363 for Maryland) for information requests and reports of hazardous products. The penalties for willful violation of the Flammable Fabrics Act are a maximum fine of $5,000 and/or a prison term of one year or

* Many large retailers will require a guarantee concerning the fabrics covered by the Act. This guarantee certifies that the fabric has been tested and conforms to the standards of the Act. Textile laboratories routinely provide these testing services.

Federal Flammability Standards

textile clothing:
requires that a piece of "oven dried" fabric, which is placed in a holder at a 45° angle and is exposed to a flame for one second, not ignite and spread flame up the length of the fabric in less than 3.5 seconds for smooth fabrics or 4.0 seconds for napped.

vinyl plastic:
requires that sample when placed in a holder at a 45°angle, not burn at a rate exceeding 1.2 inches per second.

rugs & carpets:*
requires that a sample exposed to a matchlike agent dropped on the carpet not char more than 3 inches in any direction.

children's sleepwear:
requires that when five samples are suspended vertically in a cabinet and exposed to a small gas flame along its bottom edge for 3 seconds that the average char length be no more than 7 inches; that no single sample can have a char length of more than 10 inches and no single sample can have flaming material on the bottom of the cabinet 10 seconds after the ignition source is removed.

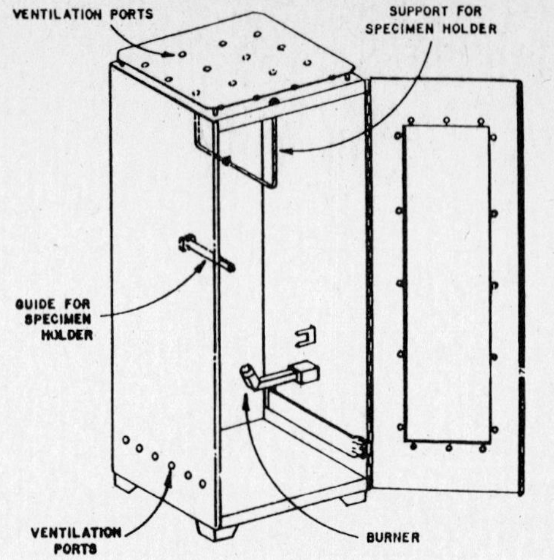

VERTICAL TEST CABINET FOR CHILDREN'S SLEEPWEAR

* Small rugs (no greater than six feet on a side and a square footage of 24 feet or less) do not have to meet the flammability standard if labeled with: **Flammable (Fails US Department of Commerce Standard FF −2−70): Should Not be Used Near Sources of Ignition.**

figure 2-3 Federal flammability standards

less. Before criminal prosecution is commenced, the CPSC will seek a cease and desist order for violations of the Act.

CARE LABELING OF TEXTILE WEARING APPAREL

Anyone selling items of clothing or piece goods should check into the Care Labeling of Textile Wearing Apparel regulations. This rule governs anyone selling items of clothing across state lines and simply requires that information about the care and maintenance of the article of clothing be "permanently affixed" to the garment. For sample labels, see Figure 2-4.

FEATHERS, BONES, AND CLAWS: RESTRICTIONS ON THE TAKING AND USE OF PROTECTED WILDLIFE AND PLANTS

If feathers and bones are in your line of business, this section is for you. Both state and federal laws affect this area. As discussed earlier in this chapter, the federal laws cover goods that travel in *interstate* commerce. Wildlife that migrate across state lines are also covered by federal laws. State laws (which sometimes include more species than the federal laws) govern transactions regarding nonmigratory species that occur within the state. Your state fish and game office should have available information on the state laws and regulations in this area.

The federal laws that restrict the sale or possession of items containing parts of protected wildlife and plants can be divided into two groups. The first totally prohibits the killing, use, or sale of items containing parts of the protected species (the Migratory Bird Treaty Act and the Bald and Golden Eagle Protection Act). The second group of laws prohibits the killing, use, or sale of items containing parts of the protected species unless obtained according to specific regulations issued pursuant to these laws (the Endangered Species Act and the Marine Mammal Protection Act).*

This area is presently full of controversy. Only the facts concerning the requirements of the current laws are presented here. We take no position on the questions of whether the government should regulate this area or whether the current laws are enlightened or properly and fairly enforced.

MIGRATORY BIRD TREATY ACT

The most stringent of the wildlife protection laws are the Migratory Bird Treaty Act and the Bald and Golden Eagle Protection Act. These laws essentially prohibit *any* taking or sale of *any* part of *any* bird protected by the two laws.** It does not matter if you found the eagle feather beside the powwow grounds or that the red-tailed hawk's claws came from a bird that had been electrocuted by the power lines behind your house, or that the feather fan had been in the family for at least twenty years. You *cannot sell* protected feathers, period! These two laws simply outlaw *any* sale of any feather or other part of a protected bird by *any* person.

BALD AND GOLDEN EAGLES PROTECTION ACT

However, Native Americans can possess and exchange protected feathers if the feathers are used in religious and cultural activities. Feathers for these religious objects can be obtained by Native Americans from wild migratory game birds which are legally taken during open season and additionally from the U.S. Fish and Wildlife's eagle depository in Pocatello, Idaho.

CEREMONIAL USE OF FEATHERS BY NATIVE AMERICANS

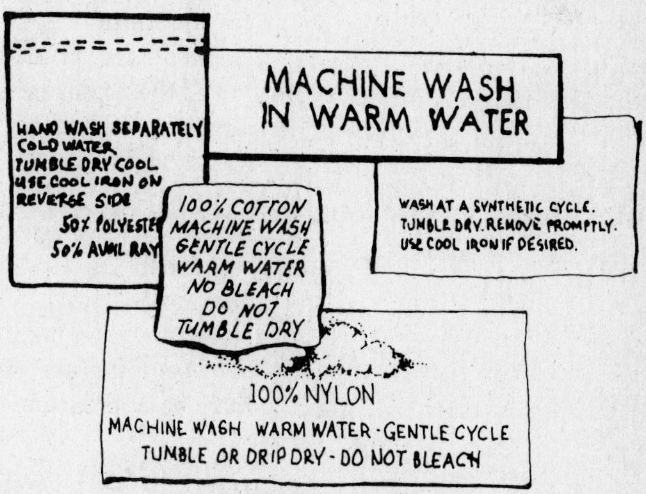

figure 2-4 Care labels

* Endangered and threatened plants can be taken but not sold or transported in interstate commerce. Don't forget to check the state law regarding protected plants.

** Taking of these birds is allowed by special permit obtained for scientific, educational, or public purposes.

BIRDS NOT PROTECTED

The law does not cover feral pigeons, starlings, English sparrows, domestic fowl: chickens, turkeys, ducks, geese, and guinea fowl; and resident game birds: pheasant, grouse, quail, and wild turkeys. However, most states do have laws concerning their resident birds and these laws should be checked. Migratory game birds—ducks, geese, et cetera—are covered by the law but can be legally hunted pursuant to local regulation and their parts sold, but only for use in down products and fishing flies.

PENALTY

The penalties for violation of these laws are a maximum fine of $2,000 and/or maximum time of two years for violation of the Migratory Bird Treaty Act and $5,000 maximum fine and/or one year of prison time for violation of the Bald and Golden Eagles Protection Act. A current list of the protected birds can be obtained from the U.S. Department of the Interior's Fish and Wildlife Service.

ENDANGERED SPECIES ACT AND MARINE MAMMAL PROTECTION ACT

The Endangered Species Act and the Marine Mammal Protection Act essentially prohibit the interstate sale, or transport of any items made of protected animal parts which were not obtained according to the regulations as well as any selling of the protected wildlife which is not according to the law. The complete list of protected wildlife and plants can be obtained from the U.S. Department of Interior's Fish and Wildlife Office. It is illegal to sell a wallet made from an alligator skin not taken according to the very long rules concerning the killing of the American alligator. Further, according to the recent ruling of the U.S. Supreme Court, it is illegal to construct a dam which will wipe out a protected snail-darter fish population. A wall hanging using the skull of a gray wolf (a protected species) would be illegal to sell. The zoology department of the local college or university may be helpful in identifying any parts of unknown wildlife that may be on the endangered species list. Alaskan Native Americans are exempt from the coverage of these two laws, providing that their taking of the protected species is for subsistence reasons.

The teeth, bones, and ivory of the protected marine mammal (polar bear, manatee, dugong, walrus, and sea otter) can be collected for personal use if the proper authorities are contacted and can even be sold if the agent contacted gives her or his approval.

PENALTY

Under the 1978 amendments to the Endangered Species Act, antique articles made of parts of protected species (except scrimshaw) are exempted from coverage by the Act *if* made before 1830. The penalties for violation of these laws are a maximum fine of $20,000 and/or one year in jail.

GOLD, SILVER, TOYS, CHILDREN'S FURNITURE, CURRENCY, STAMPS, ET CETERA

There is no requirement that Raymondo the Jeweler stamp his jewelry with a karat or sterling stamp. But if he decides to stamp his jewelry with information concerning the content of gold or silver, then he must follow the rules of the Falsely Stamped Gold and Silver Act.

STERLING SILVER

COIN SILVER

ALLOWABLE VARIATION

Essentially, this law prohibits the sale in interstate commerce* of any silver or gold item which is marked as containing a higher grade of silver or gold than the item actually contains. The law then defines "sterling" as silver which contains at least 925 parts per thousand of pure silver and "coin" as silver which contains at least 900 parts per thousand. The item can legally deviate from this standard by not more than 4 parts per thousand when considering the piece without the solder and 10 parts per thousand when considering the piece with the solder.

GOLD

ALLOWABLE VARIATION

For a gold piece, the allowable deviation from the number of karats stamped on the piece is one-half of a karat excluding the solder and one karat when considering the solder. Gold flatware and watch cases can only deviate 3 parts per thousand not including solder. The allowable variation in gold objects will change on October 1, 1981, when the variation allowed is 3 parts per thousand without solder and 7 parts per thousand with solder included. The standard for flatwear and watch cases remains the same.

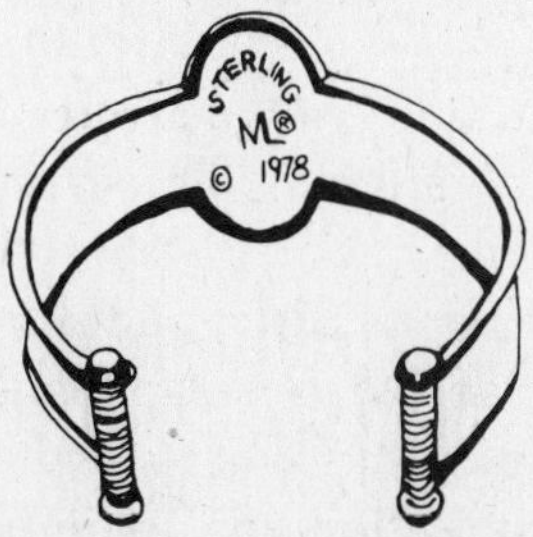

Another rule that Raymondo must consider when deciding whether to stamp his jewelry is the requirement that any item stamped with a karat, sterling, or coin stamp must also be stamped with a trademark registered with the federal trademark office.**

GOLD AND SILVER PLATE

PENALTY

Gold- and silver-plated items, if stamped at all, must clearly indicate the item as "plate." Further, the words *sterling* and *coin* cannot be used on plated items. The penalty for a violation of the Falsely Stamped Gold and Silver Act is a maximum of three months in jail and/or $5,000.

CONSUMER PRODUCT SAFETY COMMISSION

The Consumer Product Safety Commission has as its primary goal the reduction of injuries associated with consumer products. The Commission is attentive to consumer problems and at the date of this writing is available by telephone at 800/638-8326 (free) except for Maryland residents who must call 800/492-8363 (also toll free). CPSC oversees the administration of five laws:

- Consumer Product Safety Act
- Federal Hazardous Substances Act
- Flammable Fabrics Act
- Poison Prevention Packaging Act of 1976
- Refrigerator Safety Act

Besides the Flammable Fabrics Act, which was discussed earlier in the section on fibers, fur, and textiles, of most concern to the craftmaker and artist are the first two laws.

* See the discussion of the requirement of interstate commerce in the introductory paragraphs to this section on the Restrictions on Materials.

** See the discussion of obtaining a trademark in Chapter 3, "Copying."

CONSUMER PRODUCT SAFETY ACT

The Consumer Product Safety Act prohibits the marketing of a product which creates a substantial risk of injury to the public or which violates one of the Commission's standards. The Act operates on the basis of consumer complaints as well as self-policing and reporting by the sellers, who usually agree to repair, replace, or refund the money paid for the defective product.

FEDERAL HAZARDOUS SUBSTANCES ACT

Another law implemented by the Consumer Product Safety Commission is the Federal Hazardous Substances Act. This law deals with any consumer product which is toxic, flammable, corrosive, irritating, pressurized, et cetera. Under the authority of this law, the CPSC has issued regulations governing many areas including children's rattles, electric toys, cribs, high chairs, walkers, nursery furniture, playground equipment, bunk beds, electrical equipment, lead paints, and so forth. If you are working in any of these areas, call the Consumer Product Safety Commission and request that they send you the fact sheet on the product that you are interested in.

LABEL FOR PROTECTION

According to a staff member of the CPSC, 95 percent of the injuries that occur in this area could be avoided by proper education and labeling. Simple use instructions like "COOL IT before plunging in water" or "WARNING: Keep away from children and other small people" will save you from problems and legal entanglements and your customer from unnecessary injury.

REPRODUCTION OF U.S. STAMPS, COINS, OR CURRENCY

There is no longer an absolute prohibition on the reproduction of U.S. postage stamps, coins, or currency. Reproductions of these items can be printed in black and white (except for postage stamps, which can appear in color) if the copy is less than three-fourths of the actual size of the stamp, coin, or currency. The reproductions cannot be used for advertising purposes, and the plates for the prints must be destroyed after use. Finally, the law allowing the limited reproduction of these items requires that the reprints appear in a bound publication, not in individual prints.

FEDERAL TRADE COMMISSION TRADE PRACTICE RULES

The Federal Trade Commission has issued federal trade practice rules governing a number of businesses, some of which are in the craft area. These rules generally prohibit fraudulent and unfair business practices. Others set specific standards, such as the rules on shrinkage of woven cotton yard goods. The list below shows the Federal Trade Commission Practice Rules which pertain to crafts and are available from the Federal Trade Commission, Washington, D.C. 20580.

LIST OF FEDERAL TRADE COMMISSION TRADE-PRACTICE RULES THAT REGULATE CERTAIN ARTS AND CRAFTS BUSINESSES

- Jewelry
- Shrinkage of Woven Cotton Yard Goods
- Millinery
- Feather and Down
- Upholstery and Drapery Fabric
- Branding of Content of Leather Belts
- Ladies' Handbags
- Mirror
- Portrait, Photographic
- Household Furniture

SOURCES:

pg. 29 Current Supreme Court definition of obscenity: *Miller v. California*, 413 U.S. 15 (1973), Rehearing denied, 414 U.S. 881 (1973).

pg. 30 Anti–Vietnam flag sculptures O.K.: *United States ex rel. Radich v. Criminal Court of the City of New York*, 385 F. Supp. 165 (1974). Convictions for commercial use of flags upheld: *Halter v. Nebraska*, 205 U.S. 34 (1907).

pg. 32 *New York* magazine did not invade privacy: *Murry v. New York Magazine Company*, 27 N.Y.2d 406, 267 NE 2d 256, 318 N.Y.S.2d 474 (1971).

pg. 33 California libel law: California Civil Code, Section 45.

pg. 34 *Goldwater v. Ginsburg*, 261 F. Supp. 784 (S.D.N.Y. 1966, aff'd 414 F. 2d 324 2d Cir. 1969), cert. denied. 396 U.S. 1049 (1970), rehearing denied. 397 U.S. 978 (1970).

pg. 34 Deputy sheriff accused of bribery: *St. Amant v. Thompson*, 390 U.S. 727 (1968).

pg. 34 Lawyer versus John Birch Society: *Gertz v. Robert Welch, Inc.*, 418 U.S. 323 (1974).

pg. 34 *Firestone v. Time, Inc.*, 424 U.S. 448 (1976).

pg. 37 Wool Products Labeling Act of 1939: Title 15, U.S. Code Annotated, Sections 68–68j. The regulations issued pursuant to that law are in Title 16, Code of Federal Regulations, Sections 300.1–300.35.

pg. 39 Fur Products Labeling Act: Titlc 15, U.S. Code Annotated, Sections 69–69j. The regulations issued pursuant to that law are in Title 16, Code of Federal Regulations, Sections 301–301.49.

pg. 39 Regulations concerning pointing, dyeing, bleaching, and otherwise artificially coloring fur: Title 16, Code of Federal Regulations, Section 301.19.

pg. 40 Textile Fiber Product Identification Act: Title 15, U.S. Code Annotated, Sections 70–70k. The regulations issued pursuant to that law are in Title 16, Code of Federal Regulations, Sections 303.1–303.45.

pg. 41 Flammable Fabrics Act: Title 15, U.S. Code Annotated, Sections 1191–1204. The regulations issued pursuant to that law are in Title 16, Code of Federal Regulations, Sections 1602–1632.

pg. 42 Care Labeling of Textile Wearing Apparel: Title 16, U.S. Code of Federal Regulations, Sections 423.1–423.2.

pg. 43 Migratory Bird Treaty Act: Title 16, U.S. Code Annotated, Sections 703–711. The regulations issued pursuant to the law are in Title 50, Code of Federal Regulations, Sections 20.1–21.46.

pg. 43 Bald and Golden Eagles Act: Title 16, U.S. Code Annotated, Sections 668–668d. The regulations issued pursuant to the law are in Title 50, Code of Federal Regulations, Sections 22.1–22.32.

pg. 44 Endangered Species Act: Title 16, U.S. Code Annotated, Sections 1531–1543. The regulations issued pursuant to that law are in Title 50, Code of Federal Regulations, Sections 10.1–10.22 and 17.1–17.23.

pg. 44 Marine Mammal Protection Act: Title 16, U.S. Code Annotated, Sections 1361–1407. The regulations issued pursuant to that law are in Title 50, Code of Federal Regulations, Sections 10.1–10.22 and 18.1–18.33.

pg. 45 Falsely Stamped Gold and Silver Act: Title 15, U.S. Code Annotated, Sections 291–300.

pg. 45 Consumer Product Safety Act: Title 15, U.S. Code Annotated, Sections 2051–2081.

pg. 46 Federal Hazardous Substances Act: Title 15, U.S. Code Annotated, Sections 1261–1274.

pg. 46 Reproduction of U.S. postage stamps, coins, or currency: Title 18, U.S. Code Annotated, Section 504.

Chapter 3
Copying

BACKGROUND

This chapter discusses copyright, patents, design patents, trademarks, trade secrets, unfair competition, fakes, and forgeries. How to protect your work from copying and how to control the use of your work are the big subjects presented here.

DEFINITIONS

Definitions of these subjects give you an overview of what is ahead.

A *patent* protects inventions, and sometimes designs, as well as hybrid plant varieties. It is granted by the government. *Design patents* are granted for shorter periods of time, for original ornamental designs for articles of manufacture, such as jewelry, furniture, fabrics, vehicles, and industrial equipment.

A *trademark* is a protected symbol or mark used to identify and distinguish goods.

Copyright provides protection and a remedy if others copy your original work—literary, artistic, musical, et cetera.

A *trade secret* is any formula, pattern, device, or compilation of information which is used in one's business and is kept secret, giving you an advantage over your competitors.

Unfair competition covers fraudulent conduct, such as palming off or sale of goods as those of another.

A *fake* or *forgery* is a misrepresentation—a work that purports to be something other than what it is.

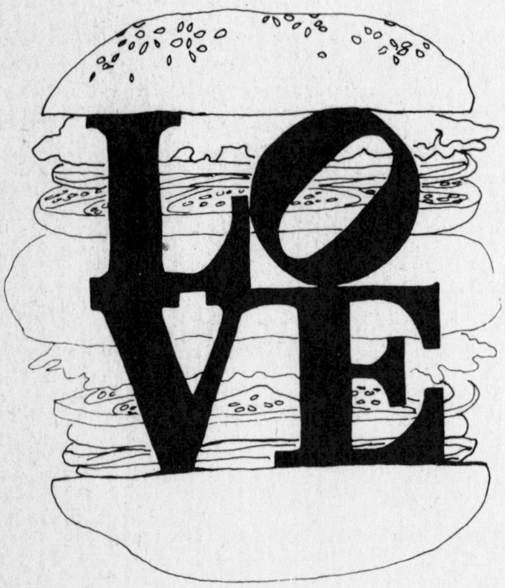

LOVEburger

COPYRIGHT

"MAY WE INTRODUCE COPYRIGHT"

Though this protection is inexpensive and easy to obtain, copyright has not been used extensively by artists and craftmakers. Now more and more artists and craftmakers are using the copyright notice on their work to retain control over their work as well as to retain a future financial interest in it. The lack of control and loss of potential profits for uncopyrighted works is illustrated by the commercial use of Robert Indiana's uncopyrighted serigraph *Love*. His design was freely used by others in jewelry, cards, posters, stamps, a box cover, and other commercial products. The *Love* design is reproduced without Mr. Indiana's permission because the design lacked a copyright notice and accordingly passed into the public domain for anyone to use freely.

The message for you is to copyright and not to copy wrong, to watch agreements and sales receipts so you do not give away copyrights unless you intend to, and to remember that even a copyrighted work can be used in certain situations without permission.

Register of Copyrights
Copyright Office
Library of Congress
Washington, D.C. 20559

Please send me the following information:

- a copy of the Copyright Revision Act of 1976.
- All current circulars
- Announcement of regulations
- regulations
- annual reports
- one each of necessary registration forms.

I would like to be put on the mailing list for future releases in the above areas. Thank you.

Sincerely,
Alice
P.O. Box 733
Albuq., N.M. 87104

figure 3-1 Sample request letter for copyright information

LIMITATIONS TO THIS CHAPTER

The first part of the chapter explains general copyright practice but does not deal with all the nuances, ambiguities, and vagaries of copyright law in each particular situation. If you are a writer, read this and read Chapter 7, "Especially for Writers." You will have to be patient as you read this chapter, for it is difficult to explain each concept completely at the time it arises. We suggest rereading this chapter a few times.

In case of infringement or copyright questions or troubles, always consult a knowledgeable lawyer. Also, remember that the 1976

Copyright Revision Act has not been interpreted by many court decisions. This means we will discuss the basic requirements of this new law, but that interpretations of the meaning of certain points in the new law are yet to be handed down by the courts. Be sure to write to the Copyright Office for a packet of free information on the federal copyright law and for registration forms. (See figure 3-1.)

HISTORY

A word to the wise:
If you don't love history, skip this.

Copying is an old practice. St. Benedict's rules included copying as a virtuous activity. There is an old story of St. Columbo who copied Abbot Finnian's Psalter, whereupon the Abbot demanded the copy and was refused. The problem was referred to the Irish King Diarmid in his palace at Tara, A.D. 567, who in settling the disputed property

"TO EVERY COW HER CALF"

rights, ruled in favor of the Abbot, saying, "To every cow her calf," and accordingly to every book its copy. The first recorded instance of copyright occurred in Venice in 1469. John of Spira received an exclusive five-year right to print the Epistles of Cicero and Pliny.

PRINTING PRESS

The invention of the printing press was regarded as an advance in the art of copying and was vigorously opposed by the scribes. In 1476, Caxton established a press in Westminister, England. Mass confusion followed regarding the products of the new device, as well as proclamations, decrees, and laws relating to copying. By the mid-sixteenth century, the leading printers in London had formed the Stationer's Company, and the Catholic Queen Mary in 1556 gave them a monopoly on printing to control the spread of Protestantism. Thus, the English history of copyright is intertwined with literary censorship. After 274 years of confusion, the first copyright statute was adopted by Parliament in 1710 and called "An Act for the Encouragement of Learning."

Summarized, the Statute of Anne provides:

THE FIRST COPYRIGHT STATUTE, 1710

> Whereas printers . . . have of late frequently taken the liberty of printing . . . books . . . without the consent of the authors . . . to their very great detriment and too often to the ruin of them and their families . . . the author of a book shall have the term of fourteen years. . . . [E]very such offender . . . shall forfeit one penny for every sheet which shall be found in his . . . custody. . . .

This Act was the model for most copyright legislation and for the first time, an author's rights were given legal protection.

OTHER COPYRIGHT ACTS

CONSTITUTIONAL BASIS FOR PATENTS AND COPYRIGHTS

The American Colonists adopted state copyright laws and then a United States Constitutional provision, which gave Congress the authority to enact national copyright (and patent) laws. Article I, section 8, clause 8 provides: "The Congress shall have the power . . . To promote the Progress of Science and useful Arts, by securing for limited Times to Authors and Inventors the exclusive Right to their respective Writings and Discoveries."

STATUTE OF 1790

The first federal copyright act was enacted in 1790. This 1790 Act was amended at fairly regular intervals until the Copyright Act of 1909, which remained the basic law (referred to as the old law) until January 1, 1978, the effective date of the new law. The new law formally is called the Copyright Revision Act, but we will refer to it as the new law.

COPYRIGHT REVISION ACT OF 1976

HISTORY OF NEW LAW

The old law, rooted in the old English legal principles on literary property, failed to keep pace with modern technology and new communication techniques—communication satellites, cable television, computers, video tape, records, photocopying machines, etc.

The evolution of the subject matter under the federal copyright law can best be illustrated by a chart:

- 1790: maps, charts, and books
- added 1802: historical or other print or prints
- added 1831: musical compositions
- added 1865: photographs and photograph negatives (because Mathew Brady's photos of the Civil War were attaining fame)
- added 1870: paintings, drawings, chromos, statuettes, statuary, models or designs of fine art
- rewritten 1909: a major consolidation of the above statutes. All the above plus composite and encyclopedic work, directories, gazetteers, periodicals, newspapers, lectures, sermons, addresses, dramatic or *dramatico-musical* compositions, works of art, reproductions of works of art, drawings or plastic works of a scientific or technical character, and pictorial illustrations
- added 1912: motion pictures
- added 1971: sound recordings
- changed 1976: Copyright Revision Act. Original fixed work which can be perceived including: literary works, musical works (including accompanying words), dramatic works (including accompanying music), pantomime and choreographic works, pictorial, graphic, and sculptural works, motion pictures, and other audiovisual works and sound recordings.

What is a copyright, how do you get it, when do you get it, and what do you get? Both the old and new law will be discussed. Generally, the old law covers works "published"* before 1978 and the new law covers works either created or "published" after January 1, 1978.

* *Publication* is a technical term discussed later in this chapter.

REASON FOR NEW LAW

Also there was confusion between what was known as common law copyright in the state, and federal copyright law. American copyright practice was out of step with that of the rest of the Western World. Congress wanted one copyright system that would keep pace with the new technology, modernize and standardize protection, and preempt the state from legislating in this area, so it passed the Copyright Revision Act.*

WHAT IS COPYRIGHT?

DEFINITION

Copyright is a remedy given by the law to the "authors" of literary, dramatic, musical, artistic, and other intellectual works when the author's copyrighted work is copied. *Author* is a technical term which refers to the creator of intellectual property, whether it be a writer, musician, artist, or craftmaker. The Author can also be a purchaser, heir, or other who acquires the creator's rights. The essence of copyright is the right of the author to protect and control the reproduction of his or her created work.

COMMON LAW COPYRIGHT

Under the old law, there was dual protection. The first was called "common law copyright." It existed from the moment of creation and continued to "publication." This would protect any work, such as old letters or unpublished manuscripts, from unauthorized copying before publication or disclosure. Once the work was made public without a copyright notice on it under the old law, it then passed into the public domain and could be freely copied by anyone.

> Memorandum of Law
>
> DATE: December 2, 1979
> FROM: MB of Blirp and Blirp
> RE: Batiks of M.G.
>
> Client wants to know if batiks that she exhibited in 1975 without any copyright notice at several art festivals in metropolitan shopping-center malls can now be copyrighted if she has not sold them.
>
> Under the facts of this case, client's situation would be covered by the old law.
>
> Under *Letters Edged in Black Press, Inc. v. Public Building Commission of Chicago*, 320 F. Supp. 1303 (N.D.Ill. 1970), the answer is no. In that case, Picasso designed a monumental sculpture for the plaza of the Chicago Civic Center. After Picasso donated the design for the sculpture, the Commission began a publicity campaign to publicize the Chicago Picasso. This included press shows, distribution of photos to the

* The revision resulting in the new law started in 1955 with numerous studies, drafts, and negotiations. The Register of Copyrights, Barbara Ringer, speaking on the new law commented that "practically everything in the bill is the product of at least one compromise, and many provisions have evolved from a long series of compromises reflecting constantly changing technology, commercial and financial interests, political and social conditions, judicial and administrative development, and—not least by any means—individual personalities. . . ."

> public, and display of the model at the Tate Museum. Neither the model nor the photographs had the copyright notice attached.
>
> Later the sculpture itself was dedicated with a copyright notice and registered with the copyright office. The court held that as a result of the publicity the Chicago Picasso was in the public domain *prior* to the attachment of a copyright notice on the monumental sculpture and anyone could copy the work without paying the owner of the work.

If the work bore a copyright notice, the federal law gave the author a remedy if the work was copied. The dual system of common law copyright protection before publication and federal law protection after publication has now been replaced by a single federal system for all fixed work, published or unpublished, which makes federal protection available from the moment of creation.

WHO CAN GET A COPYRIGHT

The ownership of the copyright initially belongs to the person who has created the work, except in the case of employees. Traditionally, the common law copyright passed with the sale of the creation, unless a written agreement provided that the author retained the copyright. The new law provides that the creator retains the copyright unless it is conveyed in a signed writing.

SALE OF COPYRIGHT WORK

GROUP EFFORT

What if more than one person contributes to a single work? The creators are co-authors and co-owners if the work is indivisible. This is called a joint work. The court-made law provides that the co-owners shall have free use of jointly owned property, subject to the duty to account for profits. Since you can't infringe your own copyright, unresolved problems between co-owners of a copyright are handled by filing a lawsuit for an accounting.

In a divisible work, a series of separate weavings displayed together, as part of a single work, for example:

- each creator can obtain individual copyright for each part.
- one can obtain copyright in the name of all.
- one can obtain the copyright in trust for the rest.

"WORK FOR HIRE" RULE

An important exception to the general rule that the creator owns the copyright concerns works created by an employee for an employer. Then the employer is presumed to have the copyright for the employee's work.* Thus, the new law continues the general rule that "work for hire" belongs to the employer where the work is made by an employee within the scope of employment. But the new law carves out an exception to this rule for a small group of "work for hire" where the author is treated as the creator of the works *unless* the parties expressly agree otherwise in writing. This exception,

EXCEPTION TO "WORK FOR HIRE"

* See discussion in Chapter 1, "Legal Steps in Surfacing Your Business," concerning the distinction between employee and independent contractor status.

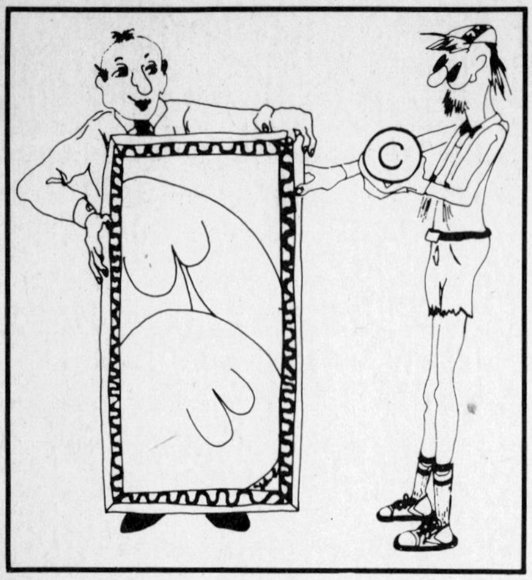

Artist keeps copyright

granting the employee copyright, embraces a number of situations or categories of work:

- work ordered or commissioned as a contribution to a collective work
- part of a motion picture or work for other audiovisual use
- translations
- supplementary works
- compilations
- instructional texts
- atlases

Under this rule, if a painter teaches drawing classes in the art department at POW University and also writes a how-to-draw book, the copyright belongs to the painter, not the employer.

Let's restate the new rule: When you sell a work with the proper copyright notice, you retain the right to copy it, as long as you have not transferred the copyright in writing and the work was not work for hire.*

WHAT CAN BE COPYRIGHTED

Under the new law, you can copyright any "original work of authorship fixed in any tangible medium of expression" which can be perceived and communicated directly or through any mechanical means or device. Any minimal expression of originality is okay so long as it's reduced to tangible form. There are seven broad categories of "original works of authorship" fixed in tangible form that can be copyrighted:

SUBJECT MATTER OF COPYRIGHT

- literary works
- musical works (plus accompanying words)
- dramatic works (plus accompanying music)
- pantomimes and choreographic works
- pictorial, graphic, and sculptural works
- motion pictures, other audiovisual works
- sound recordings

The category of "pictorial, graphic, and sculptural works" includes "two-dimensional and three-dimensional works of fine, graphic, and applied art, photographs, prints and art reproductions, maps, globes, charts, technical drawings, diagrams and models." Three factors—fixed in a tangible form, creativity, and originality—are requirements for statutory copyright protection. Thus, an idea cannot be protected by copyright until it is fixed in final form.

FIXED IN A TANGIBLE FORM

The following drawing by Author Blue's four-year-old has the necessary creativity and originality to be copyrighted. Creativity refers to the work's nature, and originality refers to the creation by the author using his or her own skill, labor, and judgment. For instance, such unoriginal objects as butterflies, cocker spaniels, and flowers made into original art creations have been held copyright-

CREATIVITY AND ORIGINALITY

* Unless it falls within the exceptions to the work-for-hire rule as explained previously.

able, as well as the artistic arrangement of panels on gift wrap. On the other hand, an arrangement of plastic flowers and a scaled-down reproduction of an Uncle Sam bank that had passed into the public domain did not have the necessary creativity and originality to qualify for copyright protection. Where works of art are reproduced, the first work already has creativity so the reproduction only needs to be original to be copyrightable.

INDEPENDENT CREATION

Creation of the same work by two persons independent of each other gives protection if others *copy* the copyrighted works, but not as between the two creators.

Alice's Allegory # 7

or

Independent Ideas

Alice designed a pipe, calling it strike-it-easy, in the shape of a coiled Rocky Mountain rattler, and put the copyright symbol, her name, and date on the head of the rattler, and sold it to a young man on his way to Nepal for four years. Alice was at an arts and crafts fair in Bisbee, Arizona, the next year and saw an identical piece with a copyright notice dated a year later by another artist named Bohoe. Bohoe stated he had never seen or heard of Alice's piece either through a Nepalese-bound young man or anyone else and he had the idea on his own. Who has the copyright? Both have a valid copyright, for each of the works was original and creative.

Tweety crying

UTILITARIAN ART OR APPLIED WORKS OF ART

You can copyright artwork (having pictorial, graphic, or sculptured features) that is embodied in useful articles. The artwork must be separately identified from and exist independently of the article's utilitarian aspect; for example, designs painted on cups and bowls, a batiked bird on a scarf. The new law incorporates the old case of *Mazer v. Stein,* which was an infringement case involving applied works of art. There, copyrighted statuettes of male and female dancers were used as manufactured lamp bases. The copyright of the statuettes was upheld by the court even though they were used as an item of utility. If you copyright a design of prickly pear cactus bordered by Indian baskets on a handwoven rug, then you get protection from someone copying exactly *that design* but you cannot keep persons from making floor rugs or from using any variation of prickly pear cactus–Indian basket design.

In a recent lawsuit, Albert Gilbert, a well-known wildlife artist, had painted *Cardinals on Apple Blossoms* and National Wildlife Art Exchange had acquired the copyright on the painting. The Franklin Mint Corporation commissioned Gilbert to paint four wildlife pictures, one of which was entitled *The Cardinal.* The appellate court held there was no infringement by the new painting because the new painting was a variation on a theme and there were distinguishing differences of line, color, body position, foliage, and general composition.

Alice's Allegory # 8

or

"Oh those Pig Hunters"

Alice was one winter day glazing and painting a design on an enormous serving platter which was a piece commissioned by the Wild Turkey and Pig Hunters of Hobin. The design was a complicated collage of turkeys and wild pigs from birth to old age in a wide variety of natural scenes. On the back she put the copyright notice, the date, and her full name. The sales receipt stated "Platter sold to Wild Turkey and Pig Hunters of Hobin on 1/2/78 for $250." A month later, Alice received a Seedy catalogue in the mail which she had sent for because their advertisement in *Father Meed News* stated "Beautiful textiles depicting nature's wild bounties." To her dismay, she found yardage entitled "Wild Turkeys and Pigs of North America" at $10 per yard which was the exact duplicate in repeats of her platter. She discovered on contacting the platter purchasers that the design had caught the fancy of the Grays and they had photographed the platter and sold the photo-design to Seedy to raise money for their nonprofit corporation, which was publishing a book tracing the origins and treatment of wild turkeys and pigs in North America.

Alice excitedly went to see her family lawyer, who in turn put Alice in touch with a copyright lawyer in the big city who said: "Well, my dear, you indeed have a case of copyright infringement, for when you transferred the platter, you did not transfer the copyright unless you did so in writing, and the receipt does not indicate a transfer. The first thing we need to do is register the work and deposit copies with the Copyright Office. If we register within three months of publication, then the court could award you attorneys' fees and statutory damages."

WHAT CANNOT BE COPYRIGHTED

Copyright protection does not extend "to any idea,* procedure, process, system, method of operation, concept, principle, or discovery. . . ."

A LEGAL RULE

Also, copyright is not generally available for works by the United States government; for obscene, libelous, and immoral work on public policy grounds; for minimal work (names, slogans, titles, lettering, coloring); for blank forms; for business operations or procedures; and for ideas or procedures for doing, making, or building things. The exclusion of government works from copyright protection covers works produced by officers and employees as part of their duties, but it does not necessarily cover work prepared under a contract or grant.** So, if you contract to photograph the work of U.S. Indian Arts and Crafts Board, be sure you get the government to agree in writing that you have the copyrights if there are any to be had. Various government agencies have differing policies about individuals' ability to copyright works prepared with the assistance of federal grant money. It is wise to have a statement of such policy at

* If you want to protect your idea, do not disclose it. If you do, then contract first. For example, you can offer to disclose your idea to a person or company provided they will not make use of the idea until a mutually agreeable price is reached.

** The United States government has been requiring contractors with it to copyright the work in the contractor's name and then assign the copyright to the government. So you need to check to see if the work has been copyrighted in that fashion.

the outset. As a matter of practice the Copyright Office registers "obscene" works, since it does not want to make decisions on what is obscene. But, if someone infringes your "obscene" work and you sue the infringer, then the alleged infringer can raise a defense that there is not a valid copyright because the work is obscene. In a recent case involving the movie, *Behind the Green Door*, a court ruled that the movie was obscene; hence no valid copyright and no infringement!*

COPYRIGHT OF "OBSCENE" WORKS

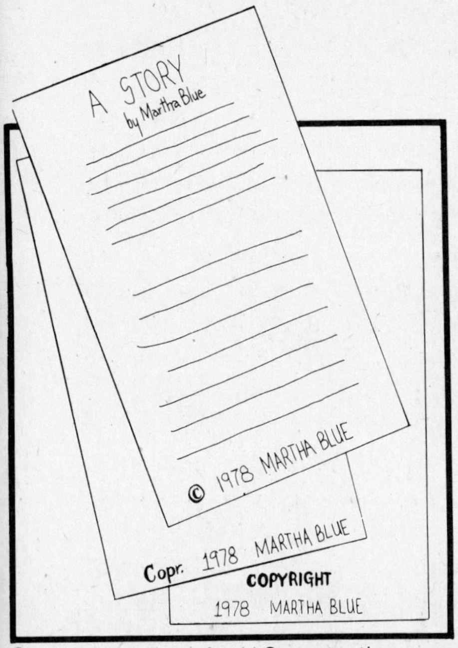

Copyright notices for U.S. protection

TIMING—WHEN TO COPYRIGHT

The term *publication* is a technical term in the world of copyright. Under the old law, "publication" occurred generally if the work was sold or distributed to the general public or displayed in a public place with no restrictions. Under the new law the date of "publication" becomes less important for it simply serves to establish time limits for registration. If a work is not registered within three months of "publication," and there is a subsequent lawsuit for infringement, the infringer would not be liable to reimburse the plaintiff's attorney's fees and to pay statutory damages.

In addition the five-year period to cure the omission of the copyright notice is determined from the date of publication.

PUBLICATION

The new definition of publication is ambiguous. The new law states that "public performance or display of a work does not of itself constitute publication . . ." but "the offering to distribute copies . . . to a group of persons for the purposes of . . . public display, constitutes publication."

Protect your work. Don't exhibit, display or sell your work without properly affixing a copyright notice to the work.

REQUIREMENTS OF COPYRIGHT NOTICE

CONTENTS

A copyright notice must contain three things:

- the copyright symbol "©" or the word "copyright" or the abbreviation, "copr."
- the year of first publication of the work
- the name of the copyright owner

SYMBOL FOR INTERNATIONAL PROTECTION

If you want some international protection, then you use the copyright symbol "©," the name of the owner and the year of first publication. For protection in the Western Hemisphere you must add the words "all rights reserved."

INTERNATIONAL PROTECTION

© 1978 Martha Blue—Marion Davidson
All Rights Reserved

As stated above, the year of "publication" of your work is generally the year you present your work to the public for sale, rental or

* See the discussion of obscenity in Chapter 4, "Legal Restrictions on Content and Materials."

DATE OF NOTICE

lease.* If this date is unclear to you, then simply put the year of completion of your work on the copyright notice. Even if an earlier year or the wrong name is put in the copyright notice, it is likely you will receive all the protections of the Copyright Act.

NAME

Put your first and last name on the notice of copyright (Hortense Mendleschmidt). However, it is acceptable to put your professional name (Yellow Bird) or symbol (H M), if you are known by these.

PLACEMENT OF NOTICE

The copyright notice must be placed on the work so that it is not concealed from view upon reasonable inspection. The notice can be placed on the front, back, or base of a work as well as on the frame or mounting. For jewelry and other works too small to house all the information required by the copyright notice, a tag can be firmly attached to the piece with the required information. To protect the designs on yard goods or decorative papers, place the notice every so often on the selvage or in the design itself. If this is not possible, put the notice on a tag which must be attached both to the material and the spool. It is sufficient that the notice be placed on only one of two earrings or other paired items.

REMOVAL OR DESTRUCTION OF NOTICE

If the copyright notice is removed or destroyed without your approval, never fear, copyright protection is still available. In a case involving yardage, the copyright notice had been printed on the selvage edge of patterned cloth. The selvage was cut off in making dresses and the yardage copied. The court said that the removal of the copyright notice did not matter and the copyright protection was not lost.

OMISSION OF COPYRIGHT NOTICE CAN BE CURED

Under the new law, the omission of copyright notice from works publicly distributed by the owner does not invalidate the work's copyright if:

- the omission is from a small number of works
- the registration of work is made within five years of publication and a reasonable effort is made to add notices to copies distributed
- the omission of notice violated a specific written provision that the work distributed bear notice (as in a publishing contract, where there was a requirement for notice that was not fulfilled)
- the notice is removed, obliterated, or destroyed without the copyright owner's permission

Thus, the situation presented in the old Picasso case would not have disastrous outcome today, since as of January 1, 1978, the omitted copyright notice can be added later. Under the old law, if the copyright notice was omitted from the work, you could not go back and cure the omission.

It does not matter if the omission was partial, total, unintentional, or deliberate. At the time of this writing, what is a "small number" of works or "reasonable effort" to add notice to all copies

* In compilations, derivations, or works using previously published material then the year of the first publication of the compilation or derivation work is sufficient. The date may be omitted where art work is reproduced on greeting cards, postcards, stationery, jewelry, dolls, toys, or any useful articles.

is still unclear and awaiting interpretation by the courts. Don't make trouble for yourself, put the full notice on your work when it is completed.

REGISTRATION

Publication with the complete notice gives the owner a valid copyright in the work *without* registration and deposit of copies. But, if you pick up a *Cheap Prints Catalogue* and see an exact copy of your copyrighted painting *The Ghost at Coalmine Canyon* being offered for sale as a reproduction, you cannot file a suit for infringement until you have a Certificate of Registration, and you may lose some of the benefits of the Act.

REGISTER PRIOR TO FILING SUIT

The simplest way to register and at the same time get the most protection is to deposit two copies* of the work along with the application and fee with the Copyright Office within three months of publication. This procedure also meets the copy deposit required for the Library of Congress collection.

DEPOSIT FOR LIBRARY OF CONGRESS COMBINED WITH REGISTRATION

Under the old law, deposit of copies for the collection of the Library of Congress and for purposes of copyright registration were taken as the same thing. The deposit of copies for the Library of Congress, Section 407 of the new Act, may be required where the work is published in the United States with a notice of copyright, even if the copyright owner does not seek to register the work with the Copyright Office. Under Section 408 the copyright owner may be subject to certain penalties for failure to deposit following written demand by the registrar of copyrights. Deposit for Library of Congress can be combined with registration. But you can use the deposit accompanying an application for registration with the Copyright Office (Section 408) to satisfy the Library of Congress deposit provisions (Section 407). You only have to register with the Copyright Office:

- if you want to take advantage of the five-year savings clause, that is, you have omitted the copyright notice and after curing the omission you must register
- if the Copyright Office demands it
- as a prerequisite to an infringement suit
- if you want statutory attorneys' fees and damages (file within three months of publication) awarded in an infringement suit
- if you want presumptive proof that you have a copyright, and the facts stated in the application are true

EFFECTIVE DATE OF REGISTRATION

The effective date of copyright registration is the day on which an acceptable application, deposit, and fee have all been received in the Copyright Office. A delay in the effective date of registration can have serious consequences—for example, loss of statutory dam-

* See later discussion of the deposit requirements, including acceptable copies. Some categories of material are exempt from the deposit of copies requirement, and identifying material may be deposited instead.

ages and attorneys' fees if work is not registered within three months of publication.

The application form consists of a single sheet, with spaces to be completed on the front and back. Detachable instructions are part of the form. There is a continuation sheet to use where more space is necessary.

Most applications will be submitted on one of these forms:

TYPES OF FORMS

- Form TX: for published and unpublished nondramatic literary works
- Form PA: for published and unpublished works of the performing arts (musical and dramatic works, pantomimes and choreographic works, motion pictures and other audiovisual works)
- Form VA: for published and unpublished works of the visual arts (pictorial, graphic, and sculptured works)
- Form SR: for published and unpublished sound recordings
- Form RE: for claims to renew copyright in works copyrighted under the old law

Two other forms are provided for special situations:

- Form CA: for supplementary registration to correct or amplify information given in the Copyright Office record of an earlier registration
- Form GR/CP: an adjunct application to be used for registration of a group of contributions to periodicals

Write the Copyright Office, Library of Congress, Washington, D.C. 20559 for free copies of the forms. Information specialists will answer your questions from 8:00 A.M. to 7:00 P.M. (703/557-8700). See Appendix 3-1 for a discussion of Forms TX, VA, and GR/CP.

GROUP REGISTRATION

You can register "a group of related works" under a single registration. The legislative report on the new law included as examples a group of related jewelry designs, a group of photographs by one photographer, and a series of related greeting cards. Registration of a group of works under a single registration saves time, money, and paperwork. As of this writing,* it appears that a weaver who had completed several tapestry studies in white could photograph them and place the pictures together on a composite sheet, fill out one application, send all this with the $10 fee, and meet the deposit and registration requirements.

DEPOSIT REQUIREMENT

In general, the material to be deposited is one complete copy of an unpublished work and two complete copies of a published work. There are some exceptions. One copy of greeting cards, postcards, stationery, labels, ads, scientific drawings, and globes may be deposited. Since actual copies of certain two- and three-dimensional works such as jewelry, ceramics, sculptures, and so forth would be

* Check with the Copyright Office for a copy of their final regulations on registration for a group of related works.

impractical, a substitute for an actual copy, called identifying material, is allowed.

If the work is published as a reproduction, you'll have to send two actual reproductions, or one, if an unpublished production. For works published in five copies or less or in limited, numbered editions, you may deposit one copy (outside the numbered series, but identical) or identifying reproductions. For unpublished pictorial and graphic works you can also use identifying materials. Generally for the artist and craftmaker the substitute can be photographs, slides, or drawings. The photographs or transparencies (slides) should meet the following requirements:

- they should be in the actual colors of the pictorial or graphic work.
- they should be complete, that is, clearly show the work.*
- slides must be at least 35 mm and mounted if 3 by 3 inches or less.
- photographs should be not less than 5 by 7 inches or more than 9 by 12 inches—preferably 8 by 10 inches.
- the title and one or more dimensions of the work should be indicated on one copy.
- The image must be at least 4 inches if less than life-size.**
- The position of the copyright notice must be shown on one copy.***

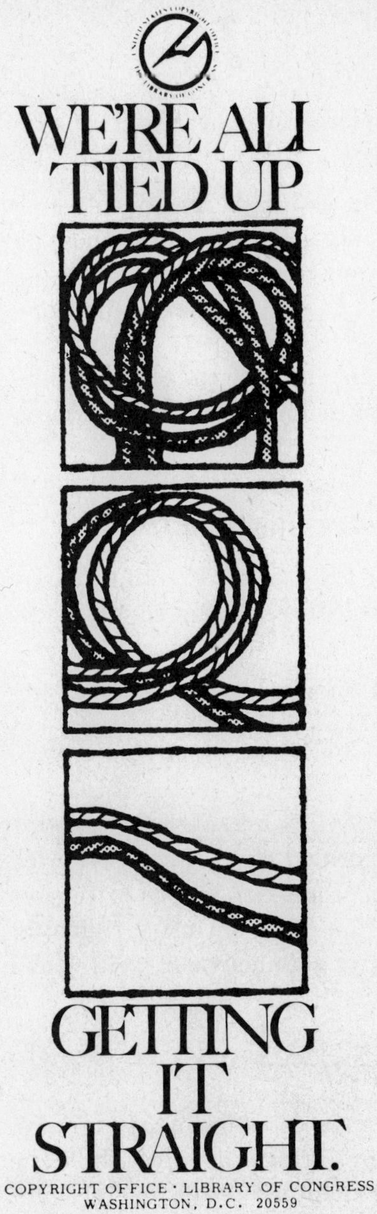

You should send in one package with the proper postage, the application, deposit, and required fees.

If this process seems confusing to you, you are not alone. The public and the employees of the Copyright Office had ample opportunity to become familiar with the procedural requirements of the 1909 Copyright Act. As a result of the 1976 revisions, new forms and new procedures became mandatory, and there were ensuing complications. In the summer of 1978 the Copyright Office sent out a public notice, part of which is reproduced opposite. The notice explained that less than 20 percent of all the applications the Office had received could be acted on without correspondence to correct errors or to get missing information, and the communications had created an enormous backlog of work. The deposit requirements are in a state of flux, so watch for changes.

HOW LONG DOES IT LAST?

TERM OF COPYRIGHT

LIFE PLUS 50 OR 75/100 TERMS

Copyright protection under the new law lasts for:

- a basic term of life of the author plus fifty years after death.
- fifty years from the death of last author of a joint work.

* If a design on a cup is being copyrighted, for example, the design should be clear.

** Does not apply to slides.

*** If the size or the position of the copyright notice makes it difficult to see the notice, then you should attach a drawing showing the exact appearance, notice content, its dimensions, and its specific position.

- the shorter of seventy-five years from publication or one hundred years from creation for works for hire or anonymous and pseudonymous works.
- life plus 50 or 75/100 terms for unpublished or uncopyrighted works in existence before 1978.*

EXTENSION OF TERM FOR SOME COPYRIGHTED WORKS UNDER THE OLD LAW

Under the old law the first term of copyright was twenty-eight years, renewable for an additional twenty-eight years. Now those old copyrighted works (pre 1950) which were renewed prior to 1978 will be protected for seventy-five years from the date of the original copyright; and works copyrighted between 1950 and 1977 are extended forty-seven years *if* a valid renewal registration is made by December 31 of the twenty-eighth year. For a discussion of the right of termination of a copyright see Appendix 3-2.

WHAT DOES THE COPYRIGHT OWNER GET?

The heart of the new copyright law is the grant of certain exclusive rights to the copyright owner. The exclusive rights of an author are broadly stated:

EXCLUSIVE RIGHTS OF COPYRIGHT OWNER

- to reproduce the copyrighted work in copies or phonorecords
- to prepare derivative works**
- to distribute to the public
- to perform publicly
- to display publicly certain works

For example, the creator of a batik entitled *Three Women of Africa* could sell the piece to Ms. A, assign reproductions rights to Terrible Towel Manufacturing Co., and keep the other exclusive rights for herself. The sale of any part of the copyright must be in writing and signed by the party making the transfer.

INFRINGEMENT

The new law provides that "anyone who violates any of the exclusive rights of the copyright owner . . . is an infringer of copyright." The copyright owner may file an infringement action in federal court against the infringer within three years from the date of the infringement. The following cases illustrate fact patterns of successful infringement actions: A copyrighted wall covering design consisting of a grid of bamboo poles superimposed on three stripes was infringed upon by another wallpaper with a similar design, medium, and colors, even though it had variations in size, spacing, and detail of the bamboo. A copyrighted rubber doll was protected against an infringer's doll. Even though the dolls were not identical in sculp-

EXAMPLES OF INFRINGEMENT

* All pre–January 1, 1978, created but unpublished works are guaranteed copyright protection, until December 31, 2002, and if published prior to that date, the term is extended to 2027.

** Writers traditionally assign these rights to publishers.

tural detail, it was still apparent that the infringer's doll was derived from the creator's.

INFRINGER MUST HAVE HAD ACCESS TO WORK

One thing the copyright owner must show in an infringement action is that the infringer somehow had access to the work, and, indeed copied it. An independent creation of an identical work is not an infringement.

The major defense to infringement is the fair-use doctrine, a doctrine which was developed by the courts under the old law and which has been made an express part of the new law.

Fair use* allows others to use your copyrighted work without your permission. It is permissible to copy a small part of it for criticism and comment, scholarship, research, news reporting, and teaching (including multiple copies for classroom use). If you are unsure whether your proposed use is unfair or if you want to do a substantial amount of copying, then you should get permission from the copyright owner.**

FAIR-USE DEFENSE

Courts consider these factors in each case to determine if the use is fair:

- purpose and character of use (whether of a commercial or noncommercial nature)
- nature of copyrighted work
- amount and substantiality of portion used in relation to the whole of the copyrighted work
- effect of use on potential market for value of copyrighted work

If the use was not fair and there is infringement, then the court can:

- halt the infringer's activities
- in extreme cases impound and destroy copies, plates, et cetera of the infringer
- award damages
- award costs and attorneys' fees

Generally, there are three methods of measuring damages in a suit for copyright infringement:

- the copyright holder's out-of-pocket loss
- the infringer's profit
- damages provided by law (statutory damages)

Under statutory damages the minimum award is $250 and the maximum award is $10,000 for each incident of infringement. If the infringement is willful then the statutory damages can be increased to $50,000, but an *innocent* infringer could end up paying as little as $100 in statutory damages for each act of infringement.

Although filing for a copyright is relatively simple, an action for infringement is complicated, so see a lawyer.

* For more information on fair use, see Chapter 7, "Especially for Writers."

** See Appendix 3-3 for a sample permission form. For a small fee, the reference division of the Copyright Office will search its own records to determine the ownership of a copyright. See Circular 22 for information.

Alice's Allegory # 9

or

Coping with Copyright

After consulting with her lawyer Alice put the copyright notice on all her work, but only registered the scenarios on her production pieces, for example, her superficial forest of hearts and rainbows. For each scenario she sent photographs along with the fee and application within three months of completion. She hand-lettered a plaque for her studio wall:

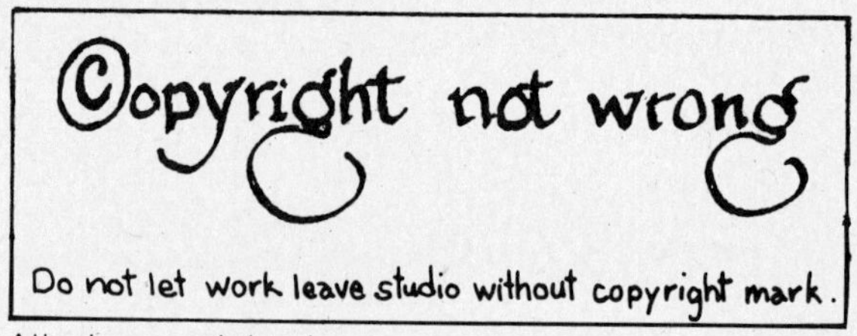

Alice's copyright sign

PATENTS

PATENTS Protection from copying is, in certain situations, provided by patents.

Dear Ms. Spinner:

Thank you for your recent inquiry about whether you could get a patent for your gerbil-powered spinning wheel and your solar-operated, vegetable-dye-extractor bath. I can't tell if you could patent either of these inventions, but if you will read the enclosed information on patents, you will get some information on patent history, the patent lingo, the steps in obtaining a patent, and where to find legal assistance. Unfortunately, patents are often overlooked by the creative person. Often artists, potters, weavers, and woodcarvers invent processes, equipment, or improvements in doing their work. Sometimes a spouse, lover, housemate, or friend executes the idea, and if it works, pretty soon other artists or craftmakers want to use it.

Beware of patent marketing companies. Don't send your idea to some person or company unless you indicate in writing that the idea is not to be used or disclosed without mutual agreement of the parties. Frequently, early contacts between an inventor and a prospective purchaser of the idea are accompanied by nondisclosure agreements, in which the person to whom the invention is shown agrees not to make it public. If you get a patent, you could sell it to a company or let someone else develop it for you under some profit-splitting arrangement. Some patents are the subject of litigation after issuance and you may want a big company involved in protecting that patent. Good luck.

From,
The Chatty Lawyer
Syndicated Column

INTRODUCTION

DEFINITION A patent is an agreement between an inventor and the public (represented by the government) that permits the inventor to make, use,
HISTORY and sell an invention for a certain period. Early "patents" were

granted around the year 600 B.C. in the Republic of Sibari in southern Italy. There, cooks who invented an especially choice dish were allowed exclusive use of the invented dish for one year in order to encourage others to invent new recipes.

In the fifteenth century the Venetian Republic began a regular system of providing grants and privileges to persons who originated and discovered new techniques. In 1624, the first British statute was adopted; then various colonies in the United States began to issue patents. In 1790, the first American patent statute was adopted.

PATENTED ITEMS

After a flurry of patent activity in the United States, the first commissioner of patents, Henry L. Ellsworth, in his 1843 annual report stated, "The advancement of the arts from year to year, taxes our credulity and seems to presage the arrival of that period when human improvement must end." Quite to the contrary, patents have run the gamut from A to Z. For instance, patents have been obtained for the zipper (which was discovered by two violinists), the coat hanger, DDT, foam rubber, insulin, solar devices, the incandescent light bulb, television, zerography, steamboats, and the telephone. Recently, we saw and talked to a craft street vendor who had a patent on a self-leveling plant shelf.

PHILOSOPHY OF A PATENT

By obtaining a patent, the inventor is granted a right for seventeen years to exclude others from making, using, or selling the defined invention in the United States. In return, the public receives a full disclosure of the invention, which then fosters technical progress.

GETTING A PATENT

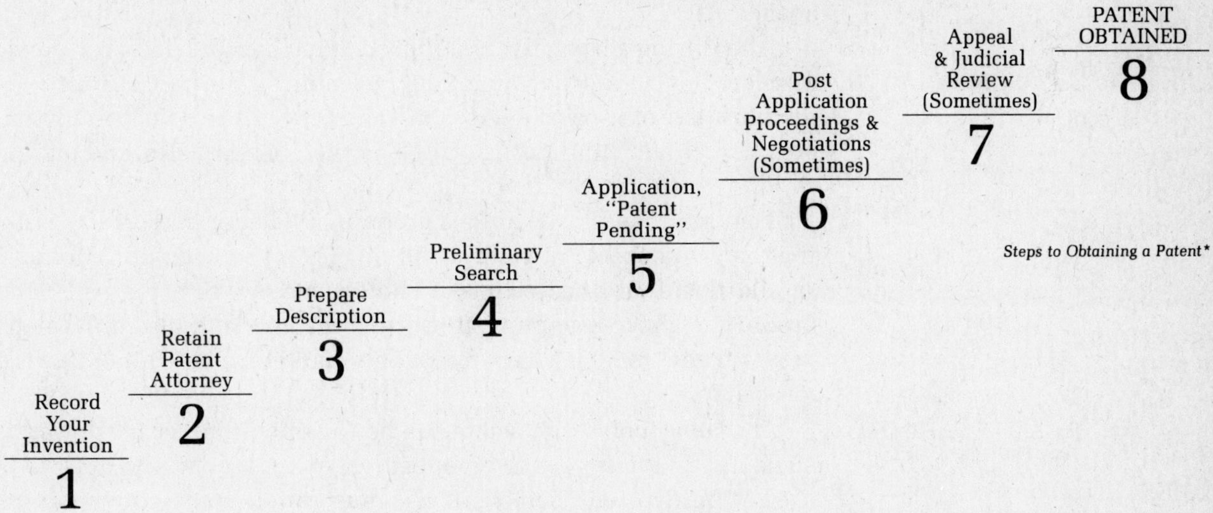

*Steps to Obtaining a Patent**

RECORD KEEPING

First put your ideas on paper and have them witnessed by an outsider capable of understanding them *at the earliest possible moment.*

* The U.S. Patent and Trademark Office, Washington, D.C. 20231 has a pamphlet called *General Information Concerning Patents* which you can send for.

Keep a bound notebook. Make your entries chronologically. Don't leave blank pages in the notebook. If you have not worked for several days, make an entry to that effect. If you attach a photo or drawing to the notebook, make sure you write the identifying remarks on the additions, so that they are placed on both the addition and in the notebook.

Accurate, on-the-spot record keeping will help you prove you invented the item first. This record keeping gives you evidence of creation plus a basis for the patent search and even preparation of the patent application. Remember the old saying in the patent world: When a man becomes an inventor, he is a dead witness.

RETAIN AN ATTORNEY

Obtaining a patent requires the services of a patent attorney. The attorneys' fees will rarely be less than $1,000. The Patent and Trademark Office as well as your State Bar Association can provide you with the names and addresses of patent attorneys and agents (who are not attorneys) but who are licensed to prosecute patent applications before the Patent and Trademark Office.

IDEA BROKERS

Be very cautious of idea brokers—they have been criticized by the press, involved in numerous lawsuits, and investigated by the Federal Trade Commission. The fraudulent idea brokers give you a glowing report on your invention, ask for $1,000 to $2,000 from you in order to obtain a patent, and do nothing. On the other hand, there are invention brokers who work solely on a contingent fee basis, with any charge consisting of a part of the patent earnings. Before parting with any of your money, check out the company or person with your Attorney General's Office and government regulatory agencies.*

WORKING WITH YOUR ATTORNEY

After hiring a lawyer you will need to tell him or her if you know of related devices or whether your invention is an improvement or modification of a prior device, and if so, what the patent numbers are. Also provide the attorney with any literature, articles, and publications relating to the invention, or any other invention like it.

Your attorney should make a preliminary determination concerning the patentability of your invention. Then you and your attorney should decide if you can make enough money from the patented product to make patenting it worthwhile. An automated Tibetan prayer wheel may not have much of a market in the United States, for example.

WHAT CAN BE PATENTED

The subject of a U.S. patent can be "any new and useful process, machine, manufacture, or composition of matter, or any new and useful improvement thereof." It also must satisfy the requirements of *utility, novelty*, and *nonobviousness*. Some classes of subject matter cannot be patented: printed matter, naturally occurring substances

* See Chapter 8, "Obtaining Legal Assistance," for a discussion of state and federal regulatory agencies.

such as elements, methods of doing business, ideas, scientific principles, and mental processes.

Even if your invention is a proper subject for patent, you may be denied a patent because you have not met other technical objections to the issuance of a patent, such as anticipation, prior printed publication, public use, on sale one year prior to date of patent application, abandonment, prior foreign patenting, prior inventor, noninventor (applicant did not invent), priority, and obviousness. These are technical terms which your own patent attorney will explain to you.

DESCRIPTION AND SEARCH

Once a complete description of the invention is developed, a preliminary search, called a patentability search or "prior art search," is made at the U.S. Patent Office to determine if the invention is old or obvious. This is a search* by a patent lawyer or an associate to determine whether the invention is patentable. The searcher tries to find the patents closest to the invention. Then the patent attorney should be able to decide if the invention is patentable or not; and if patentable, the scope of patent protection. If you can get a patent, then you should reevaluate whether it is financially worth pursuing a patent.

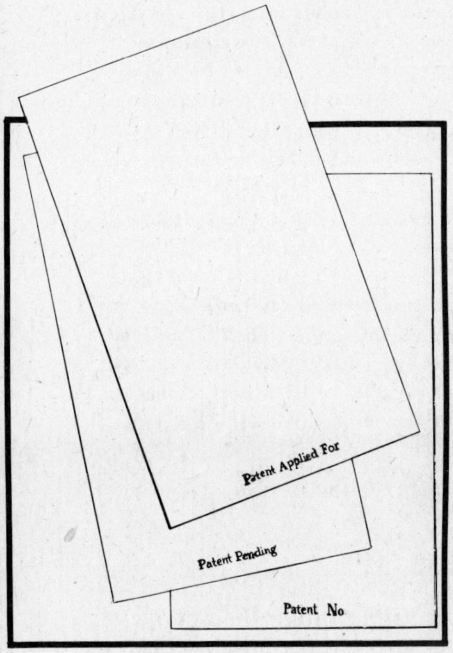

If so, the next step is to prepare and file a patent application along with the filing fees of $65. Some of the patent application documents require fine technical writing and illustration. Usually a draft patent application is done by the attorney for the inventor to review, and then the draft is revised for the final application. A "Patent pending" mark may be put on an invention only after the application has been filed.** It only serves to give the public notice that someone utilizing the invention after the patent issues runs the risk of infringement. Before a patent issues, anyone may make, use, or sell the invention without liability. Times for issuance of patent vary.

AMENDMENTS

INTERFERENCE PROCEEDINGS

An examiner with the Patent Office reviews the patent application and often will reject all or part of a patent claim, saying that the prior art teaches the claimed invention. The claim can be amended, and the amendments relate back to the original filing date of the patent application. In about one out of twenty applications, interference proceedings start. This means that more than one inventor has filed a patent application on the same invention. There are two important dates in interference proceedings: the date of conception*** and date of filing the patent application.

* There are many kinds of searches that are done. One estimate on the cost of a recent search was $200.

** If you put the "Patent pending" mark on your invention before filing, you are guilty of a misdemeanor and subject to a $500 fine for each violation.

*** The uncorroborated testimony of the inventor is not worth much as far as the conception date. That is why record keeping is important.

About 50 percent of all patent claims are finally rejected by the patent examiner, and often these claims are more favorably received by the Patent Office Board of Appeals. Remember, during the processing of a patent application there is some "horse trading," for often the claim is overly broad in a patent application. This means that the Patent Office will allow you to keep part of your claim if you agree to delete other parts of the claim.

APPEALS

ABE LINCOLN, HIMSELF A PATENTEE, SAID, "THE PATENT SYSTEM ADDED THE FUEL OF INTEREST TO THE FIRE OF GENIUS"

Alice's Allegory # 10

or

Alice's Brainstorm

One day Alice had Romero build her this fantastic potter's wheel that she had dreamt about, and it was like no other. For one thing, it was powered by solar energy and its alternate energy was a motion machine operated by a three-year-old child. Then feeling moved to words, Alice wrote a monograph on developing tools and equipment for craftmakers. At the next craft fair, Alice and Romero sold a lot of pots because they demonstrated their new wheel and gave out copies of their monograph.

Mr. Noit came up to them at the crafts fair and said, "I don't see any 'patent pending' sign on this. Gee, I've had the same idea as this." He talked awhile and left. Alice called her lawyer and said, "How can we protect this?" He gave her the name of a patent attorney, Pat Bond, and Romero and she talked him into doing a trade of pots and half cash for a patent application. Mr. Pat Bond told them: "Write up your invention; this is called a description. Put in enough sketches so that its structure is apparent. State briefly how it works, what its advantages are, and its uses. Then bring it into me and we will do a patent search."

DESIGN PATENTS

You can protect your design by design patent rather than copyright. Design patents have been granted for designs in wearing apparel, fabrics, lampshades, jewelry, a round box with decorative features, a reclining chair, outward configurations of lawn mowers, shoulder rope for a military uniform, and a lamp with metal sleeves. Design patents can be obtained by: "Whoever invents any new, original, and ornamental design for an article of manufacture. . . ." In order to be a valid subject for a design patent, the design must be:

STATUTORY DEFINITION OF DESIGN PATENT

ELEMENTS OF A DESIGN PATENT

- new or novel—a different design from others
- original—with the author
- ornamental—the product of authentic skill and artistic conception
- inventive in character—beyond the skill of an ordinary designer

The design is the visual features of an object which can be the applied surface ornamentation or the work's shape or both. The purpose of the design patent law is to encourage the decoration of manufactured articles. A design patent application follows the same steps as patents for inventions, but the filing fee is only $20. The issuance fee depends on whether you elect a three and one-half-, seven-, or fourteen-year term of protection.

Sometimes you should get a design patent instead of a copyright. For instance, a court recently concluded that plaintiff's creation of a design for distinctive footwear ("mitten toe socks" and "glove socks") was not infringed by defendant's manufacture of socks with compartments for toes. The court noted that copyright of the legwear drawings protected the *expression* of the idea, but the general concept could get protection only through a patent. Can you get both a copyright and design patent in one work? Prior to 1978 you could. For instance, the designer of a novelty watch bearing a caricature of Spiro T. Agnew applied for, and finally received both a copyright and a design patent. It is unclear under the new law if you can still get both.

DESIGN PATENT OR COPYRIGHT?

In a recent case under the old copyright law, the plaintiff developed a kite design that could be manufactured out of only one piece of fabric, and in the process of applying for a patent, the Patent Office printed a written description of the kite in its official journal. A publishing company reproduced the patent text in one of its publications. The plaintiff had not copyrighted the text but argued that he had protection under common law copyright, and the court said that he did for he had not published the work by just describing its use in a patent application. Under the new copyright law there also would probably be no publication, because the patent statutes require publication of patent applications in a government journal, and there is no commercial distribution there for the creator. Since the kite design was unpublished under the new law, it would have copyright protection and there would be infringement.

The following chart will give you an idea of how the two protections compare:

COMPARISON OF

COPYRIGHT	*DESIGN PATENT*
• courts often find infringement	• courts rarely find infringement
• cheap and simple to get (use for seasonal items)	• long and expensive to get (not good for seasonal items)
• protects against slavish copying	• broader protection from copying
• protects against persons who have access	• protects against persons who each reached idea on own
• no invention requirements	• invention requirements
• term: life plus fifty years	• term: maximum is seventeen years

Generally, for the artist and craftmaker it is simpler and cheaper to get protection with a copyright.

WHEELING AND DEALING A PATENT

If you do have a patent, you may be stuck in a big-guy/little-guy situation. You may not have the money to market the invention or defend it. For instance, Alexander Graham Bell defended his patent

USE A LAWYER FOR SALE OR MARKETING AGREEMENT ON PATENTS

in many suits. If you turn to a big guy with your patent, be sure to use the services of a competent lawyer to negotiate any agreement regarding the patent. Some alternative arrangements would be:

- sell the patent outright.
- enter into a development and marketing arrangement under a profit-splitting agreement.
- give a company the patent to develop and market for a specific time, with ownership and partial profits (royalty) to come back to you.

PATENT INFRINGEMENT

PATENT INFRINGEMENT

DAMAGE AWARD

The unauthorized making, using, or selling of your patented invention during its term gives you the right to bring an infringement action. You have six years from the date of infringement to file a suit. It is not uncommon for the validity of a patent to be tested through litigation. The court can stop the infringement and award money damages. You should see a patent lawyer if you have this problem. Patent litigation is costly and complex.

TRADE SECRETS

Alice's Allegory # 11

or

The Sky Blue Trade Secret

Alice's friends, Marlene and Dave the Batikists, had long had a secret process for obtaining sky blue in their batiks. It was a carefully guarded secret and all their assistants were warned not to reveal it, but the young man, George, who helped remove the wax became involved in the process when the batikists had a very large order for a batiked mural for the ceiling of a Moroccan restaurant called Henry-Lamb-Eggplant. Now curious George did not forget the process and showed it to some commercial department store batikists—competitors—who called Marlene when they were drunk and said, "Wow, your sky blue process is great and now we have got the secret from our spy, and we have made 100 batiks using it."

Marlene and Dave sought help from their family lawyer to stop George and the rip-off batikists from using their trade secret.

WHAT ARE TRADE SECRETS

PROTECTED TRADE SECRETS

Besides protection under patent law, one may have a common law right in an invention that the state courts will protect through the theory of trade secrets. A trade secret is information generally not known in a trade. Trade secrets which have been protected by the courts are chemical formulas, customer lists, customer credit ratings, blueprints, architectural plans, patterns, unpatentable or unpatented designs, inventions, advertising slogans, and other information. Examples of long-standing trade secrets are the formulas for Coca-Cola and Smith's Black Cough Drops (which is over one hundred years old). Trade-secrets protection can last longer than the seventeen years of a patent. Some trade secrets have died away—for example, knowledge of pigment compositions by Old Master painters. The

Romans controlled the entire line of possessors of a trade secret by slavery and the Anglo-Saxons used guilds. In modern times you can file a lawsuit against a person who discloses or uses your trade secret without your permission. Usually the person would have acquired the secret improperly either by theft or by receiving the information in confidence with the understanding that he or she would not disclose the information.

CONTRACT TO PROTECT TRADE SECRETS

If you think your business involves valuable trade secrets, then watch the number of persons you share the secret with and have employees at the time you hire them sign a written contract that they will not disclose the secret.

UNFAIR COMPETITION

Another source of protection from misuse of your work by others is the remedy of unfair competition. Unfair competition has been found by the courts in the following cases:

EXAMPLES OF UNFAIR COMPETITION

- passing off a product of another as yours
- false or misleading advertising
- running down your competitor's goods or reputation
- copying or simulating a trade name
- trade secrets in unpatented and unpatentable items
- interference with the business growth of another
- unfair use of written works
- obstruction of competitor's suppliers
- bribing customers of competitors
- unfair usage of imported products
- boycott
- price wars
- unfounded patent litigation

If you think that you have a claim for unfair competition, ask yourself the following questions:

- has the design of the offending article been taken from yours?
- has the offending work been compared to your original work?
- does the overall appearance of the offending copy strike you as an attempt to pass it off as the original?
- does the copy have the same design but inferior workmanship and are the materials the same as the original?
- has there been trade libel or price cutting?

An example of unfair competition would be a pumpkin-shaped, machine-woven, quilted tea cozy produced by Palm Off, Inc., that is the exact replica of yours except that it uses synthetic fibers instead of handspun, vegetable-dyed wool. It is advertised as "A $10.95 Exact Replica of the Famous Wovenwork's $49.95 Pumpkin Tea Cozy." If you think you have a case of unfair competition, see a lawyer for advice and assistance.

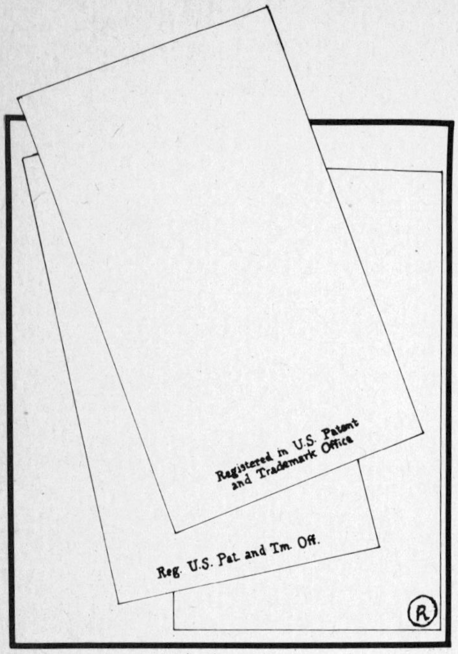

Trademark registration

TRADEMARK

> A clothier in Gloucestershire sold very good cloth so that in London if they saw any cloth of his mark they would buy it without searching thereof; and another who made ill cloth put the clothier's mark upon it without his privity, and an action was brought by him who bought the cloth for this deceit and adjudged maintainable.

Goodwill and trademarks have always been closely related. Symbols have been used as a means of giving information about the maker of goods. Examples from history include the marking of Etruscan cheese with the sign of the moon, marks on pottery found at the ancient sites of Ur, and the granting to George Washington of a trademark for his particular brand of flour.

There are both federal and state trademark statutes. If your business does not have nationwide scope or potential, then the state registration (if your state has a trademark or trade name law)* will be simpler, cheaper, and probably adequate for your needs.

The advantages of a federal trademark are:

- more protection than under common law
- nationwide protection
- coverage for a broad class of symbols
- possibly a treble damage award if you win a suit for infringement
- attorneys' fees if infringer acts in bad faith

DEFINITION

A trademark is a visible symbol identifying and distinguishing your goods from similar goods of others. It can be a word, name (Sunoco, Kodak), phrase, sign or symbol (flying red horse, muscular arm with hammer), or all of these. Federal trademarks are available only for marks used in commerce between states, or with foreign nations or Indian tribes. The federal law concerning trademarks is called the Lanham Act.

LANHAM ACT

REQUIREMENTS FOR REGISTRATION OF A TRADEMARK

A mark must be distinctive to be registered, and generally marks that are descriptive, deceptively misdescriptive, surnames, and geographical marks *are not* registrable. "Sawmotor," an oil additive for auto engines, was not registrable. "Old Country," a soap manufactured in the U.S., and "Syrup of Figs," a medicine containing few figs, were not registrable. You establish your rights in a trademark by adopting one that appears, after preliminary research, not to infringe on an existing trademark and by using it on goods in trade for a period of time. Only then may federal registration be sought. An informational pamphlet and applications can be obtained from the Patent and Trademark Office, Washington, D.C. 20231.

APPLICATION PROCESS

After your application is filed, it is examined, and if it is found not entitled to registration, then you are notified that you have six months to respond. There can be reexaminations and interference proceedings, as with patents. However, if you file an affidavit of in-

* A sample trade name registration form for Arizona is reproduced in Appendix 3-4.

TWENTY-YEAR DURATION PLUS RENEWAL

contestability (a statement that the work has been used for five years prior to registration and that there have been neither adverse decisions regarding the ownership of the mark nor proceedings involving it), then no interference proceedings are allowed. If you achieve trademark registration, it is for a twenty-year term with additional twenty-year renewal terms. Upon receipt of trademark registration, you must put the notice of trademark, an *R* in a circle ®, or "Registered in U.S. Patent and Trademark Office" or "Reg. U.S. Pat. and Tm. Off." after every use of the trademark word or symbol.

If you are considering a federal registration of your trademark or a lawsuit for trademark infringement, then you are involved in "big business" and can afford a competent lawyer.

Let's use an example illustrating some of the subjects discussed in this chapter. The creator of Free-of-Moths, which professes to keep weavers' wool free of moths, has developed an information card to be attached to the product. A patent application has been filed and is pending before the Patent Office. The card carries the trademark "Free-of-Moths," which is registered as indicated by the ® adjacent to the trademark. The content of the card is the proper subject matter for copyright registration, which copyright is indicated at the bottom of the card and is owned by the sole proprietor, Martha Blue, of the Free-of-Moths business.

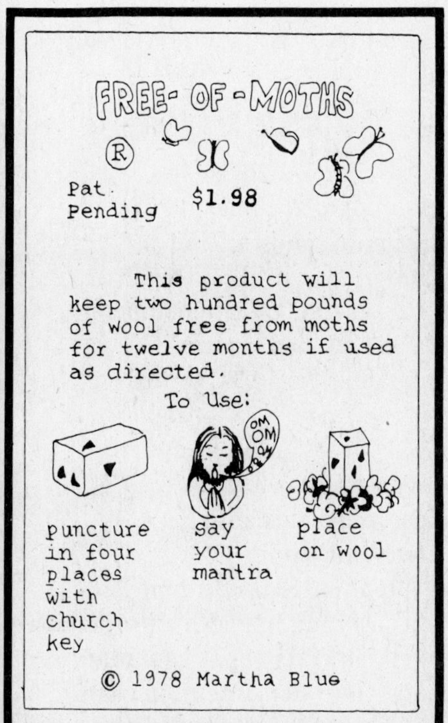

FAKE OR FORGED ARTS AND CRAFTS

Last, but not least, you should exercise caution if your own work is copied from others' work.

More than collectors are concerned about fake or forged arts and crafts. As a result of the Indian arts and crafts boom, the distribution of forgeries has reached epidemic proportions, and many groups—Native Americans, state attorney generals, and so forth—have acted to stem the tide of fakes that have been flooding the market place. The Zuni Tribe has taken action to stop a major nationwide department store from selling fake "Zuni" jewelry.

This section is informative to the forger regarding the consequences of his or her forgery, and the purchaser of the forged work or others affected by the forgery concerning what help is available.

Generally, fakes and forgeries can be divided into three categories:

- deliberately fabricated work—this is work which is created to be sold as the product of another, e.g., Mexican-made rugs and sold as Navajo rugs; old ivory carved and sold as ancient Eskimo art
- exact replicas which are sold as originals—this is work that is executed in the style of a certain artist and sold as that artist's work, e.g., David Stein painted in the style of old masters and forged names to his works
- altered art—the work is changed in order to enhance its value, e.g., when *The Misses Payne* by Sir Joshua Reynolds was restored, one of

the figures was deleted; and a plain old Mimbres pot recently had a design painted on it.

FEDERAL AND STATE GENERAL ANTIFRAUD LAWS

These general federal and state antifraud laws require proof of fraudulent or criminal intent, which is difficult to show for many forgeries because the sellers usually avoid knowledge that the work is forged or faked.

On the federal level there is the general antifraud law mentioned above and the Federal Trade Commission Act, which prohibits "unfair methods of competition in commerce and unfair or deceptive acts and practices." Under the Act it is not necessary to show actual deception. It is sufficient if the activities have a capacity to deceive. The Act is violated if there is a misrepresentation as to who created, designed, or manufactured a product. Be careful if you make "Indian goods," for the FTC has specific guidelines for Indian arts and crafts:

FTC GUIDELINES FOR INDIAN ARTS AND CRAFTS

- if sold as "Indian made," "Indian," or "American Indian," then the item must be handmade or handcrafted by Indian residents of the United States.
- if the product is made in part by machinery, then the item cannot be represented as Indian made except for those parts handmade or crafted by Indians. But if Indians played a part in the manufacture, this can be stated.
- if products contain foreign components, the country of origin must then be disclosed.

FTC COMPLAINT PROCEDURES

The FTC will not act unless the unfair competition or deceptive practices occur in interstate commerce* and concern "the public interest," that is, big-time operations. The FTC has declined to act on many of the complaints made to them because the offender's operation is too limited in scope and effect. If you have been victimized, go ahead and send your complaint letter** and ask the FTC to investigate the offender. If the FTC investigates, they may file a formal complaint, which costs you nothing, but even if they find wrongdoing, you will not get money damages. But if you are the violator, the FTC can stop your unfair or deceptive practices, plus you could get a civil penalty of up to $10,000 for each separate violation.

INDIAN ARTS AND CRAFTS BOARD ACT

Specifically directed to the Indian situation is the Indian Arts and Crafts Board*** Act which provides criminal penalties (up to $500, jail up to six months, or both) for representing goods as Indian products when the seller knew the goods were not Indian or were not Indian products of a particular tribe. Besides referring matters for prosecution, the board tries to bring the difference between genuine Indian products and imitations to public attention. By letter dated September 9, 1977, the Indian Arts and Crafts Board, in re-

* See previous discussion of interstate commerce in Chapter 2, "Legal Restrictions on Content and Materials."

** Send a copy of your letter to your friendly congressman or senator and request congressional attention.

*** The board offers a special certification mark to use in marketing for Native-owned craft-marketing enterprises with registered trademarks and high-quality products.

sponse to a complaint that certain activities violated the criminal provision of the Indian Arts and Crafts Board Act advised:

> The information you have provided does indicate a possible violation, and we have referred the matter to the Department of Justice with our recommendation that it be investigated and that criminal proceedings be instituted if warranted. However, we want to forewarn you that this provision has proven very difficult to enforce. In fact, there has not been a successful prosecution to date.

The Lanham Trademark Act discussed earlier in this chapter can provide some direct relief to a wronged individual. Under this Act, a person can recover damages if the offender has falsely represented, designated, or described goods in commerce. Also, you could get an order preventing further unfair or deceptive practices.

STATE LEGISLATION FOR INDIAN ARTS AND CRAFTS

Several states have specific legislation dealing with the protection of Native American artists and crafts persons from unfair competition, along with criminal penalties for violations of their laws. However, enforcement of these statutes has proved a problem, except for South Dakota, which has an inspection team that travels the state checking Indian articles to see if they are labeled properly. The enforcement problem is severalfold—there is no physical inspection by the state of the seller's labeling of goods because of program expense, there is no reimbursement to the defrauded purchaser, and the penalties are slight when compared with the prices charged.

ALASKAN IDENTIFICATION MARK—"AN AUTHENTIC ALASKAN NATIVE CRAFT MADE IN ALASKA"

Alaska's solution to counterfeit Native handicrafts was to allow special marks (issued by a state agency) to be placed on authentic articles of Native handicraft. There is no charge for the mark, and the work is inspected by an agent who has a permit from the Commissioner of Commerce. Recently, Alaska adopted another mark to protect handicraft items made in the state by resident Alaskans. There are criminal penalties for knowing and willful violations of these Alaska laws.

ARIZONA

Under the Arizona law it is unlawful to hold out imitation Indian arts and crafts for sale as authentic or to put a registered label on any art or craft which is not an authentic Indian work. This could be interpreted as placing a duty of checking on the dealer.

CALIFORNIA

California's law makes it unlawful to sell any article as authentic unless it is produced wholly by Indians. However, the work is recognized as authentic *if* the trademark or label is registered with the Indian Arts and Crafts Board in Washington, D.C., or with the American Indian Historical Society, Inc., in San Francisco, which is rarely done.

OTHER STATES

As of this writing, two states require that the imitation articles be segregated from the authentic work—Montana and New Mexico. New Mexico also places a duty of inquiry on the seller to discover the supplier's methods of producing the work. Many states have requirements that the seller label imitation work "not Indian made" (Minnesota), "Imitation" (Nevada, Montana), "Indian Imitation"

(New Mexico), "not genuine American Indian art or craft" (South Dakota).

State laws change frequently. The above discussion is not exhaustive, so if you make Indian arts and crafts, or sell Indian arts and crafts, we suggest that you check with the Attorney General's Office of the states where you will sell your goods to determine their law or have a legal opinion prepared concerning the requirements of the pertinent state laws.

Both New York and Michigan have enacted special laws governing the sale of inauthentic artworks. These laws generally hold the seller of a work to his or her representations concerning the history and authenticity of the artwork. As discussed in Chapter 4, "Making Contracts," several warranty sections of the Uniform Commercial Code would also apply to the sale of fake or forged arts or crafts.

OTHER STATE AUTHENTICITY LAWS

New York State also has a criminal law concerning the making or alteration of objects so that they appear rare, old, or authored by someone else or the issuance of a false certificate of authenticity of a fine work of art.

SOURCES

pg. 52 The Copyright Revision Act of 1976: Title 17, U.S. Code Annotated, Section 101 *et seq.*

pg. 52 First English Copyright Act: Act of Anne, 1710.

pg. 55 Statutory exception to Copyright Act's work-for-hire rule: Title 17, U.S. Code, Annotated, Section 201.

pg. 56 Subject matter of copyright under the revision: Title 17, U.S. Code, Annotated, Section 102(a).

pg. 57 Definition of pictorial, graphic, and sculptural works: Title 17, U.S. Code, Annotated, Section 101.

pg. 57 Classic case on copyright of utilitarian art: *Mazer v. Stein*, 347 U.S. 201 (1954).

pg. 57 Variations on a cardinal theme: *Franklin Mint Corp. v. National Wildlife Exchange Inc.*, 575 F. 2d 62 (1978) cert denied in 99 SC 217.

pg. 58 Subjects not copyrightable: Title 17, U.S. Code, Annotated, Section 102(b).

pg. 59 Obscenity not copyrightable: *Mitchell Bros. Film Group v. Cinema Adult Theatres*, C. A. No. 3-74-645-D (U.S.D. C. No. D., Texas, 1976).

pg. 59 Definition of publication in new law: Title 17, U.S. Code, Annotated, Section 101.

pg. 60 Fabric case where notice destroyed: *Peter Pan Fabrics, Inc. v. Martin Weiner Corp.*, 274 F. 2d 487 (2d Cir. 1960).

pg. 60 Omission of copyright notice: Title 17, U.S. Code, Annotated, Section 405.

pg. 62 Single registration for group-related works: Title 17, U.S. Code, Annotated, Section 408 (c) (1).

pg. 64 Exclusive rights of the copyright owner: Title 17, U.S. Code, Annotated, Section 106.

pg. 64 Infringer of copyright: Title 17, U.S. Code, Annotated, Section 501(a).

pg. 65 Fair Use: Title 17, U.S. Code, Annotated, Section 107.

pg. 65 Damages for infringement: Title 17, U.S. Code, Annotated, Section 504.

pg. 68 The subject of a U.S. patent: Title 35, U.S. Code, Annotated, Section 100.

pg. 70 Design patent: Title 35, U.S. Code, Annotated, Section 171.

pg. 71 Kite case: *Zachary v. Weston Publishing Co., Inc.*, 143 Cal Rept. 34 (1977).

pg. 73 Unfair competition is a common law remedy and is also covered somewhat by the Lanham Act: Title 15, U.S. Code, Annotated, Section 1125 *et seq.*

pg. 74 Trademark: Title 15, U.S. Code, Annotated, Section 1065.

pg. 74 A case heard in the court of common pleas in 1591, the thirty-third year of the reign of Elizabeth I from *Two Hundred Years of English and American Patent, Trademark and Copyright Law*, a Bicentennial Symposium presented by the American Bar Association Section of Patents, Trademark, and Copyright Law, August 9, 1976.

pg. 75 See the excellent article by Leonard D. Duboff, "Controlling the Artful Con: Authentication and Regulation," 27 *Hastings Law Journal* 973.

pg. 76 The federal general antifraud statute: Title 18, U.S. Code, Annotated, Sections 1341, 1343.

pg. 76 Federal Trade Commission Act: Title 15, U.S. Code, Annotated, Section 45.

pg. 76 Federal crime re fake Indian arts and crafts: Title 18, U.S. Code, Annotated, Section 1159.

pg. 77 Lanham Trademark Act: Title 15, U.S. Code, Annotated, Section 1125.

pg. 77 State statutes regulating Indian arts and crafts: Alaska Statutes Section 45.65.010–45.65.070.

pg. 77 Arizona Revised Statutes Sections 44-1231–44-1233.

pg. 77 California Business and Professional Code, Sections 17569–17569.9.

pg. 77 Revised Codes of Montana, Sections 85-301 to 304.

pg. 77 New Mexico Statutes Annotated, Sections 40-21–40-25.1.

pg. 77 Minnesota Statutes Annotated, Sections 325.41–325.43.

pg. 77 Nevada Revised Statutes, Section 598.050.

pg. 78 South Dakota Codified Laws, Sections 37-7-1–37-7-2.1.

pg. 78 State art authenticity laws: New York General Business Laws, Section 219b-e; Michigan Complied Laws, Sections 442.321–442.324.

pg. 78 Criminal law concerning forgeries: New York Penal Law, Section 170.45.

Chapter 4 Making Contracts

WHAT IS A CONTRACT

Alice's Allegory # 12

or

Find the Contracts Hidden Below

Alice fueled up old Viola the VW for a trip into town to drop off some bowls and mugs at the Artists Coop. She dusted off her going-to-town costume and hoped that the hot-air balloons would be rising along the way.

Alice had breakfast at Mother Nurture and Son with a strawberry smoothie and the revitalizing combination of Mu-Ginseng tea to percolate her through her errands. She dropped off the pottery at the Coop and picked up all the local artsy gossip. Then to Bart's Art Supply, where Alice placed an order for some special glazes that Bart didn't have in stock. With fortunate timing, Alice drove home in the setting sun.

The first step in understanding the basic law of contracts is to perform this simple exercise: sit up straight, close your eyes, and EXORCISE all prior notions that you have concerning the law of contracts such as: all contracts must be written; you never made a contract in your life; contracts must be typed, on white paper, and be notarized; all contracts last forever; making a contract involves too much red tape; and so on. The discussion of the law of contracts that follows is a general one. State law varies in this area so check with your local legal eagle for the provisions of your state's contract laws.

EXORCISE

WARNING

Alice made at least four contracts on the day described above. The first was a gas contract with Rainbow Hill Axon; the second was a breakfast contract with Mother Nurture and Son; the third was a consignment contract with the Artists Coop; and fourth was the special-order contract with Bart.

DEFINITION

DEFINITION

Quite simply, a contract is an exchange of promises between two or more people which is enforceable by law. Had Alice forgotten to pay Mother Nurture, Mother could successfully sue her for the price of the breakfast. Although Alice did not say, "I hereby promise to pay Mother Nurture $1.50 if she delivers to my table a smoothie and tea," and although Alice and Mother Nurture did not sign a written contract, an agreement was made by implication and is legally enforceable.

IMPLIED CONTRACT

The abstract-contract-theory-in-the-sky requires five essential ingredients to make a legally enforceable contract:

- offer
- acceptance
- consideration
- competence
- legality

OFFER An offer sounds like: "I will pay you $75 for a set of that wonderful green stoneware." An acceptance sounds like: "O.K." In some situations, the only way you can accept an offer is by taking action. A reward for a lost llama is this sort of offer. Consideration is what the parties to the contract promise to give each other, and it usually has a dollar-and-cents value. Sometimes consideration can take the form of refraining from action. "I will give you $10 if you stop smoking cigarettes," for example.

ACCEPTANCE

CONSIDERATION

ACCEPTANCE OF AN OFFER

Usually offers may be withdrawn at any time before acceptance. But once an offer is accepted, a contract is formed and the offer cannot be withdrawn. If Alice had changed her mind and decided to order the "Good Morning Special" at Mother Nurture's, she could not withdraw her offer and make a new offer after Mother Nurture had accepted Alice's first offer and put the strawberries in the blender. Of course, if Mother Nurture was agreeable, then Alice could withdraw her offer.

WISH ≠ OFFER

At Bart's Art Supply if Alice had said, "It sure would be nice if you would order me some special glazes for that stoneware order," and Bart had said, "O.K.," there would be no contract, because Alice's statement was not an offer, only a wish. To make an offer, you must make a firm, definite promise. If there is a disagreement over whether an offer was made, the courts will look to the demonstrated *intent* of those involved. If Bart had gotten the glazes anyway, he could not force Alice to purchase them, nor could Alice force Bart to get the glazes for her, because no contract was formed. However, since Alice had made an offer—"I hereby order some special green glazes" and had agreed to pay consideration, then the contract between Alice and Bart is enforceable by either party.

CAPACITY TO CONTRACT

INCOMPETENTS

Beware of making a contract with the insane or demented, and those rendered mentally incompetent by reason of excessive use of drugs, alcohol, et cetera. These people can break their contracts even though the incompetent's failure to uphold his or her end of the bargain would bring harm and damage to you, the other party. This is because these people do not have the "capacity" to make a contract. If the person ordering the stoneware was a reeling drunk and decided to reject Alice's specially and speedily produced set of green stoneware, Alice could not get a court to enforce her contract.

MINORS

In the past, minors also were able to break their contracts, because of their youth. Today, with the growth in both the rights and responsibilities of minors, some states will hold minors to their business contracts. If contracting with a minor, find out what your state law says in this area.

LEGALITY

Contracts to break the law usually will not be enforced by the courts. So don't go to court to collect an outstanding debt from last month's poker game.

WRITTEN CONTRACTS

WRITTEN CONTRACT OFTEN UNNECESSARY

If you hadn't noticed, none of Alice's contracts involved much writing. At Mother Nurture's the waiter wrote a bill on a blank piece of paper which Alice gave to the cashier when she paid. The Artists Coop gave Alice a receipt listing the items received and the date. Bart gave Alice nothing. A contract does not have to be on paper to be enforceable. Salvador Dali verbally agreed to paint a picture of the Statue of Liberty on live television as a fund-raising gimmick and later thought better of his offer. Dali asked the court to dismiss the case filed against him, saying that the agreement to paint a picture of the Statue of Liberty was not written and therefore not enforceable. The court allowed the case to continue, saying that there could be an enforceable oral contract for personal services in this case.

Only in a few cases* must a contract be written in order to be enforceable:

CONTRACTS THAT *MUST* BE WRITTEN

- contracts for sales of goods valued at over $500
- contracts which cannot be completed within one year
- contracts for the sale of land
- leases for longer than one year

There are other situations where a writing is required to make an enforceable contract but these are not relevant to the areas covered in this book.

EXCEPTIONS TO WRITTEN REQUIREMENTS

Under certain circumstances, even oral contracts for the sale of goods valued at over $500 are enforceable. An oral contract for the sale of specially made goods valued at over $500 is enforceable if production of the special order has begun. Also, oral agreements between "merchants" (most artists and craftmakers who are earning a regular income from their work could be considered "merchants") for the sale of goods of $500 or more are enforceable *if* the oral agreement is confirmed in writing and the confirmation is not objected to within ten days of its receipt. Also, if goods valued at $500 or more are received and accepted by the buyer, pursuant to an oral contract, the agreement is enforceable even though it is not in writing.

Alice's Allegory # 13

or

Beware of Woofs in Sheep's Clothing

Nine o'clock Monday morning the telephone rang on Rainbow Hill. "Must be some eager beaver," said Alice as she jumped over the sleeping dog to get to the phone. It was Warp and Woof Woof offering a good deal on a truckload of wool. "Sure," said Alice, thinking of the wool for macrame hangers for her Fabulous Flowerpots. She hung up the phone and forgot all about her con-

* These rules vary slightly from state to state, so check.

versation while she packed up Viola the VW for a trip to her Great-Uncle's one-hundredth-birthday party.

Home again, two weeks later, Alice found a letter from Warp and Woof Woof confirming her order of wool. Having spent her last dollar on a crate of fresh apricots, there was no way she could pay for the wool.

Old Cautious, the extended family lawyer, told Alice that she did not have a long or a short leg to stand on—oral contracts for goods valued at over $500 are enforceable *if* confirmed in writing and not objected to within ten days—and that Woof Woof had her over a barrel so to speak. Cautious then negotiated a partial trade of pots for the wool bill, and Alice dazedly caught a quick ride home, far away from the madding crowd.

GET IT IN WRITING

Although a written contract is required only in a few situations, one of the messages of this chapter is to get *all* contracts in writing *now* to avoid trouble later. One reason for getting agreements in writing is the problem of proving the terms of an oral agreement in court. Many times lawsuits based upon oral contracts boil down to one party's word against the other—that is, a swearing contest.

WARRANTIES

Besides laws spelling out the requirements for an enforceable contract, state law sometimes inserts other terms into a contract. The contract terms inserted by state and federal state law ("gap fillers") are usually for the protection of consumers or to simplify the law and foster the making of good contracts. Where these laws would affect the contracts discussed in this chapter, we will examine their application.

IMPLIED WARRANTIES

Perhaps of most concern to artists and craftmakers are the laws concerning warranties. Although Larry Leatherman does not state to a customer that the leather briefcase he is selling is the "best in the West," the law implies at least three warranty terms into Larry Leatherman's contract of sale of items for personal, family, or household use, that is, consumer goods. One warranty is that the briefcase is "fit for the ordinary purposes for which such goods are used," which in the case of a briefcase is to hold business papers. Another warranty implied by the law is fitness for a particular purpose. If Larry Leatherman receives a special commission for a sword swallower's carrying case, the size should be such to handle assorted swords and other paraphernalia.

"AS IS"

OBVIOUS FLAW

You can avoid the application of these two warranty terms to your sales contracts by including the term that the goods are sold "as is" or "with all faults" in your sales agreement. Also, if a defect is clearly evident upon inspection, a split on the rim of a ceramic mug, for example, the law does not imply a warranty about this obvious flaw.

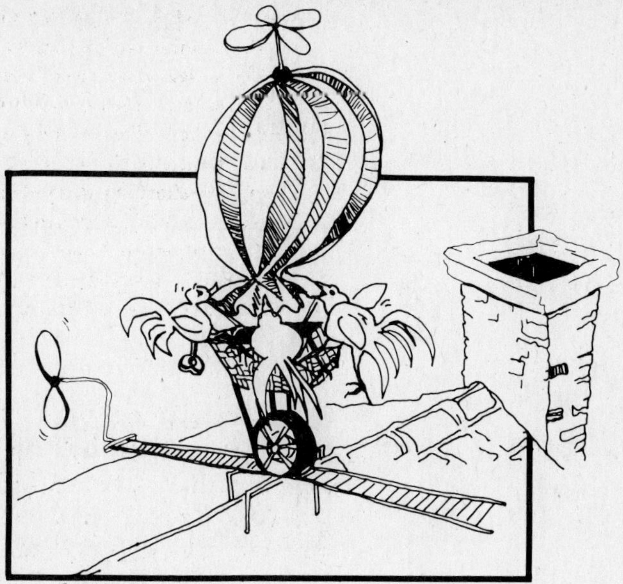

Sure it flies

WARRANTY OF GOOD AND CLEAN TITLE

Another warranty inserted by law into sales contracts is a guarantee that the seller has the authority to transfer good title (ownership) to the buyer and that the items sold are not burdened by a lien or other clouds on the title. In order to avoid the application of this warranty to a sale, the seller must alert the buyer that seller does not claim to have good title.

EXPRESS WARRANTY

The law also may turn a little of your fast-talking salesmanship into an express warranty. You may be held to guaranteeing any words, written or spoken, relating to the item to be sold. If you advertise in the *Campus Register* for individually designed and tested flying roof ornaments in all colors of the rainbow, those contraptions had better dance with delight in a high wind. Is the best salesperson a mute salesperson, then? The best salesperson is one who offers an

"OPINION"

opinion on the goods to be sold but does not promise or state marvelous things that are not true.

WARRANTY OF AUTHORSHIP

By placing your name on your work, you "expressly" guarantee your authorship of the piece. Because of the problem of fakes in art, New York and Michigan have special laws governing the authenticity of artwork.

FORMALITIES

FORMALITIES OF MAKING A CONTRACT

Contracts come in all shapes and sizes, and with the exception of agreeing to break the law, you have pretty much free rein in drafting the terms of your contract. The language of the contract should be clear and mandatory. Take a tip from Horton and mean what you say and say what you mean. A written contract need not be a formal typewritten document with notarized signatures. A signed, handwritten statement of the essential points of the agreement is a fine contract. In most states, a signed letter containing the terms of the contract binds the signer of the letter. Beware of the fine print on the back of your suppliers' purchase orders. Sit down, put on your reading glasses, and scrutinize each paragraph. If you object to any of these contract terms, make a written objection to the supplier or you will be held to those terms.

For some contracts, the assistance of a lawyer will be required. See Chapter 8, "Obtaining Legal Assistance," for more information on when and how to get a lawyer.

A CONTRACT FOR EVERY OCCASION

DIRECT SALES

DEFINITION

Many artists and craftmakers prefer to sell directly to their customers. This arrangement is the most lucrative, the least risky, and puts the creator in touch with his or her audience. Direct sales account for the majority of transactions for many artists and craftmakers and take place in a variety of settings—craft fairs, studios, mall shows, in the street—and are contracted with a variety of customers—individuals, museums, galleries, schools, banks, et cetera.

In many cases, the only documentation of a direct sale is a receipt with price, date, and sales tax listed. For the Rainbow Company's sale of three hand-glazed clay flowerpots, the sales receipt shown in Figure 4-1 is a perfectly adequate record of the transaction.

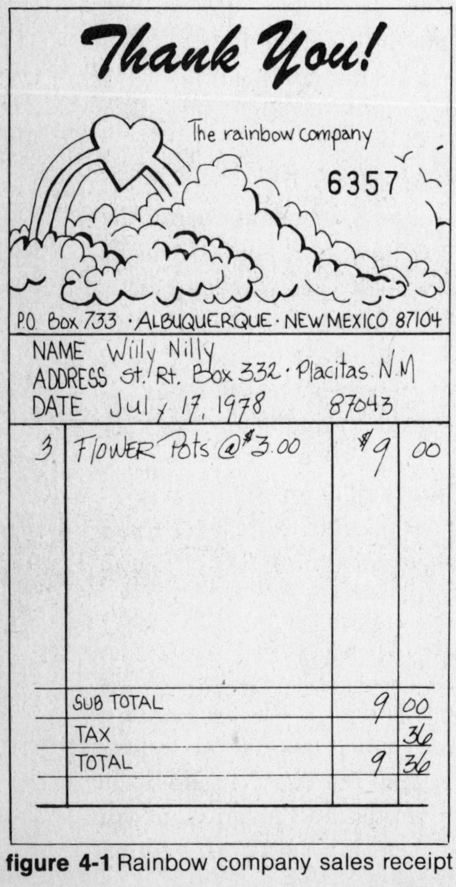
Thank You!

The rainbow company

6357

P.O. Box 733 · ALBUQUERQUE · NEW MEXICO 87104

NAME Willy Nilly
ADDRESS St./Rt. Box 332 · Placitas N.M 87043
DATE July 17, 1978

3	Flower Pots @ $3.00	$9	00
	SUB TOTAL	9	00
	TAX		36
	TOTAL	9	36

figure 4-1 Rainbow company sales receipt

Alice's Allegory # 14

or

Sadder but Wiser

One fine windy fall day, Alice sat dreaming on Rainbow Hill with stars in her eyes and wind in her hair. Since such a marvelous convergence of the elements is apt to produce brilliant inspirations, Alice had one—porcelain bath-towel racks.

Being prone to follow where inspiration leads, Alice found Romero lying under Viola the VW and told him to come and help on this great inspiration.

Alice sold out her entire collection of her handsome porcelain bath-towel racks at the next arts and crafts fair to Knew Contractors, who were producing handcrafted houses and wanted Alice's racks for every nook and cranny of the bathing grottos. Romero said he wouldn't mind delivering the racks, because he wanted to check out the design of Knew's solar spaces.

Late that night when everybody slept, a tornado whirled out of nowhere and took all of the porcelain bath-towel racks to the land of Oz. Alice was also blown away because she had already spent Knew's check on the beautiful stained-glass window that she had been coveting for years. And she knew that Knew knew that the risk of loss was on seller till receipt by buyer.

For other transactions, like Alice's unfortunate sale described above, the seller and the buyer should discuss various issues involved in the sale and resolve each of the issues and write down the terms. Even a sale or gift to a friend that involves special terms should be memorialized on paper. Better to negotiate now than to lose a friend later over a disagreement on what exactly were the terms of the sale. It does happen, you know. Appendix 4-1 contains a direct-sales contract for reference in sales made directly to customers.

This next section will discuss the various issues that should be considered when negotiating a direct-sale contract and will be followed by a checklist enumerating each of these issues.

NAMES AND ADDRESSES

Besides providing the buyer and the seller with each other's name for future reference (contact for shows, Christmas cards, future sales, lawsuits, etc.), it is important to obtain the seller's name and address in the event you need to recall the work or for some other reason notify the purchaser.

PRICE

The price of the work being sold is a basic consideration under the payment terms of the contract. If the customer is going to make payments over time, or trade for the work, then these details should be hammered out and put in writing. If the sale provides for installment payments, the agreement should state that transfer of title will occur upon completion of the payments and that until full payment, the artist retains a security interest in the work. By retaining a security interest, the artist can "repossess" the work if the purchaser fails to make payments. Also, the artist's security interest in the work would protect the work from seizure by purchaser's creditors.

SECURITY INTEREST

Because of the high prices that some modern art is bringing on resale, some artists include in the sale contract a clause which entitles them to a percentage (usually 15 percent) of any increase over the original price at the time of resale. Appendix 4-2 contains a copy of the Artist's Reserved Rights Transfer and Sale Agreement, second edition, which gives the artist 15 percent of any resale profits. This contract, drafted after discussions with artists, dealers, lawyers, collectors, and others is relatively new and somewhat controversial. California recently passed a law governing the resale of an artwork for $1,000 or more, which requires that the artist receive 5 percent of the gross resale price provided that the resale price exceeds the purchase price. Of course, this law covers only resales in California or by a California resident.

RIGHT TO PERCENTAGE OF RESALE PROFIT

In the sale of a work, the artist, craftmaker, or writer automatically retains the copyright *unless* the contract specifically states otherwise. Also the creator may sell part of the copyright and retain the

COPYRIGHT

balance, which Arnold Artist did when he simply sold the right to produce postcard copies of his work.*

The simplest sale with the simplest logistics is cash and carry. However, this is not always possible.

> Memorandum
>
> TO: Wood Shaver File
> FROM: MBD
> RE: Drafting Contract for Client to Use in Sale of Large Cherry Desk
>
> After interview with client, contract for sale of cherry desk should include special terms concerning:
>
> 1. delivery
> 2. risk of loss
> 3. insurance
>
> Wood Shaver and his buyer have made the following arrangements, which should be included in the contract:
>
> 1. Delivery: Since Wood Shaver has truck, he will deliver desk to buyer's home at Peaceful Mountain Top, Vermont, after buyer has paid purchase price.
> 2. Risk of Loss: Risk of loss to pass to buyer upon delivery of the desk, even though payment received prior to delivery.
> 3. Insurance: Since risk of loss is on Wood Shaver, then he will insure the desk until delivery.

DELIVERY

If a contract does not state who is responsible for delivery, the buyer would have to make these arrangements, provided the seller made the work available to the buyer and told the buyer how to pick up the work.**

RISK OF LOSS

If a contract does not say anything about who is out of luck if the work is damaged before it reaches the buyer, the seller loses. If the seller has agreed to deliver by carrier, then risk of loss is on the seller until the buyer receives or the post office or the shipping company has notified the buyer of the arrival of the goods.

INSURANCE

If the seller has agreed to arrange for shipment of the goods, then the seller also is responsible for arranging insurance during shipment even if he or she had not specifically agreed to do this. It should be noted here that most shippers do not provide *complete* insurance coverage. If the parties wish to obtain *complete* coverage while the work is being shipped, the sale contract should specify who should obtain and pay for such coverage. Open your returning artwork from a faraway show at the post office and get the clerk to sign a description of any damage.

The final groups of rights that could be included in a sales contract—acknowledgment of authorship, artistic integrity, exhibition

* For more information on copyright, see Chapter 3, "Copying."

** See Figure 4-2 for a sample letter notifying a buyer of where and how to pick up the work purchased.

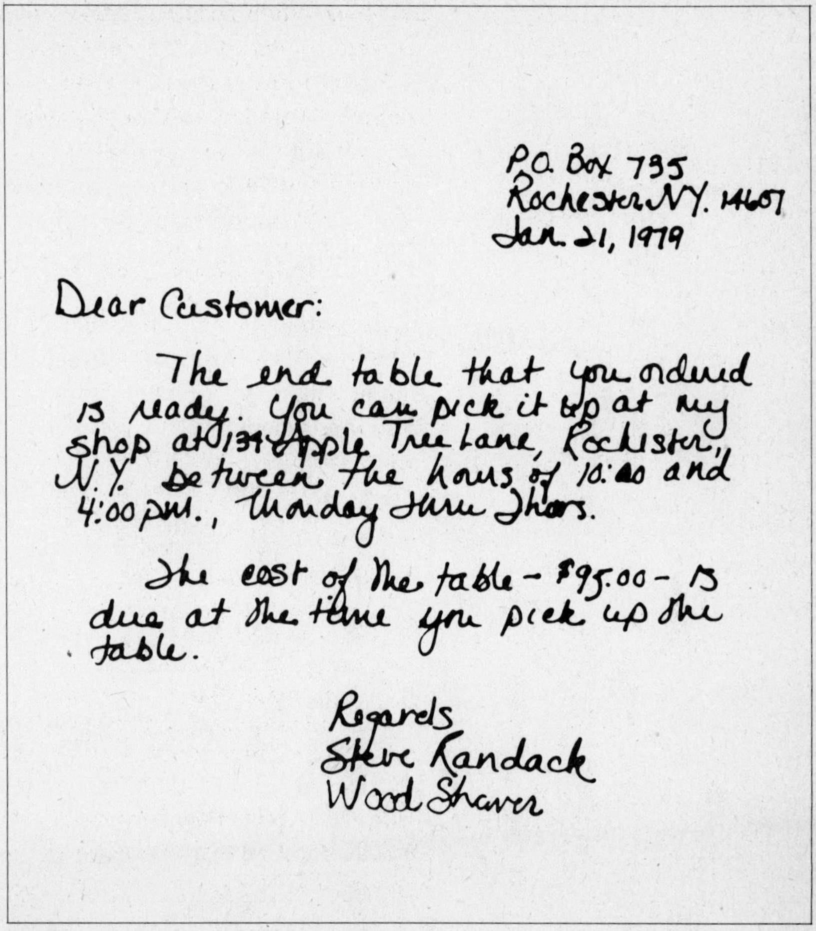

P.O. Box 735
Rochester N.Y. 14607
Jan. 21, 1979

Dear Customer:

The end table that you ordered is ready. You can pick it up at my shop at 134 Apple Tree Lane, Rochester, N.Y. between the hours of 10:00 and 4:00 pm., Monday thru Thurs.

The cost of the table - $95.00 - is due at the time you pick up the table.

Regards
Steve Randack
Wood Shaver

figure 4-2 Buyer notification letter

ARTIST'S RIGHTS

rights—are sometimes called artists' rights or *droit morale.* Some of these rights are guaranteed by law in over sixty countries of the world. With one exception,* artists and craftmakers have none of these rights in the U.S.A. unless the contract of sale spells out these protections.

ACKNOWLEDGMENT OF AUTHORSHIP

In several instances where artists have demanded acknowledgment of their authorship, the courts have decided that an artist is *not* entitled to have the authorship attributed to him or her unless the contract of sale so specifies. Some time ago, Vargas sued *Esquire* magazine for carrying some of his drawings without attributing the work to Vargas. He lost.

ARTISTIC INTEGRITY

A clause in the sales contract concerning artistic integrity would protect an artwork from mutilation or destruction and would give the artist the right to repair or restore a work that he or she sold. Without

* The recently passed California Art in Public Buildings Act requires that the state respect the moral rights of the participating artists. This includes the requirement that each work "is properly maintained and is not artistically altered in any manner without the consent of the artist." The act also provides that the artist has the right to acknowledgment of authorship.

such a provision, artists have no way, after sale, to prevent their work from being destroyed or probably even mutilated.* The contract of sale should require the artist's consent before any alteration or destruction of the work occurs and provide that the artist be notified in the event of the requirement of repairs or restoration so that artist has an opportunity to perform the repairs for a reasonable fee.

EXHIBITION RIGHTS

The exhibition clause could give the artist the right to retrieve the work for an exhibit for certain periods of time, like six weeks, every few years.

To prepare for the negotiating session when you are making an agreement governing the direct sale of art or crafts, (and to ensure that all the major questions are covered in your agreement), use the following checklist:

CHECKLIST—DIRECT-SALES AGREEMENT

	Artist	Purchaser
1. Name:	____________	____________
Address:	____________	____________
	____________	____________

2. Payment:

Amount: __________ Terms: __________ Due Dates: __________

Right to __________% resale profits: [ ] yes [ ] no
Security Interest Retained until paid in full: [ ] yes [ ] no

3. Identification of Work:

Title: ____________________ Date: __________

Medium: ______________ Description: __________

4. Copyright:
[ ] Retained by Artist (automatically)

[ ] Other (explain) ____________________

5. Delivery:
[ ] Responsibility on Purchaser
[ ] Responsibility on Artist

6. Risk of Loss Prior to Receipt by Buyer:
[ ] On Purchaser
[ ] On Artist

[ ] Other (explain) ____________________

Provision of ____________________

7. Full insurance coverage prior to receipt by Buyer on:
[ ] Purchaser
[ ] Artist

[ ] Other (explain) ____________________

____

* An artist sued to remove the paint placed over his fresco commissioned by the Rutgers Presbyterian Church. He lost.

8. Acknowledgment of Authorship Required:
   [ ] yes
   [ ] no
9. Artistic Integrity:
   a. Restoration and repair rights in Artist:
      [ ] yes
      [ ] no
   b. Protection from mutilation or destruction:
      [ ] yes
      [ ] no
10. Exhibition Rights:
    [ ] Artist's right to regain work at no cost to Buyer for ________ days every ________ year(s), for purpose of exhibition

SALES THROUGH GALLERIES

Most artist-gallery relationships are based upon consignment arrangements. Consignment means that the artist retains title to his or her work during the time the work is at the gallery. When the work is sold by the gallery, the title passes directly from the artist to the buyer. Since the gallery both has possession of your work and also acts as your agent to the public, choice of the right gallery is very important and should be carefully made.

CHOOSING A GALLERY

A gallery should be honest in its dealings, financially sound, and acceptable as your representative to the public. Some artists and craftmakers feel a most important point in a gallery choice is the possibility of an open and comfortable working relationship with the gallery.

Since it is possible, except in New York, California, Connecticut, Michigan, and Texas,* that an artist's works on consignment at a gallery could be taken in court proceedings brought by the creditors of the gallery, it is important that a gallery be investigated before placing work on consignment there. This is especially important if you are placing works with an out-of-state gallery, because of the added difficulty of resolving differences across state lines. The best reference, of course, for your potential gallery are other artists and craftmakers who have dealt with the gallery. Also, the American Crafts Council in New York City provides a reference service for craftmakers interested in checking out a gallery. The ACC also keeps track of complaints made about galleries. The local Better Business Bureau may have information on the gallery, especially if artists had complaints about it in the past.

CHECKING OUT A GALLERY

Since the gallery's records establish the prices paid for the work and the commission taken by the gallery, it is important that the gallery keep accurate and complete records of all its transactions and that these records be available for inspection by the artist.

GALLERY RECORDS

* These states have enacted special laws concerning the relationship of the gallery to the artist. These laws specifically exempt works of art on consignment in a gallery from seizure by the gallery's creditors or when the gallery declares bankruptcy.

ART IS BIG BUCKS

The size and annual gross of arts and crafts galleries are as varied as the sandal sizes in a Franciscan Monastery. In 1975, it was estimated that the art galleries in New York City alone grossed in excess of $200 million. Art can mean big bucks, and like it or not, the art gallery is the broker of this sometimes lucrative business.

ARTIST-GALLERY LEGISLATION

Any business based upon sale of another's work has the potential for abuse. Some art dealers in New York who failed to remit regular payments to their artists caused such an uproar among artists that the state legislature passed special laws to protect artists from art dealers and to prosecute art dealers should they wrongfully withhold the artist's portion of the sale proceeds. The recent legal contests between artists or their heirs and galleries concerning the works of Franz Kline, William de Kooning, and Mark Rothko further illustrate the potential for controversy in the artist-gallery relationship. An ounce of prevention is worth a pound of cure. Don't wait until you are a "successful" artist before you consider negotiating a written contract with your galleries.

NEGOTIATING A DEAL

Associating with a gallery is a serious step in an artist or craftmaker's life. It may take three or four meetings to negotiate a mutually satisfactory agreement. At the final negotiating session, be prepared: know what terms you want in the agreement; have a contract with you that reflects your wishes, and if you want the gallery to use a special sales contract when they sell your work, have a copy of that with you too. For many artists and craftmakers, negotiations are easier and more successful if you use a friend or attorney to help you.

After agreeing with the gallery on the terms of the contract, change the form contract to reflect the negotiated settlement; cross out clauses not applicable and add any additional terms; date the document; and then both parties should initial all changes and sign their names.

CHECKLIST—ARTIST-GALLERY AGREEMENT

	Artist	Gallery
1. Name:	____________________	____________________
Address:	____________________	____________________
	____________________	____________________

2. Appoint of Gallery as Artist's Agent:
[ ] yes [ ] no
[ ] in ____________________ geographic area
[ ] in ____________________ media area
[ ] for all works
[ ] for all works except:
[ ] commissions [ ] studio sales [ ] trades
[ ] juried shows [ ] gifts
[ ] for those works chosen by Gallery

[ ] for those works agreed to by Artist and Gallery

[ ] other ______________________________

3. Delivery and Return:
   a. Responsibility of delivery—costs and insurance on:
      [ ] Artist [ ] Gallery
   b. Responsibility of return—costs and insurance on:
      [ ] Artist [ ] Gallery
4. Selling Price Set by:
   [ ] agreement between Artist and Gallery with __________ percent commission
   [ ] Gallery; Artist to receive agreed-upon net price
   [ ] Gallery may discount __________ percent from agreed-upon price in sales to museums, galleries, decorators, and architects
5. Commissions due Gallery on:
   [ ] all sales by Artist
   [ ] all sales by Artist arising from Gallery contact
   [ ] Gallery sales only
6. Payment:
   [ ] within thirty days of receipt
   [ ] within thirty days of receipt of an installment payment; the entire payment to Artist until his or her percentage is paid in full
   [ ] Gallery agrees to bear all losses due to the failure of customer's credit
7. Approval Sales:
   [ ] yes, for __________ days [ ] no
8. Assurances:
   [ ] Artist warrants that work is an original, owned and executed by him/her
   [ ] Artist will deliver at least __________ works every __________ month(s)
   [ ] Gallery will promote Artist's work
9. Exhibition:
   [ ] Gallery agrees to arrange exhibition(s) of Artist's work of ______ days in length, cost of exhibition paid by ______________
   [ ] Artist shall be consulted concerning the details of the exhibition including other exhibitors, program design, etc.
   [ ] ______________________ will pay for costs of framing, etc.
10. Statements:
    [ ] Shall be made every _______ month(s) and shall include:
       [ ] works sold
       [ ] date, price, and terms of sale
       [ ] purchaser's name and address
       [ ] commission due Gallery
       [ ] location of all unsold works not at Gallery
11. Sale Contract:
    [ ] special contract for sale of work required
12. Copyright:
    [ ] Artist retains copyright (automatically)
    [ ] other ______________________________

13. Loss or Damage:
    [ ] Gallery responsible for providing insurance coverage from date of delivery to date of removal at __________ percent of the agreed price
    [ ] Gallery insurance covers loss from
        [ ] fire [ ] theft [ ] negligence
        [ ] acts of God
14. Termination:
    [ ] right of either party to terminate within __________ days of giving notice to the other
    [ ] must wait ninety days from date of exhibition to terminate
15. Contract Disputes:
    [ ] settled by arbitration
    [ ] winner entitled to attorneys' fees
    [ ] ______________________ state law governs contract

This checklist presupposes that the gallery will be taking the work on consignment. If you are lucky enough to be selling direct to a gallery, use the direct-sale-contract checklist in the previous section as well as any of the artist-gallery contract terms that would be applicable.

Not all artists or craftmakers have the luxury of dictating the terms of a gallery agreement. Many times the starving artist will have little choice in the terms of a contract with a gallery, because the bargaining power of the parties is unequal. If you must use the gallery's contract form, isolate three or four key issues and try to negotiate the changes in the contract that you feel are essential. Figure 4-3 is an old Wood Shaver–gallery agreement that has been revised to be a little more favorable to the artist.

PROTECT YOURSELF WITH A FINANCING STATEMENT

At the conclusion of all artist-gallery negotiations and contract signing, you and the gallery representative should fill out and sign a "financing statement."* File a copy of the financing statement with the Attorney General or the state or county office that records such documents. The financing statement should be filed in the state or county where the gallery is located. Figure 4-4 is a copy of the financing agreement that Wood Shaver filed to protect his works on consignment to Bark Arts Gallery.

This additional step in the standard procedures for artist-gallery contracts protects the artist's work from seizure by the gallery's creditors. Without filing a financing statement, your carefully drawn tri-panel might vanish under the arm of one of the gallery's creditors without even so much as a thank-you.

* If the gallery is located in California, Connecticut, Michigan, New York, or Texas, you may not have to file a financing statement to protect your work on consignment to a gallery. Each of these states has passed a law concerning special treatment for artists' works on consignment. Since these laws vary somewhat from state to state concerning what is covered by the law (crafts) and any requirements for getting this special treatment (special signs, etc.), check this to see exactly what your artwork consignment law is. Chapter 8, "Obtaining Legal Assistance," gives the address of Volunteer Lawyers for the Arts, which should be able to help.

RECEIPT AND CONSIGNMENT AGREEMENT

BARK ARTS

Date: July 15, 1978

Received from:

Name of artist: Wood Shaver

Address: P.O. Box 735
Rochester, N.Y. 14607 phone: ________

The following items:
(title, medium, size) Price

		Price
3	1) SMALL OAK BOXES	$15.00 EACH
1	2) CHERRY DINING TABLE	$250.00
	3)	
	4)	
	5)	
	6)	

The items listed on this receipt are placed on consignment with BARK ARTS for sale and the terms of this agreement between the artist and BARK ARTS are as follows: 40%

For the service of promoting and selling the artist's work, BARK ARTS will receive a commission on each item sold. ~~will set the retail price for each item, which will determine the commission. The commission on any item will be no less than 30% nor more than 50% of the retail price; and the average commission from all items on consignment will approximate 40%. When an item is sold the artist will receive, as payment, the amount of the price indicated on this form.~~ A.S. S.R. Payment to the artist for any sale made during a month will be sent to the artist on the last day of that month.

Reproduction rights on each of the listed items are reserved by the artist.

BARK ARTS will take every precaution to protect the items entrusted to it under the terms of this agreement; however, BARK ARTS will not be held responsible for items should they be lost, stolen or damaged.

The artist may remove the listed items from BARK ARTS at any time for any reason, thereby terminating this agreement.

Prices listed above will be the one retail sale price. Bark Arts to receive 40% A.S. S.R.

Steve Randack
artist's signature
(Wood Shaver)

[signature]
for
BARK ARTS

figure 4-3 Artist-gallery agreement

Alice's Allegory # 15

or

Bald der Dash and his Scented Dome

While at the Fall arts and crafts fair in Tucumcari, a representative of a Dallas gallery saw Alice's handsome porcelain bath-towel racks and was so excited that he hit his bald head on a hanging pot full of scented geraniums. Rubbing his now scented dome, he introduced himself as Bald der Dash and told Alice that he would take all the bath-towel racks that she had and more.

Alice was excited by the gallery's interest and told Mr. Dash that she would be happy to sell him her entire porcelain bath-towel bar supply and

Financing Statement

Name of Gallery (debtor) *Arnold Supreme d/b/a Bark Arts*
Address: *P.O. Box 35*
New Hope, Pa.

Name of Artist (secured party) *Steve Randack*
Address: *d/b/a Wood Shaver P.O. Box 735*
Rochester, New York 14607

This financing statement covers the following types of property whenever acquired by Gallery: *wooden furniture and other carvings including boards, boxes, plates, etc.*

Arnold Supreme d/b/a Bark Arts
Signature of Authorized Gallery Representative

Steve Randack d/b/a Wood Shaver
Signature of Artist

July 30, 1978
date

figure 4-4

even give him a discount. "No," Mr. Dash was not interested in purchasing but rather in a consignment arrangement.

"Well," said Alice, "that changes things somewhat," and sent Romero to look for her good friend Negotiator as she whipped out her handy-dandy-big-gallery-little-artist contract. And after two hours of tea, conversation, frowns, compliments, insults, meaningful glances, et cetera, the three arrived at this:

NAME:	*Alice*	*Bubbly Bath Boutique, Inc*
ADDRESS:	*P.O. Box 733*	*Big Town Mall*
	Albuquerque, NM	*Mesquite, Texas*
PHONE:	*None*	*214-993-7300*

Artist and Gallery agree to make a consignment contract effective *Oct 15*, 19 *78*. The terms of the agreement are:

NAMES

For a discussion of the name term of the contract, see the section on names in the direct-sales section of this chapter. The parties to a

EFFECTIVE DATE

contract usually can insert an effective date before or after the date of actual signing. Most times, the effective date is the same as the date of signing.

AGENCY

1. Artist appoints Gallery to act as his/her exclusive agent in the exhibition and sale of Artist's Ceramic (medium) work in the Dallas (geographic) area.

By naming the gallery as agent, several important things are accomplished. First, the gallery must keep the best interest of the artist in mind at all times and act accordingly. As agent, gallery must place the advantage of the artist before its own. Also, the agent gallery can make agreements with customers on behalf of its artists.

Alice limits the scope of Bald der Dash's Bubbly Bath Boutique's exclusive agency to the Dallas area and to Alice's ceramic works.

ARTWORKS COVERED

2. The artist will deliver the following number of his/her works in the Ceramic medium (a) to the Gallery:

[ ] all works
[ ] all works except for gifts, trades, commissions, juried shows
[ ] those works selected by Gallery
[×] those works agreed to by Artist and Gallery

Your gallery can be the only source for the distribution of your work. If you are giving a gallery such an exclusive on your work, it would be wise to exempt from coverage any works that you wish to give or trade. This term in the contract also exempts commissions, studio sales, and works submitted to juried shows. Although Alice has granted Bald der Dash a geographic exclusive, she is not granting him the right to sell all her works. Mr. Dash can sell only those works that he and Alice agree upon.

3. Artist will be responsible for delivery including costs, complete insurance coverage, and risk of loss.

Gallery will be responsible for return of works including costs, complete insurance coverage, and risk of loss.

DELIVERY

RETURN

Many times, the first delivery of works has already occurred when the contract is signed. However, most artist-gallery relationships extend over a period of time, and the question of who bears the responsibility of future deliveries should be settled at the outset. In Alice's contract, she agrees to provide delivery and the gallery agrees to return all unsold items. In the event that a loss occurs during delivery or return and the insurance does not cover the entire amount of the loss, this term clarifies who bears the loss.

ARTIST'S WARRANTIES

4. Artist states that she/he created and owns all the works delivered to Gallery.

GALLERY RECEIPT

5. Gallery acknowledges receipt of the work described in the List of Works. A supplemental List of Works concerning any additional works delivered to Gallery will be provided by artist and acknowledged by Gallery.

In these two sections of the agreement Alice authenticates her creation of and title* to the works being placed with the gallery and the gallery acknowledges receipt of the works listed on the List of Works.**

SALE PRICE

6. Gallery will sell the Works at the price listed on the attached List of Works. Gallery may discount 10 percent in sales to museums, galleries, decorators, and architects.

COMMISSION

7. Gallery will receive 30 percent commission on the sale price of:
   [ ] all sales by Artist
   [×] all sales by Artist arising from Gallery contact
   [ ] Gallery sales only

In this contract, Alice sets the prices that the gallery will charge for her work and the gallery takes an agreed-upon percentage as a commission. Another way to reach the price and commission is for the artist to state the amount he or she wants to receive for the piece and to allow the gallery to set any selling price. This "net price" method is usually less beneficial to the artist.

Galleries acting as the exclusive agent of artists many times require that they receive a percentage of *any* of the sales made by the artist. Here Alice and Bald der Dash agree that the gallery will receive a commission on all sales made either by the gallery or by Alice if the sale was as a result of the customer's contact with the gallery.

PAYMENT

8. Payment of each party's percentage share will be made within thirty days of the date of receipt of payment from the customer. All proceeds from installment payments will be made first to Artist until his/her share is paid in full. The Gallery agrees to guarantee the credit of its customers, and to bear all losses due to the failure of the customer's credit.

This clause basically places the burden of credit sales on the gallery by providing that the artist receive his or her entire share of the sale price before the gallery receives its commission. Also, the gallery would be the loser if a customer defaulted on payments, because the artist would be entitled to his or her full share of the sale price regardless of the fact that the customer did not pay the gallery.

PROMOTION AND EXHIBITION

9. Gallery will pay for the cost of framing or any other expenses necessary in preparation for display or sale of work. The Gallery will make a reasonable effort to promote the Artist and to sell his/her work. The Gallery will hold at least 1 exhibition(s) of artist's work of at least 1 week(s) in length each 2 year(s). Artist will

* For more information on warranty of good title and authorship, see the discussion of warranties in that section of this chapter.

** A sample List of Works accompanies a sample agreement between Artist and Gallery, Appendix 4-3.

be consulted concerning the details of the exhibition including any promotional materials, other exhibitors, and arrangements. Responsibility for the costs of the exhibition will be agreed upon in advance. Neither party may obtain reimbursement for these costs from the other without prior approval.

This section is very important if you have signed an exclusive agency contract for a period of time. This section would protect you from having all your works collecting dust in the gallery's basement. Also, this section requires that the gallery arrange a special exhibition of your work. The clause provides that the costs of such an exhibition be divided between the gallery and the artist and agreed upon by both. Further, the section provides that the artist will be consulted concerning the promotional materials used by the gallery.

STATEMENT

10. Gallery will give Artist a statement every two months, beginning with Dec 1, 19 78. This statement shall include:
    - [×] works sold.
    - [×] date, price, and terms of sale.
    - [×] commission due to the Gallery.
    - [ ] name and address of each Purchaser.
    - [×] location of all unsold works not at Gallery.

    Artist and Gallery will have the right to inspect the other's financial records concerning transactions covered by this agreement.

ACCOUNTING

The requirement that the gallery provide a regular statement of account ensures the artist that the gallery will maintain orderly records of sales, commissions, and works on hand. For an active account, a monthly statement would be appropriate.

11. The Gallery will use the sale contract which is attached to this agreement for all sales of artist's work governed by this contract.

DIRECT-SALES CONTRACT

If you wish the gallery to use a special contract for sales of your work, then attach a blank of your direct-sales contract form to the artist-gallery agreement and provide the gallery with copies of the contract.

COPYRIGHT

12. As provided in the Copyright Revision Act of 1976, the Artist retains all copyrights in the works delivered to Gallery. Gallery will prohibit the public from copying Artist's Works, except for publicity purposes. All reproductions of Artist's Works in Gallery publications and publicity by others will be accompanied by a complete notice of copyright including the copyright symbol, the Artist's first and last name, and the year of first publication.

This section restates the rule of the new Copyright Act which provides that unless a copyright is expressly transferred to buyer it is retained by seller. This section presupposes that the artist has placed a copyright notice on all the works delivered to the gallery. It also seeks to avoid copyright infringement by requiring that the gallery prohibit the public from copying the artist's works and that the gallery place a complete copyright notice beside any reproduction of the artist's work.*

LOSS OR DAMAGE

13. Gallery is responsible for providing insurance coverage from date of delivery to date of removal. Works will be insured at ________ percent of the retail sale price. Insurance shall cover fire, theft, loss, damage from negligence in the Gallery and outside Gallery premises when under Gallery control.

INSURANCE

Some galleries have no insurance coverage at all, and most gallery insurance policies do not insure the works for the selling price. You could pay for this additional coverage through your own insurance policy. Also, find out if the gallery's insurance covers your work while under gallery control, no matter where it is located—show, home of prospective buyer, in transit, et cetera. Usually, gallery insurance becomes effective when the work is received by the gallery.

TERMINATION

14. Unless already terminated, this agreement will terminate one year from its effective date. Artist or Gallery may terminate the agreement by giving the other party written notice thirty days prior to the date upon which the party wishes to terminate. The agreement may not be terminated for ninety days following a solo exhibition of Artist's work by Gallery.

This term allows either party to be released from the contract after giving thirty days notice to the other. Because of the investment of time and money in an exhibition, the agreement cannot be terminated for three months after such an exhibition. If allowed to run its course, the agreement automatically will terminate in a year's time. At that time, renewal or renegotiation may be in order.

BOILERPLATE

15. This agreement represents the entire contract made by the parties. Its terms cannot be modified except by a written document signed by the parties. Neither party may assign any of the rights or responsibilities contained in the contract without the consent of the other party. Such consent shall not be unreasonably withheld. If any part of this agreement is held to be illegal, void, or unenforceable, this shall not affect the validity of any other part of the contract.

This clause cites terms, normally found in all contracts—integration, nonassignment, and severability. The written document represents the total agreement and can be changed only through another written document signed by the parties. The assignment term pre-

* For more information on copyright, see Chapter 3, "Copying."

vents either artist or gallery from getting someone else to perform their responsibilities without the written consent of the other party to the contract. The final clause states that if a court rules that one section of the contract is no good, then the contract still stands minus the offending section.

GOVERNING LAW

16. This Agreement shall be governed by the law of the state of ________.

Since New York, California, Michigan, Texas, and Connecticut have the most progressive laws concerning artists and galleries, you should provide that the laws of one of those states apply to any disputes arising under the contract, if either of the parties lives or works in one of those states. Otherwise, choose the law of your state.

Signed this 15 day of August, 1978.

ARTIST Alice

GALLERY By Bald der Dash
(Signature of Authorized Representative)

Since the gallery was in Texas, Alice did not need to file a financing statement to protect her porcelain bath-towel racks from Bald der Dash's creditors because of Texas' special protection of art on consignment provided by the Texas Art Consignment Law.

COMMISSIONS

Alice's Allegory # 16

or

She Had a Dream

The matriarch of the local house of worship Claire Voyant dropped by Alice's hilltop home one wintery day. "I have a dream," she said, "of the most beautiful chalice in all of the country." Alice not being a religious sort wasn't sure just what a commission of the most beautiful chalice in the country involved. "Tell me more," suggested Alice. The matriarch was so enraptured by her chalice fantasy that Alice had to cough a few polite coughs to bring Claire Voyant back to earth. The matriarch pressed her hand on Alice's forehead and said, "Now I shall transfer my vision to your brain." And she did.

Special problems are posed by commissions. On some level the artist or craftmaker must produce a work satisfactory to the customer. Since it is not always possible to satisfy a customer's wishes, a commission agreement should contain a discussion of what happens if the customer is not satisfied.

UNDERSTAND CUSTOMER'S WISHES

Since not everyone has Claire Voyant for a customer, the essential problem in a commission agreement is the customer's communication of his or her idea of the design to the artist. In a large commission, the best way to deal with the problem of satisfying the customer is to provide a design study for the commission proposed by the customer. If a design study would take time and/or materials, it would be best to negotiate a design contract with the customer.* This agreement should include means of payment for the design—hourly, set sum for an agreed-upon number of sketches—and who gets the design sample. The contract also should provide that the artist receive the payment whether or not the customer decides to order the proposed piece.

DESIGN STUDY

PART PAYMENTS AND APPROVAL

As work progresses on the commissioned piece, arrange for a timetable, part payments, and the customer's approval of the work completed at the time of the payment. Also, the commission contract should not agree to "satisfy the purchaser" but to produce a "satisfactory" work.

OTHER COMMISSION CONTRACT TERMS

Provide for a dissatisfied customer in the commission contract. Determine if the artist can retain the payments already made, the work itself, the copyright, and if the artist can complete and sell the work in the event of dissatisfaction by the purchaser. Your commission contract should also contain any special terms of sale such as those discussed in the section of this chapter on direct sales. If you use a special sales contract, attach a copy to the commission agreement.

VERBAL COMMISSION AGREEMENTS

Even though a commission contract may be for a work valued at over $500, such an agreement could be considered a personal services contract, not one for the sale of goods, and as such, the verbal contract is enforceable. So be careful.

CONTRACTS WITH MUSEUMS

CHARITABLE PURPOSE

Since the stated purpose of most art museums is to further the education and welfare of the people, museums usually enjoy a preferred legal status. For example, a law in New York state protects from seizure by creditors all fine artworks on loan to any nonprofit art museum there. Most museums are usually exempt from paying sales tax because of their nonprofit status. Because the role of an art museum is to promote the public welfare, certain of their practices are supposed to be more enlightened than those of the art galleries discussed earlier. Keep this special status in mind when dealing with these institutions. It could help.

LIABILITY FOR DAMAGE

Contractual arrangements between museums and artists usually involve either a loan of a work for exhibition or sale/gift to a museum. Absent an agreement to the contrary, a museum is only liable to the artist for loss of or damage to a borrowed piece when the damage arises from the museum's negligence. There is no protection for damage to a loaned piece because of non-negligent fire, flood, or acts of God. However, most museums do use contracts that pro-

* See Appendix 4-4 for a form agreement for the design of a commissioned artwork.

LOAN TERMS

vide added protection to the artist by including a clause that requires the museum to take the same care of a loaned piece as it takes of its own works. Further, many museum agreements insure the loaned work in an amount specified by the lender from the time it leaves the lender's until its return. Unless the artist has extensive insurance coverage, an insurance clause should be required. Other terms customarily contained in a museum contract are receipt, length of the loan, description of the work, any special precautions for preservation and safety of the work, responsibility for return, publicity, reproduction, and framing.*

RESTRICTIONS ON GIFT

A sale or gift to a museum is like any other direct sale discussed earlier in this chapter. The checklist for a direct-sales agreement in this chapter should be consulted prior to negotiating the sale or gift.** Unless the artist or craftmaker is quite well known, most museums will not buy or even accept a gift accompanied by restrictions or conditions. If you donate your work to a museum or give the museum a break on the price, consider including a clause in the sale contract that would give you the right to buy back your work if the museum decides to sell it. The Joint Artist-Museums Committee has recommended that a museum not sell or otherwise dispose of a gift without prior consultation with the artist.

BUY-BACK RIGHT

PUBLISHING CONTRACTS FOR ILLUSTRATORS AND PHOTOGRAPHERS

Alice's Allegory # 17

or

And Yet Another . . .

Alice's porcelain towel racks were so mind-blowing that *Art Vark* magazine wanted to pay Alice for some photographs of these magical devices to appear in their upcoming article entitled "The Crafty Home," scheduled for the spring spectacular issue.

Soon after Alice had produced the requested photographs, a letter arrived in the mailbox at the bottom of Rainbow Hill containing a "Grant of First-Time Magazine Rights" for Alice's signature. Alice sighed a knee-deep sigh and walked up the hill stopping at Karmic Hollow to meditate over this newest problem in her life.

This section will discuss contracts to provide artwork or photographs for a book or magazine. Negotiating a contract for the publication of a book is discussed in Chapter 7, "Especially for Writers."

Negotiating a contract with a publisher is a classic David and Goliath situation. With such bad odds to start with, there is no point in worsening the situation by giving up the little protection you

* See Appendix 4-5 for a sample museum contract.

** For the tax consequences of an artist's gift to a museum, see Chapter 5, "Federal Income Tax."

GET IT IN WRITING

have by making an oral agreement with a publisher. It is far better to be aware of the bitter truth from the start than to be surprised and outraged a year later when you see your drawing in an advertisement for breath deodorizer.

NEGOTIATING THE PUBLISHING CONTRACT

Ninety-nine percent of the time your publisher will present you with a form contract for your signature. Sometimes you will be able to negotiate a few changes. Some artists' groups are working on form publishing contracts for graphic artists, but these efforts are only just beginning. Before you sit down to the negotiating table, it is advisable to have obtained and scrutinized the publisher's form contract and to have written down your suggestions for changes. This section will discuss the basic terms contained in most publishing contracts with visual artists and indicate the various issues contained in each clause. Appendix 4-7 contains a contract form used by a major publisher.

DESCRIPTION OF WORK

DEADLINES

Usually the first term of a publishing contract describes the work to be done by the artist. This section of a contract should contain a *clear* description of the work required by the contract—the size, number, medium, and subject matter. Also, the deadlines for delivery of the preliminary and final work and any penalties for delay are usually set forth here. This term usually specifies that the work be "satisfactory" to the publisher. If possible, insert the word "reasonably" before the word "satisfactory" to avoid a publisher's rejection of the work for no good reason.* This term also should require that the artist consent to any changes in the work made by the publisher, but the publisher probably will want to require that the artist not withhold consent unreasonably.

ARTIST'S CONSENT TO CHANGES

SUBSIDIARY RIGHTS

The next term in most publishing contracts describes exactly what rights the publisher receives from the artist. Traditionally, the publisher got "all rights" sometimes described as "exclusive world rights in perpetuity." These rights fall into two categories—the basic right of the publisher to publish and sell the work and the subsidiary rights to the work. Subsidiary rights include paperback, book club, foreign, reprint, and performing rights.

COPYRIGHT

RETURN OF ORIGINAL

RESERVATION OF RIGHTS

Several limitations are now being placed on the grant of "all rights" by those negotiating with publishing companies. Nowadays, artists try to retain the copyright to their work so they can control the publisher's use of their work.** Also artists usually include a term guaranteeing the return of their work after its use by the publisher or within an agreed-upon period of time if not used. Another clause limiting the publisher's rights is one which retains for the artist all the rights that are not specifically transferred to the publisher. Another limitation that could be placed on the grant of all

* For more information on the "satisfactory" problem, see the section of this chapter on commissions.

** For more information on copyright, see Chapter 3, "Copying," and Chapter 7, "Especially for Writers."

RESTRICTION OF USE

rights to the publisher is that the use of the work be only for purposes related to the publication of the book or magazine.

MAGAZINES

Many times magazine publishers only want the first-time magazine publication rights with the artist retaining all other rights. Other magazine contracts provide that all the rights granted by the contract will revert back to the artist after the first publication of the work.

PAYMENT

ADVANCE NONREFUNDABLE

"KILL FEE"

Payment for your work is either by means of a one-time fee or an advance and royalties. Your contract should state that any advance by the publisher is not refundable and also is not chargeable against other work contracted for by the same publisher. If a publication contracts for work that is not used, then many magazines will pay the illustrator a "kill fee" for their efforts to produce the work.

ROYALTIES

If you will be getting royalties, it is important which dollar figure your royalty percentage will be based on—the retail price or the publisher's net price. If the royalties are based upon the lower figure—the publisher's net price—your royalty percentage should be greater than those royalties based upon the retail price. If it is possible that the work will be reproduced in another form, you should agree both on the basic royalty percentage and on the percentage of income from sale of subsidiary rights.

WARRANTIES

INDEMNIFICATION

Most contracts will contain a clause where the artist agrees that the work produced is original and neither libelous, nor obscene, nor invades the subject's privacy. Here the artist usually agrees to pay any costs of the publisher resulting from lawsuits contesting the artist's work. If lawsuits arise concerning any of the matters covered in the warranty clause, most contracts provide that the artist will pay *all* the publisher's costs. The Authors Guild's model contract limits the author's liability only to the publisher's costs arising from final court judgments after appeals have been taken. Since you agree to indemnify the publishing company for any costs, include a term giving you the right to have a lawyer of your choosing participate both in any litigation concerning your work and any settlement offers.

EXCLUSIVE

CREDIT

Some contracts will prohibit the artist from selling artwork to competing publishers. You should also agree whether you will be given credit for your work and the manner in which credit will be given.

TERMINATION

If the publisher does not publish the work within an agreed-upon period of time or does not maintain the work in print, the artist should have the right to terminate the contract and regain all the rights transferred to the publisher. Also, the artist should be able to terminate in the event of the publisher's bankruptcy or insolvency.

AGENTS, REPRESENTATIVES, AND DISTRIBUTORS

Photographers, illustrators, artists, craftmakers, and writers all may use agents to sell their work. The relationship with an agent is very similar to the artist or craftmaker's relationship with a gallery. For information on author-agent relationships, see Chapter 7, "Especially for Writers."

Choice of an agent is *very* important. Many artists and craftmakers have been taken by a fast-talking agent who is here today and gone tomorrow with all the artist's work. And it is hard to track them down because an agent usually doesn't have a gallery or a showroom. Get the names of other people your agent has represented and check the person out before you place yourself in his or her hands. Larry Laidback has nothing but praise for his agent who sets up shows and sells Larry's work ten times faster than Larry can. Different strokes for different folks.

BEWARE OF FLY-BY-NIGHT AGENTS

AGENT CONTRACT

An agent usually takes a percentage on the work he or she sells for you. Many times representatives will want their percentage (10 to 50 percent) before the customer has paid the bill, which could pose a problem.

The individual requirements of each type of business have resulted in customary terms for agency contracts in that business. The best way to discover the special points in an agency contract for your area is to contact someone who has already dealt with an agent.

Issues arising in any agreement with an agent include: commission, exclusivity, and method of payment. Make sure the figure upon which the commission is based is clear; if the sale price includes special costs to the photographer, for example, does the agent still get a commission based upon the total sale price? Does the agent have the exclusive right to sell all the artist's work or can the artist or someone else also sell the work? Can the agent handle other work that competes with the work already represented by the agent? Does the customer pay the agent or the artist? Make sure that your agency contract covers questions like those listed above. Also make sure that the exact powers of the agent are spelled out, because absent limiting language, an agent can make agreements on your behalf that bind you. See the checklist for an artist-gallery agreement in this chapter for other issues that should be considered when contracting with an agent.

SHOWS

Art shows run the gamut from craft fairs to museum-sponsored competitions, mall shows, street fairs, juried shows, and others. Each show has its peculiar way of doing things, so read all the promotional literature carefully and obtain answers to any questions that you might have.

Any organizer of an art show—juried or not—is bound by the guarantees made in the show's promotional material. If you arrive at a mall show only to discover the "free" booth space requires a $50 rental fee, the Consumer Fraud Department of the State Attorney General's Office should be contacted, since a large group of people

PROMOTER'S ADVERTISING

were misled by the false advertising of the promoter. Suing the show's organizers is also available as a remedy but is usually too expensive and time consuming for this sort of problem.*

INSURANCE

Another special consideration for shows is who bears the costs and insurance for items shipped to a show for judging and/or sale and also for those items returned. Stories of damage to works shipped to a show are plentiful, so make sure that someone insures your creation in transit and while in the show. Also agree that if your work is damaged, you will have the right to substitute another for the duration of the show. Besides the considerations discussed above, sales at a show are like any direct sale, and that checklist should be consulted. Many artists and craftmakers prefer selling at shows because they can keep the middle man out.

CHECKS

Another problem that comes up at shows is payment by personal check. Make sure the check is made out to your "bank account" name. Check for the customer's address and that the correct amount has been written on the check. You may want to verify the customer's address with a driver's license. If you feel uncertain about the check, ask for a check-guarantee card. Note the date and the maximum amount guaranteed.

PRINTS

WILL THE REAL FINE PRINT PLEASE STAND UP

In recent years, a special wrinkle has developed in the area of fine print sales. A booming art market resulting in an astronomical rise in both the price and sales of prints and the development of sophisticated photomechanical reproduction techniques has caused John Q. Public to wonder just what is behind those high price tags—etching, woodcut, lithograph, seriography, engraving, or what? In some instances unscrupulous dealers have grossly overcharged for reproductions, or peddled editions said to be limited, but which contain as many prints as the stars in the sky. As a result, legislation regulating the advertising and sale of prints has been passed in California, Illinois, New York State, and New York City. The laws in California and Illinois are quite similar and essentially require that certain disclosures be made upon the offering or sale of any signed, numbered, or limited edition print. Appendix 4-6 contains a sample print documentation form which meets the disclosure requirements of California and Illinois. If the seller of a print does not have the necessary facts to provide all the information required, then the seller must state so with regard to each disclosure requirement. A comparative synopsis of these laws appears below. A careful record of the printing process for each edition will protect the artist from complaints of fraud.

FINE PRINT LAWS

* For more information on remedies for rip-offs, see the section in this chapter on enforcing your contracts.

FINE PRINT LAWS

	California	*Illinois*	*New York*
COVERAGE			
Date	Prints sold after July 1, 1971	Prints printed after July 1, 1972, and sold by noncreator	Prints sold after January 1, 1976
Value	Over $25 unframed Over $40 framed	Over $50 unframed Over $60 framed	
PENALTY	Print's value + interest three times value if willful violation	Same as California + misdemeanor with $1,000 maximum fine	Print's value, damages, and criminal violation
ENFORCEMENT	Within one year of discovery or three years of purchase	Same as California	
INFORMATION REQUIRED	• name of artist • year printed • if limited edition: no. signed or numbered no. unsigned or unnumbered no. any other proofs no. in total edition • status of plate • if other editions: series no. of current editions total size of all other editions • number of any prior states of same impression and relation to current edition • if posthumous or restrike edition or if plate reworked • name of printer	• name of artist • year printed • type of print • total size of limited edition • status of plate • if other editions: no. of editions series no. of current edition • if posthumous or restrike edition and if plate reworked • name of printer	Any alteration of the plates
OTHER			"signed" means by artist's own hand

After years of argument over what sort of print law to pass, the New York State Legislature enacted a law which requires that a "signed" print be personally signed by the "artist's own hand" and provides that any sale of prints made from altered plates is illegal unless the alteration is clearly disclosed. Since the artist's signature indicates the artist's approval of the print as authentic, an artist could be held liable for signing a print which could defraud the public either as to the printing process or the number in the edition.

New York City's Consumer Protection Law Regulation 30 provides that it is a deceptive sales practice to sell or offer for sale, as a limited edition, goods that are indeed not issued in the quantity indicated.

Because of the booming print market, many artists find themselves contracting for the production of prints of their work. Generally there are three ways to have your work printed:

- contracting with a printer
- co-publishing with a print workshop
- accepting a commission for a print

CONTRACTING WITH PRINTERS

The first arrangement is fairly straightforward with the artist retaining all the rights and making all the payments. Be sure that the printer keeps sufficient records so that you can properly document the print upon sale as required by the laws of California and Illinois.

The co-publishing arrangement is quite simple. The artist provides the original image and time in the printshop and the print workshop provides the equipment, each party taking half of the prints. The commission arrangement is similar to the commission contract discussed earlier in the chapter. Payment is either by flat fee or a royalty percentage. Under this arrangement, the artist usually gets a few artist's proofs. Under any of these arrangements, be sure to reserve the right to approve the final print. Also provide in the agreement that the print contain a copyright notice and, if possible, that you retain the copyright.

SELLING PHOTOGRAPHS

INTRODUCTION

Selling a photograph is pretty much like selling a painting or weaving or other form of art or craft. This section on contracts for photographers supplements the information presented earlier in the chapter. Whether you are a photographer or a potter, the basic terms of a commission agreement are the same. Ditto contracts with galleries, museums, agents, publishers, and so forth.

The special terms contained in a contract for the sale of a photograph arise from the nature of the photographic medium—the photographing of a subject and the subsequent making of prints from the transparency. A body of law and custom has grown up around the handling of both the print and the negative as well as the subject matter. This section will discuss an assortment of these special photographic facts.

The basic question that must be clearly answered in any agreement concerning the sale of a photograph is what *exactly* is the photographer selling and customer buying. The problems that occur in this area usually result from too vague a sales agreement—"Sure, I'll sell you this photograph." So be very clear about exactly what you are selling.

EXCLUSIVE RIGHTS

The magic words used to express the sale of *all* rights to a photograph are the words *exclusive rights*. The customer then has the right to unlimited use of the photograph including the right to:

- the photograph itself.
- reproduce the photograph.
- crop or retitle the photograph.
- copy the photograph in another medium.
- make any other use of the photograph.

COPYRIGHT

It is not clear at this time if the copyright would be included in the list of "exclusive rights." If you do not wish to sell the copyright, indicate in your contract that "artist retains copyright."

"FIRST RIGHTS" "ONE-TIME RIGHTS" LIMITED EDITION

Most times a customer only receives the right to a limited use of a photograph—basically the right to rent the photograph. Magazines will usually buy "first rights"—the right to be the first to publish the photograph. Similarly, when a customer buys "one-time rights," the photographer retains all rights to the photograph except for the right of the customer to use the photograph one time. If the photograph is sold as part of a limited edition, then the customer has the right to possess one print out of the total number in the edition—no more and no less.

CUSTOMER'S RIGHTS

Without a contract concerning the sale of photographs, the courts look to the relationship between the photographer and customer for guidance in determining who owns what. If the photographer is "employed" by the customer, then the customer has all the rights to the photographs taken, except for the possession of the negatives. Only if the photographer is free-lancing and covering all expenses, does he or she have full rights to the photographs taken.

CREDIT LINE CROPPING RETITLING

Other items in a photography contract that limit the customer's use of the photograph could be a term requiring that the customer give the photographer credit for the photograph and a clause prohibiting customer from cropping, retitling, or otherwise changing the photograph.

Two other legal questions that occur in photography contracts arise from the possibility of a lawsuit based either upon the invasion of the subject's privacy or upon the libelous use of a photograph. If you wish to read more about invasion of privacy, libel by photography, or obtaining a release from the subject, see the sections on these topics in Chapter 2, "Legal Restrictions on Content and Materials."

INDEMNIFICATION

Because of the possibility of these lawsuits, many magazine publishers will require that the photographer idemnify (pay any costs) incurred by the publisher in defending a lawsuit brought because of the photograph. This puts a heavy burden on the photographer, who can least afford such an expense. The photographer should make sure that, if he or she is sued because of the customer's use of the photograph (retitling, placement, etc.), the customer will indemnify the photographer.

VALUE OF LOST PHOTOGRAPH OR TRANSPARENCY

Another special problem for photographers is establishing liability and valuing a photograph or transparency should the customer lose or damage the work prior to purchase. First, the parties should agree that the risk of loss is on the customer while the photographs are in the hands of the customer prior to sale or approval. Without this agreement the risk of loss remains with the seller until the sale is completed. So when submitting photographs or transparencies to a customer on approval, obtain a receipt which lists the number of photographs or transparencies delivered and states that the customer is liable for any loss. Also agree on a dollar value before the prints or transparencies are released, because of the difficult task of placing a value on the lost photographs. Without such an agreement the value would be based upon the selling price of a similar work by the photographer or if there is no similar photograph, the cost to the photographer (transportation and materials) to replace the lost photograph. Man Ray received $15,000 for eleven transparencies lost by the American Museum of Natural History. A similar valuation problem occurs when film is lost or damaged by the processor or shipper.*

CONTRACTS CONCERNING "OBSCENE" MATERIAL

A final area of problems for photographers concerns the enforcement of a contract deemed by the courts to concern the production of "obscene" material. Many courts will not enforce a contract which is considered to deal with obscene materials. For a discussion of the current legal definition of the word *obscene*, see Chapter 2, "Legal Restrictions on Content and Materials."

ENFORCING YOUR CONTRACTS

INTRODUCTION

Memorandum

TO: Bigodi Bigthumb File
FROM: MBD
RE: Letter Received from Client (attached below)

DO: Contact client to come in as soon as possible to discuss strategy of locating adverse party and regaining jewelry or its equivalent.

Hiring a lawyer and rushing to court is not the only way to deal with a problem like Bigodi Bigthumb's. The Better Business Bureau of Winslow may be concerned about the town's image and could be helpful. The State Attorney General's Office in Phoenix may have a new attorney who is especially concerned about the illicit practices of Indian traders. Maybe the trader met with a fatal accident on the Interstate and his estate will take care of all the business debts.

Sometimes a problem may arise from a simple misunderstanding or lack of communication. If the problem is fairly straightforward or too insignificant to warrant the assistance of an attorney, start the

FIRST THINGS FIRST

enforcement process with a telephone call to the person in charge of the business.** Have the documents (receipts, contracts, etc.) concerning the problem in front of you during the telephone call so that you can refer to them. State your case and listen carefully to the response and take notes. Remember that your presentation of the facts can be crucial to your case. If a telephone call does not take care

* Also beware of the processor's contract clauses attempting to limit their liability for lost or damaged film to the cost of the film itself.

** Douglas Matthews' book, *Sue the B*st*rds*, Dell, New York, 1975, has a good chapter on the steps to take before you go to court.

> Hello. How is my lawyer? I have been thinking about you. I am fine. I am having some troubles, though. My sister left some rings and bracelets at a new trading post in Winslow for them to sell for me, and the store closed. Nobody around. I hope that you can help me. Let me know.
>
> Bigodi Bigthumb
> Little White Cone
> Arizona

figure 4-5 Bigodi Bigthumb letter

DEMAND LETTER

of the problem, immediately send an "I am serious about this" letter. In the letter, state the facts of your case and what you want from your opponent. Save copies of this letter as well as *all* other documents relating to the transaction in question, no matter how spindled, torn, or mutilated. See Figure 4-6 for a sample demand letter.

TIMING

In contemplating your strategy, you should not wait so long to go to court that it is too late. All states have laws concerning the time within which a lawsuit must be filed. This is called a statute of limitations. A suit for the breach of a written contract must be filed within two to ten years from the time of the breach, depending on your state's law. For the breach of a contract involving the sale of goods, usually the lawsuit must be brought within four years of the breach.

HELP FROM PRIVATE AND GOVERNMENTAL AGENCIES

If you still have no success, then consider the possibility of filing a complaint with an agency that handles the sort of complaint that you have. Agencies that provide assistance to shortchanged consumers can be grouped into three basic categories:

- private organizations
- local and state government agencies
- federal agencies

PRIVATE ORGANIZATIONS

You will find the Better Business Bureau and a Chamber of Commerce in most fair-sized cities. How effective these organizations are depends on local staffing, membership, and about whom you are complaining. The Better Business Bureau might be helpful in arbitrating a disagreement with a gallery concerning the correct amount of the gallery's commission because the BBB's basic concern is to maintain a good image of local business. In over one hundred cities, the Better Business Bureau provides free arbitration services for aggrieved consumers. However, the adversaries must voluntarily submit themselves to the arbitration proceeding because the Bureau has no powers to require a merchant to submit to arbitration.

Sometimes an effective place to make a complaint, especially concerning a practice that effects a group of people, is the con-

37 Starlit Acres
Espanola, N. M. 87342
April 27, 1979

Jack Splatte
Mirror Image
24 Hyperson Mall
Albuquerque, N. M. 87125

Dear Jack,

I have called several times to talk to you about the payments that you owe me for the work that I did for you. I agreed to take half up front and the balance when the job was done. To date I have not received the second half - $150 - although I finished the work over a month ago.

I need the money that you owe me and would appreciate payment within the next two weeks. Please call me immediately if this is not possible.

If I do not receive the money owed me by May 15, 1979, I will take any steps necessary including legal action to get the money that I am owed.

I do hope we can solve this without too much trouble.

Sincerely yours,

Skip

Skip Reynaldo

figure 4-6 Sample demand letter

sumer "hotline" affiliated with the local television or radio station. This would be a good place to complain about a sales representative who showed up at the last arts and crafts fair and took your whole line of leather belts and disappeared into thin air. The television station might help you track down the thief. Also, the local Nader-supported Public Interest Research Group may be helpful for a group gripe.*

LOCAL AND STATE AGENCIES

As of the date of this writing, all states except Alabama have passed laws to protect the consumer from fraud or "deceptive sales practices." The laws authorize state funds for investigation of fraudulent practices and usually give the state Attorney General power to seek an order halting such practices. Some state laws also give consumers a right to recover cash damages if they can show that they were victims of deceptive sales practices. In most states, the state Attorney General's Office is responsible for administering these laws and would be the agency to contact for help. A mall-show promoter who did not provide the mass prepublicity campaign that had been agreed upon, or a clay distributor selling clay loaded with lime are good targets for the state consumer protection laws. Figure 4-7 is a consumer complaint completed by Bigodi Bigthumb for submission to the state Attorney General's Office.

FEDERAL AGENCIES

Many federal agencies have departments concerned with some aspect of consumer protection. The General Services Administration staffs the Federal Information Center in key cities across the country. These centers serve as the public's directory to the federal bureaucracy for the purpose of both making complaints and obtaining information. The United States Postal Inspection Service operates a consumer-protection program which assists in any mail-fraud problems. A Navajo weaver I know was helped by the U.S. Postal Inspection Service in regaining a rug she had sold through the mail to a Connecticut couple who never paid the balance due. A coordinating Consumer Affairs Office is presently located in the Department of Health, Education, and Welfare.

GOING TO COURT

SIZING UP YOUR LAWSUIT

Sometimes it is just not worth bringing a lawsuit, even though right and justice are on your side. If the only people liable for the disappearance of the best in your line of batiks are applying for food stamps, it may not make sense to file a lawsuit against them. Size up the situation—be cagey. The chart on page 118 will help size up your prospects for a successful court suit.

"YOU CAN'T SQUEEZE BLOOD OUT OF A TURNIP"

Whose name and address are you going to put on the complaint? You might have to find out who really owns the gallery by checking with the city business-license department or the state corporation commission. If the owners live out of town or out of state, this adds

* Check your local telephone book for PIRG's address and telephone number.

STATE OF ARIZONA
OFFICE OF THE ATTORNEY GENERAL
CONSUMER PROTECTION AND ANTITRUST DIVISION
124 State Capitol Building, Phoenix, Arizona 85007

(Complete this Form in BLACK INK ONLY)

Bigodi Bigthumb
Your Name

c/o Lone Mountain Trading Post
Address

Little White Cone, Arizona 86515
City State Zip

Phone: None
Home Business

29 X
Age Married Divorced Single

LAW ENFORCEMENT USE ONLY:

Department ________
D.R./Case Number ________
Reporting Officer ________
Date Received ________

CONSUMER FRAUD DIV. USE ONLY:

Complaint Received:
By mail ________ In Person ________

Date Received ________
Attorney Assigned ________
Investigator ________
Legal Assistant ________
Docket/File NO. ________

Please complete the following information concerning your problem. Our ability to assist you will depend upon your giving us a complete and detailed statement. Attach to this form COPIES of ALL DOCUMENTS, such as contracts, cancelled checks, advertisements, letters, etc., concerning your problem. (KEEP THE ORIGINALS FOR YOUR FILE) Please note: To be of the most assistance to you, we must forward a copy of this Complaint to the person or the firm complained against.

COMPLAINT AGAINST Rob Trader

ADDRESS Shikiss Trading Post Winslow, Arizona 86504
City State Zip

PHONE NUMBER ________ PRODUCT/SERVICE INVOLVED jewelry

SALESMAN ________ DATE OF TRANSACTION About Feb. 15, 1978

WAS PRODUCT OR SERVICE ADVERTISED? IF YES, INDICATE HOW ADVERTISED AND THE DATE:
No.

WITNESSES TO TRANSACTION My sister, Ella Bigthumb

HAVE YOU COMPLAINED TO THE COMPANY? yes

HAVE YOU DISCUSSED THE MATTER WITH YOUR ATTORNEY? yes

Attorney's Name and Address Elizabeth Begay, P.O. Box 306, Window Rock, Az. 86515

IS ANY LEGAL ACTION PENDING? No.

GIVE A STATEMENT OF YOUR COMPLAINT by using the back of this sheet and attaching additional sheets, if needed

My sister left some jewelry with the trader for him to sell. He closed up and I don't have my jewelry or any money for it. I sent the trader a letter. I am sending you a copy of it.

FORM No. I

figure 4-7 Consumer complaint

[Magistrate Court Rule 2]

STATE OF NEW MEXICO
IN THE MAGISTRATE COURT — No. ....

Bernalillo COUNTY

"Skip" Joseph Reynaldo, Plaintiff

against

Jack Splatte d/b/a Mirror Image, Defendant

CIVIL COMPLAINT

1. Plaintiff or Defendant resides, or may be found in, or the cause of action arose in this County.

2. Plaintiff claims from Defendant the amount of $ 150.00 Plaintiff also claims interest and court costs.

Plaintiff claims from Defendant personal property of the value of $ ...., which is described as follows: ....

3. Plaintiff's claim arises from the following event or transaction: I agreed to design and frame 10 mirrors at $30.00 each for Splatte. He paid me $150.00 but did not pay me the $150.00 balance, as agreed, upon my delivery of the mirrors.

4. Trial by jury is (not) demanded. *[If a jury is demanded, an additional cost must be paid upon filing.]*

June 1, 1979 — Joseph Reynaldo (SIGNED)

JOSEPH REYNALDO (NAME (PRINT))

37 STARLIT ACRES (ADDRESS (PRINT))

ESPANOLA, NEW MEXICO 87342 (CITY, STATE AND ZIP CODE (PRINT))

None (TELEPHONE NUMBER)

APPROVED: COURT ADMINISTRATOR & SUPREME COURT, OCTOBER 1, 1977.
FORM 1.00

figure 4-8 Small-claims-court complaint

to the difficulty of the suit. Poor defendants are the worst kind because it is usually impossible to collect a judgment from them.

THE WINNINGS

What amount will you get if you win? The amount you sue for in a contract suit is your dollar loss resulting from your opponent's failure to uphold his or her end of the bargain. If money cannot replace the loss, then sometimes a court will order that the loser perform some action like returning Bigodi Bigthumb's jewelry.

EXPENSES OF LAWSUIT

How much will the lawsuit cost? Will you use a lawyer or can

[Magistrate Court Rule 7]

STATE OF NEW MEXICO
IN THE MAGISTRATE COURT

No. ....

Bernalillo .... COUNTY

"Skip" Joseph Reynaldo ...., Plaintiff

against

Jack Splatte d/b/a Mirror Image ...., Defendant

ANSWER TO CIVIL COMPLAINT

1. The amount of damages claimed by Plaintiff is not owed because: ....

....

....

or

1. The personal property claimed by Plaintiff should not be turned over to Plaintiff because:

....

....

2. *[If applicable]* Defendant asserts the following counterclaim or set-off against Plaintiff:
Skip Reynaldo owes me $75.00 for materials, he has charged at my store.

3. Trial by jury is (not) demanded. *[If Plaintiff has already demanded trial by jury, as indicated in the complaint, a jury will be provided automatically and you need not fill in this item. If Plaintiff has not demanded trial by jury, you may do so here, but if you do you must pay an additional cost upon filing this answer.]*

Jack Splatte
SIGNED

Jack Splatte
NAME (PRINT)

24 Hyperson Mall
ADDRESS (PRINT)

Albuquerque, N.M. 87125
CITY, STATE AND ZIP CODE (PRINT)

366-9487
TELEPHONE NUMBER

(This answer must be filed with the Court on or before the date set in the Summons.)

APPROVED: COURT ADMINISTRATOR & SUPREME COURT, OCTOBER 1, 1977.
FORM 1.03

figure 4-9 Small-claims-court answer and counterclaim

you represent yourself in the local small claims court?* Is the case too big for small claims court? Can you get legal help free from a local organization?** What is the filing fee for a lawsuit? How do you serve the papers on the adverse party and what is the fee for service

* All states have a small-claims-type court. In some states these courts are called justice or magistrate court.

** Chapter 8, "Obtaining Legal Assistance," lists sources of free legal help for artists, craftmakers, and writers.

SIZING UP A LAWSUIT

		YES	NO
Adverse Party			
Available for service of papers:		☐	☐
Has Assets:		☐	☐
Recovery Expected			
Estimated Damages (or value of items regained):	________		
Plus Filing, service and lawyer's fees (if available from adverse party):	+ ________		
Minus Filing, service and lawyer's fees (if NOT available from adverse party):	– ________		
Minus Other expenses (witnesses, discovery et cetera):	– ________		
Minus Counterclaim (if any):	– ________		
Equals Total Estimated Judgment:	= ________	☐	☐
		(if higher than total estimated expenses)	(if lower than total estimated expenses)

of the papers? You may have to take time off from work. This also costs money.

LAWYER'S LETTER

At this point, you should consider the possibility of getting a lawyer to send a letter to your opponent for you. Since the time and expense of sending a lawyer's letter is far less than going to court, this step makes good sense in many cases.

If, after calculating all the angles, a lawsuit still seems sensible, it is likely that your case will never see the inside of a courtroom. Eighty to ninety percent of the suits filed in small claims court are settled before a trial is held.

SMALL CLAIMS COURT

The next step is to decide if you can and want to file suit in small claims court. Sometimes this is a quick and cheaper (lower filing fees and no attorney's fee if you represent yourself) way of getting the courts to help you with your problems.* Find out if your case can be handled by the small claims court. Telephone the clerk of the court and ask what is the maximum amount that can be sued for in small claims court. Tell the clerk the current business and home

* Free or inexpensive lawyer's advice may be available for assistance with making a claim in small claims court. Also the state Attorney General's Office may have a pamphlet with instructions on small-claims-court procedures.

address of your adversary and ask if the small claims court would cover his or her location. Stroll around the courthouse when you go

CHECK IT OUT

down to fill out the forms. Sit inside a courtroom to see what's happening there, who's there, what they are saying, who's winning, what sort of judges, and so on. If you feel comfortable with the small claims court, fill out the complaint form, file it, and pay your money. Figure 4-8 is a sample small-claims-court complaint form. The clerk will tell you how to serve the right papers on your opponent. Don't forget that your opponent will file an answer to your papers and in that answer can charge you with any debts that you may owe him or

COUNTERCLAIM

her. This procedure is called a *counterclaim.* A sample small-claims-court answer and counterclaim is reproduced in Figure 4-9. P.S. If you decide to use small claims court to enforce your contract, be sure to read Douglas Matthews' book, *Sue the B*st*rds.*

After you file the lawsuit, your opponent may finally realize that you are serious and will make a settlement offer. If you can't file your lawsuit in small claims court or you decide for some reason not to, then you will need the service of a lawyer. Read Chapter 8, "Obtain-

FREE LEGAL HELP

ing Legal Assistance," before you shop for your lawyer. Also consult that chapter for information on sources of free legal help.

SOURCES

pg. 83 Salvador Dali and the Statue of Liberty: *National Historical Shrines Foundation v. Dali,* 4 U.C.C. Rep. Serv. 71 (N.Y. 1967).

pg. 83 Enforceability of oral contracts for sale of goods valued at over $500:
- —specially made: Section 2-201(3)(a) Uniform Commercial Code.
  The Uniform Commercial Code (U.C.C.) with local variations regulates contract law in every state except Louisiana, which has adopted only part of the U.C.C.
- —between merchants and confirmed in writing: Section 2-201 (2) Uniform Commercial Code.

pg. 84–85 Implied warranties:
- —fitness for ordinary purpose: Section 2-314(2)(c) Uniform Commercial Code.
- —fitness for particular purpose: Section 2-315 Uniform Commercial Code.
- —clear title: Section 2-312 Uniform Commercial Code.

pg. 85 Express warranty: Section 2-313 Uniform Commercial Code.

pg. 85 State art authenticity laws:
- —New York General Business Law, Sections 219b-e.
- —Michigan Compl. Laws, Sections 442.321–442.324.

pg. 87 California resale royalties law: California Civil Code, Section 986.

pg. 87 Discussion of the pros and cons of artists' reserved rights, transfer and sale agreement:
- —Leonard D. DuBoff, *Desk Book of Art Law,* Federal Publications, 1977, pp. 861–863.
- —Tad Crawford, *Legal Guide for the Visual Artist,* Hawthorn Books, New York, 1977, pp. 61–66.

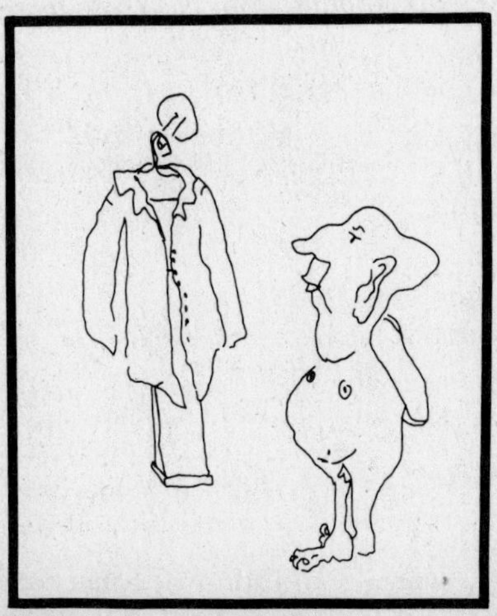

Sizing up your lawsuit

pg. 88 Delivery of goods: Sections 2-301 and 2-503 Uniform Commercial Code.

pg. 88 Risk of loss: Section 2-509 Uniform Commercial Code.

pg. 89 California's Art in Public Buildings Act:
—California Government Code, Sections 15813–15813.6.
—Hamish Sandison, "California Enacts *Droit Morale* and *Droit de Suite*," *Art and the Law*, vol. III, no. 1, March–April 1977 for more information.

pg. 89 No right to authorship; *Vargas v. Esquire, Inc.*, 164 F 2d 522 (7th Cir. 1947).

pg. 90 *Crimi v. Rutgers Presbyterian Church*, 194 Misc. 570; 89 N.Y.S. 2d 813 (Sup. Ct. 1949).

pg. 91 Special State Art Consignment Laws:
—Section 219–219(a) New York General Business Law, amended 1969; California Civil Code, Sections 1738–1738.5.
—Section 442.311–442.315 Michigan Compiled Laws.
—Texas Business and Commerce Sections 2.326(c)(4) as amended 1977.
—Connecticut Public Act 78–254.

pg. 91 Consignment and Creditors: Section 2-326 Uniform Commercial Code.

pg. 92 Prosecution of Art Dealers: Section 220 New York General Business Law, repealed in 1969 by Sections 219–219(a) because agency relationship created by law was such that the errant dealer could be prosecuted under existing criminal laws. See Legislative Memorandum of Attorney General relating to New York General Business Law, Article 12-C, Art Consignment, Misappropriation in Franklin Feldman and Stephen E. Weil, *Art Works: Law, Policy, Practice*, PLI, 1974, p. 475.

pg. 92 Artists versus galleries:
—"Estate of Franz Kline," *New York Law Journal*, March 31, 1964, p. 14.
—*Janis v. de Kooning*, 33 A.D.2d 555, 304 N.Y.S.2d 826 (1969), aff'd, 26 N.Y.2d 910, 310 N.Y.S.2d 97 (1970).
—*Matter of Rothko*, 71 Misc. 2d 320, 336 N.Y.S.2d 130 (1972) modified and affirmed, 40 A.D.2d 965, 338 N.Y.S.2d 854 (1972).

pg. 94 State art consignment laws: See citations for p. 91.

pg. 102 New York State Law protecting fine artworks from seizure by creditors while on loan to nonprofit museum: New York General Business Law, Sections 219-j–219-k.

pg. 107 Fine print laws:
—California Civil Code, Sections 1740–1745.
—121½ Illinois Annotated Statutes, Sections 361–369.
—New York General Business Law, Section 228.

pg. 110 Photographer as employee, all rights to customer; *Avedon v. Exstein, et. al.* 141 F. Supp. 278 (S.D.N.Y. 1956) Except right to store negatives: *Hockstadter et al. v. H. Tan, Inc.*, 188 Misc. 561, 68 N.Y.S.2d 762 (1947).

pg. 110 Risk of loss on seller prior to acceptance: Uniform Commercial Code, Section 2-327.

Chapter **5**

Federal Income Tax

TAX BACKGROUND

- Introduction
- Filing

STEPS PRIOR TO FILING A RETURN

- Accounting Period
- Record Keeping
- Accounting Method
- Inventories

INCOME—THINGS OF VALUE YOU GET

MONEY YOU SPEND

- Adjustments to Income
- Deductions—Schedule A
- Exemptions
- Self-Employed Business Expenses
- Prorate Certain Deductions

CUTTING YOUR TAXES (WITHOUT CUTTING YOUR THROAT)

- Income Averaging
- Shifting of Income in Family
- Installment Sales
- Buying a House and Other Tax Shelters
- Capital Assets: Depreciation and Investment Credit
- Other Tax Credits

BUSINESS AND HOBBY LOSSES

COMMON TAX RETURN ERRORS

AUDITS

SUMMARY

■ LEGAL ADVICE, NOT ON YOUR LIFE

TAX BACKGROUND

INTRODUCTION

"The art of taxation consists in so plucking the goose as to obtain the largest amount of feathers with the least amount of hissing."

—A French statesman in the Seventeenth Century

HISTORY

Historically, taxes have consisted of money, services, or payment in kind demanded by a government for its support. The normal Roman land tax was one-tenth of annual yields; the Bible speaks of the tithe (one-tenth) as the annual tax; European serfs paid their taxes by working a certain number of days for their lords; the Chinese paid entry and exit fees at their ports of entry; and nobles levied tolls on goods transported by roads or rivers that crossed their lands.

TAXATION WITHOUT REPRESENTATION

Taxes have triggered some revolutions. Some say the stamp tax plus other British duties levied by the British Parliament started the American Revolution, and presently we may be seeing the beginnings of a peaceful tax revolt in this country.

INCOME TAX RESULTS FROM INDUSTRIAL REVOLUTION

Since the old forms of taxation left untouched the sources of wealth resulting from the Industrial Revolution, the income tax seemed the only way to capture some of the wealth that was being accumulated and to give funds to improve the conditions of the poor. Historically, taxation of income was based on one's ability to pay.

TAX ROOTS

In the Middle Ages the unfairness of taxing the rich man and the peasant at the same rate was recognized: The 1377 poll tax taxed the Duke of Lancaster at a rate 520 times that of the peasant. The root of modern income tax was a 1799 English 10 percent income tax which was passed as a temporary wartime measure, as was the first personal income tax law enacted in the United States. Our tax act was passed during the Civil War and was repealed after the war. The

THE SIXTEENTH AMENDMENT TO UNITED STATES CONSTITUTION

second United States income tax law was held unconstitutional in 1895 by the United States Supreme Court and it took a constitutional amendment, the sixteenth, in order to pass the income tax law that now requires your annual tax payment.

Memorandum

TO: Rose Weaver File
FROM: MB
RE: Tax Confusion of Client

During a discussion with Rose Weaver, I asked the amount of income reported on her 1979 federal tax return. She told me she had never filed any federal tax returns on her craft business because she had been advised by wholesalers in her state that she did not have to pay any taxes as long as she was wholesaling.

I explained to her that the tax the wholesalers were referring to was *not* the federal income tax but was the state sales tax, and also explained different kinds of taxes.

Craftmakers, artists, and writers are concerned with three general categories of taxes: federal, state, and local. A simplified chart of these general tax categories follows:*

AN ASSORTMENT OF TAXES

- Federal
  - Personal income tax
    - Estimated Tax—self-employed
    - Withholding—employee
  - Self-employment tax—(social security tax for self-employed)
  - Unemployment tax
  - Corporate tax
  - Estate and gift tax
  - Federal excise tax
- State
  - Personal income tax
  - Unincorporated business tax
  - Sales tax
  - Estate and gift tax
  - Real property tax
  - Personal property tax
  - Licenses
  - Inventory tax
- Local
  - Real property tax
  - Income tax
  - Sales tax
  - Business license tax
  - Unincorporated business tax
  - Inventory tax

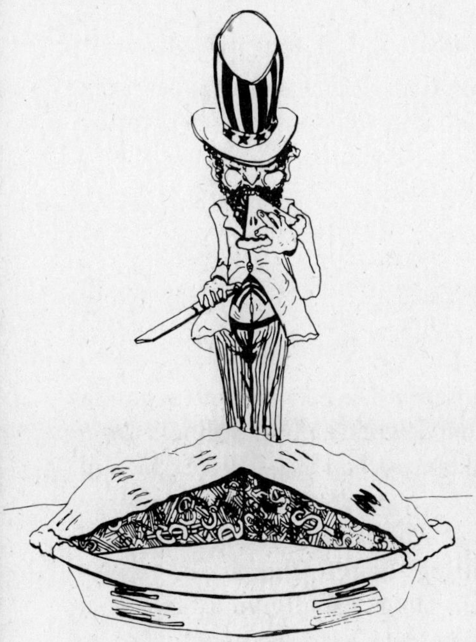
Four-month tax bite

The average taxpayer's yearly bite out of his or her earnings to pay federal, state, and local taxes is substantial. Average Q. Taxpayer works from January 1 to May 4 of the year to pay these taxes.

WARNING

Don't wait until April 15 to read this. These chapters on taxes are not exhaustive, but will give an overview of federal and other taxes, so that you have some idea of the tax consequences of certain transactions, know what records to keep, can take advantage of tax planning, and generally make some sense out of the tax-work quilt. Keeping proper records means that you can get all the tax deductions and benefits that you have coming.** Organized and detailed records mean a savings on any tax preparer's charge and your time.

KEEP RECORDS

Further, if you are audited, then you have the necessary information to back up your return. Learn one message at least from this chapter —keep complete and accurate records and keep a good diary.

We will not discuss line by line each tax form you may have to fill out, because tax forms change and tax laws are in a constant state

* Not every person would be subject to all these taxes and not every state or local government has these taxes. New Hampshire does not have income or sales tax, for instance. New York State has an unincorporated business tax, as does New York City.

** The person who "does" your taxes, whether you or someone else, *must* have checks, receipts, sales slips, diary, etc., in order to do your return.

of flux. What is a deduction or credit one year may not be the next year.

FILING

Federal income tax is due on most income, property, or anything of value you receive in a sale or exchange. A simple formula to arrive at your tax is to calculate the income you get (money and fair market value of property received) minus certain money spent (expenses or costs) and minus deductions for certain situations (i.e., dependents) equals taxable income. Then apply the applicable tax rate to your taxable income to arrive at the tax you owe and subtract any tax credits.

your income (money and fair market value of property)
− certain money spent (expenses, costs, personal exemptions)
taxable income
× tax rate
tax
− credit for certain situations (investment credit, child-care credit, etc.)
final tax liability

HOW DO YOU PAY TAXES?

You prepay taxes if you are self-employed when you pay estimated taxes, and if your are employed when tax is withheld from your check. You may pay additional taxes when you file your federal income tax return.

FILING YOUR RETURN

Filing an income tax return consists of filling out the various tax forms, signing the return, and sending them to the proper service center. The basic filing form is Form 1040. Usually your tax return (including any of the more than thirty special forms which may be part of it) should be filed at the Internal Revenue Service Center named in the directions to your personal Form 1040 or at the service center listed for your place of residence on the 1040 instruction sheet.*

WHEN DO YOU FILE?

Most people file by April 15.** The postmark date on your mailed return is the date of filing. If you file a late return, then the date IRS received the return determines the penalty. You can get an automatic extension*** for filing your federal tax return without even an

* Nonresident aliens and U.S. citizens living abroad check instructions to 1040 form for further information.

** A business electing other than the calendar year files at the end of its calendar year. A corporation files on the fifteenth day of the third month after the end of their fiscal year, and nonprofit corporations have until the fifteenth of the fifth month after the end of their fiscal year.

*** Since state income tax returns are tied to federal returns, you will need a state extension also. State income tax extensions sometimes require a reason. Check with the tax department of your state.

excuse, if you file on or before April 15 a request for an extension on Form 4868 and enclose a check for your estimated or "calculated guess" tax bill. Catch 22: If what you sent as the estimated tax owed is less than the tax liability computed on your late return, then you have to pay a 6 percent penalty on the difference, as of February 1978.

HOW MUCH DO YOU PAY?

You use tax-rate schedules to figure your tax. The tax-rate scale is graduated and increases as taxable income increases. Whether you must file depends on how much money you make.

"TAXES SHOULD BE PROPORTIONED TO WHAT MAY BE ANNUALLY SPARED BY THE INDIVIDUAL."
—*Thomas Jefferson*

WHO MUST FILE?

Generally, you must file a return if you are:	**If your gross income is at least: 1979**
Single	3,300
Single, sixty-five or over	4,300
Married	5,400
Married, one spouse sixty-five or over	6,400
Married, both spouses sixty-five or over	7,400
Self-employed	400

FILE TO GET REFUNDS

If your gross income is less than above figures, you *must* file to get a refund of any taxes withheld from your wages, and to get the earned income credit for low-income householders.

Filing a return does not mean you always have to pay taxes.* Your tax liability depends on your deductions, exemptions, and so forth, but you must file before a tax liability or nonliability can be established, or before a refund is made. We can hear you now, "Well, I won't file a return, and since I am a self-employed printmaker, who will know the difference."** There are several reasons for "going legit" and filing:

GOOD REASONS FOR GOING LEGIT

- to establish a financial record to obtain financing, loans, credit***
- to get a refund for overwithholding from a salary job
- because *if* you owe tax, the IRS can levy on your property and wages without getting a court judgment
- because the IRS can find out that you have earned income and have not reported it
- because the three-year statute of limitation (time for the IRS to take action against you) does not start running until you file, and under certain situations there is no statute of limitations for tax evasion
- because there are penalties for not filing, including prison time

* Returns are due from persons or entities that don't pay taxes. Partnerships and nonprofit corporations must file information returns but pay no taxes on these returns.

** *Newsweek*, April 10, 1978, pp. 85–86, discussed the underground economy, giving examples of persons who do not report their income. This underground economy of jobs, services, and business transactions that are never publicly recorded exists, but you take a serious chance in not reporting. Indeed, one of the people discussed in the *Newsweek* article later made it behind bars.

*** In applying for credit, loans, etc., the lender *always* requests from self-employed persons a copy of their financial statement and/or tax returns.

Remember there are ways to minimize your tax load. This is called *tax avoidance,* and it is legal. *Tax evasion* though is cheating and involves a fraudulent intent to evade taxes. The tax evader gets heavy interest, penalty charges, and maybe jail.

common violations	penalty/sentence
For unpaid tax or deficiency where taxpayer has filed a return	One-half percent per month penalty not to exceed 25 percent on the net amount of tax due; also 6 percent per year on tax due
Payment of tax with bad check	One percent of amount of check but for check under $500 penalty is the lesser of $5 or amount of check
Failure to file return	A delinquency penalty of five percent of tax due for not more than thirty days with an additional five percent for each additional month, not to exceed twenty-five percent
Failure to file information returns	$10 for each failure, not to exceed $25,000
Willful attempt to evade or defeat tax	Felony; up to $10,000 fine and/or five years in prison

FREE TAX GUIDES FROM IRS

There are numerous publications available free from the IRS, including Publication 334, *Tax Guide for Small Business,* Publication 17, *Your Federal Income Tax for Individuals.* These have completed forms in them. There are also numerous one-subject pamphlets for most forms and major deductions. Remember, these publications *do not* discuss views contrary to the IRS's official position or ambiguities in the tax law. Other useful publications are the Volunteer Lawyers for the Arts'* *Fear of Filing* and J. K. Lasser's *Your Income Tax,* published yearly by Simon and Schuster. The latter is excellent, widely distributed (e.g., in supermarkets), dull, and reasonably priced.

Alice's Allegory # 18

or

"It's all there, but . . ."

Spring had come to Rainbow Hill, although coupled with it were the usual March winds. Alice, who was busy wedging clay, stopped and thought, "Oh my dear, April 15 is only one month away. My taxes!" She left her studio and went to the house frantically searching for her records. She couldn't find them so she made herself some mu tea and did some deep breaths. Romero was not very interested in the search, saying, "Why go legit?" but Alice said, "Because I sell to an IRS agent, and besides how will we get the loan for our Tibetan prayer wheel if we can't prove what we make?"

* Volunteer Lawyers for the Arts (VLA) is discussed in Chapter 8, "Obtaining Legal Assistance."

"I know," she said rejoicing, "the only logical place, the Thai rice storage basket." She located the basket between raw cashews and the herb jars and dumped the contents on the meditation mat. She looked at the IRS 1040 and the mass and jumble of receipts on wrapping paper, paper bags, sales slips, bank statements, and her expense diary, which was a rolled Japanese scroll written from right to left. She exclaimed, "I can't do it!" as she gathered it all up and trucked into town to see a Certified Public Accountant recommended to her by Wood Shaver.

"What's your usual charge for preparing a tax return for a potter?" she asked. Mr. Figure said, "Well, about two hours at $25 an hour if you are organized." "Great," and she opened her Thai basket and gracefully spread the contents on the south half of his otherwise clean desk, saying, "I've been real organized this year and kept everything." Mr. Figure gasped and proceeded to explain what he meant by organized, but admitted he was pleased she had kept records.

Although the charge ended up to be more than $50, Alice talked Mr. Figure into a trade for a ceramic wall plaque to add luster to his rather dull office.

TAX PREPARERS

Tax preparers charge for time, so the better organized you are, the less it costs. It has been estimated that an average tax return* takes two hours, and tax preparers charge $20 to $100 per hour. Tax preparation charges are deductible. Some states have an organization of accountants, similar to VLA, called Accountants for the Public Interest, which does free work for nonprofit organizations and those without money.

There are several categories of persons who do tax returns:

- local or national chain tax preparers who may just provide a quickie service and are not specialists
- uncertified accountant, public accountant, or a bookkeeper
- a certified public accountant (CPAs)
- tax attorneys
- enrolled or ex-IRS agents—these people have passed an IRS exam Check with the national IRS office for a list.

Some tax preparers agree to accompany you to an audit at no extra charge or to pay any extra tax liability incurred because of an arithmetic error on their part, and some agree to nothing. A good tax preparer usually will know how to accurately and quickly fill out the forms to be filed with your return and should be able to direct you to tax savings based on your individual situation. Because of past abuses, the 1976 Tax Reform Act imposes certain requirements and various penalties on income-tax-return preparers. Do choose your tax preparer carefully.

While the IRS itself provides assistance in preparing tax returns, on very detailed questions they may not be helpful. In 1975, an IRS

* If your return involves unusual transactions like the sale of residence, capital gains income, or investment credit, this figure would be too low.

inspection team posing as taxpayers found the wrong tax advice was given 72 percent of the time by IRS taxpayer-assistance workers! Warning: If an IRS employee gives a wrong tax advice, the IRS isn't bound by that advice. A 1976 General Accounting Office study also found a very high rate of error on returns prepared by a national chain of tax preparers. Uncertified accountants should be more accurate than national or other local tax services. The best bet is a certified public accountant. He or she can set up your bookkeeping system so that tax preparation will be simplified (and cheaper), and is qualified to represent you at an audit and can do tax planning. Most of our clients who have been referred to a CPA save more than the CPA's fees as a result of a lower tax obligation.

TAX ADVICE

STEPS PRIOR TO FILING A RETURN

You need to decide three basic things when you start your business: your accounting period, record-keeping methods, and method of accounting.

ACCOUNTING PERIOD

ACCOUNTING PERIOD

You can use the calendar year from January 1 to December 31 or any fiscal year you might choose.* Most people choose the calendar year.

RECORD-KEEPING

The second task is setting up a general record-keeping system. Record keeping is simply the way you are going to record business activity. First, keep *any* documents indicating income or expenses including:

PRIMARY RECORDS

- invoices
- vouchers
- bills
- receipts for both expenditures and sales
- register tapes
- canceled checks
- deposit slips
- diary entries

These are referred to as "primary" or "first" records of individual transactions.** If these documents do not contain a designation of

* A fiscal year extends over any twelve-month period. You should choose the first day of a month and end on the last day of a month twelve months later. Since you have to get permission to change from a fiscal year to a calendar year, and then file an interim return, the choice of a fiscal year is important.

** No particular form is required, but records must be kept thoroughly and accurately, accessible and available, in a safe and convenient place. Artists are often self-employed individuals, and tax laws require self-employed persons to "keep such permanent books of account or records, including inventories, as are sufficient to establish the amount of gross income, deductions, credits, or other matters to be shown" on the tax returns.

the transaction, that is, date item was purchased or sold, business purpose (if not apparent), and cost, then you should put that information on the document. These primary records need to be kept in a readily accessible place, like a file folder, shoe box, cookie jar. These records will have to be sorted at least once a year, at tax time, into categories like rent, supplies, travel, medical, insurance, salaries, and so forth.

RETENTION OF RECORDS

How long should you keep your records? Since the government can challenge (audit) your tax return up to three years after your return is filed, you should keep all the supporting records, both primary and secondary, for at least that period. If you average your income, you will need four years of back records. Contracts, government documents (e.g., trademarks, copyrights), advertising materials, claims and papers regarding legal suits should be kept permanently.*

SECONDARY RECORDS, "BOOKS"

Secondary records are often referred to as *books*—a journal, ledger, single-entry book**—where primary transactions are entered and totaled. These records provide a handy way to review your financial affairs—the money that comes in and the money that goes out. There are many record-keeping methods ranging from the very simple to the complex. We'll discuss just three—two simple journals and a file-folder system—which can be used in a do-it-yourself program. Samples of two very simple single-entry income-expense journals appear in Figures 5-1 and 5-2.

		WOVENWORKS JUNE 1978	INCOME				EXPENSES
6	4	Dead Duck Gallery	300-	6	1	Studio Rent	75-
6	9	Sale Mr. Veronica	35-	6	6	Yarns - Yard Depot	60-
6	17	State Income Tax Refund	44-	6	7	Entry Fee - ADC Show	15-
				6	12	Craft Peripherds - frames	22-

figure 5-1 Single-entry income-expense, Sample #1

DATE	WOVENWORKS JUNE 1978 DESCRIPTION or PAYEE	CHECK No.	CASH IN	CASH OUT	SALES	OPERATING EXPENSES
6 1	Mr. Wall - Studio Rent	101		✓		75-
6 4	Dead Duck Gallery		✓		300-	
6 6	Yarn Depot - yarn	102		✓		60-

figure 5-2 Single-entry income-expense, Sample #2

* The *Craft Business Management* publication for April 1978 has a thorough discussion of record retention. Available from American Craft Enterprises, Inc., P.O. Box 10, New Paltz, NY 12561.

** If you are going to use a double-entry system, which according to accountants is the only way to tell whether your books are in balance, see an accountant to set these up.

Or you could mark a file folder (with double pockets) for each month and put sales or other documents indicating income on one side and the documents showing the money you paid out on the other. Some calendars have pockets designed for this purpose. At the end of the month write down on one sheet the items and amounts paid out, and in another column the items and amounts received. Now with the figures totaled, you have at a glance a summary of your month's activities, that is, profit or loss. This is essential for business planning. Note that most business advisers suggest that you plan a year at a time—say you decide $100 a year is your budget for advertising, then if you spend that $100 on advertising in the first four months, your plan is in trouble.

BUSINESS AND PERSONAL CHECKING ACCOUNTS

Separate your business income and expenses from your personal income and expenses. Deposit all business income and receipts in a separate bank account. Pay all business expenses by check. Establish a petty cash fund for small expenses but support those cash payments by documents—for example, $2 receipt from hardware store for nails for picture frames. Note on all checks what item is paid for (it may not be self-evident that a check to Acme Art Supply for $22 is for canvas) and on all deposit slips the source of income. When you want money for your personal use, then write a check to yourself from your business account and deposit it in your separate personal account. Use your personal account to pay personal, nonbusiness obligations. We mean what we say—kept separate checking accounts and record your withdrawals for personal use from your business account.

For example, Crazy Mary's Quilts was audited by IRS, and her use of one checking account without any secondary records led to a large tax liability. Then Crazy Mary set up two bank accounts. On December 10, 1979, she had the following transactions: she had $1,000 in her business account, $10 in petty cash, $200 in her personal account and $400 of personal bills to pay. Of that, $100 was rent and half of that rent was for studio space. For the thread (47 cents worth) that Mary needed that day at T.G.I.F., she used petty cash and saved the receipt. She wrote a business check to herself for $300, marked "Withdrawal—Crazy Mary" and put it in her personal account. She paid her personal expenses, including all the rent (part personal, part business) from her personal account. In her secondary records she reflected that portion of the rent that was the business share.

Some accountants recommend voucher checks—when you write a check, it automatically makes copies. The original check goes to the creditor, one copy gets attached to the receipt, and the other copy is kept in chronological order. There are also other types of checking account systems you could discuss with your accountant.

SUFFICIENCY OF CANCELED CHECKS

Are canceled checks sufficient documentation of an expense? Some IRS offices say *it depends* on the item of expense and the

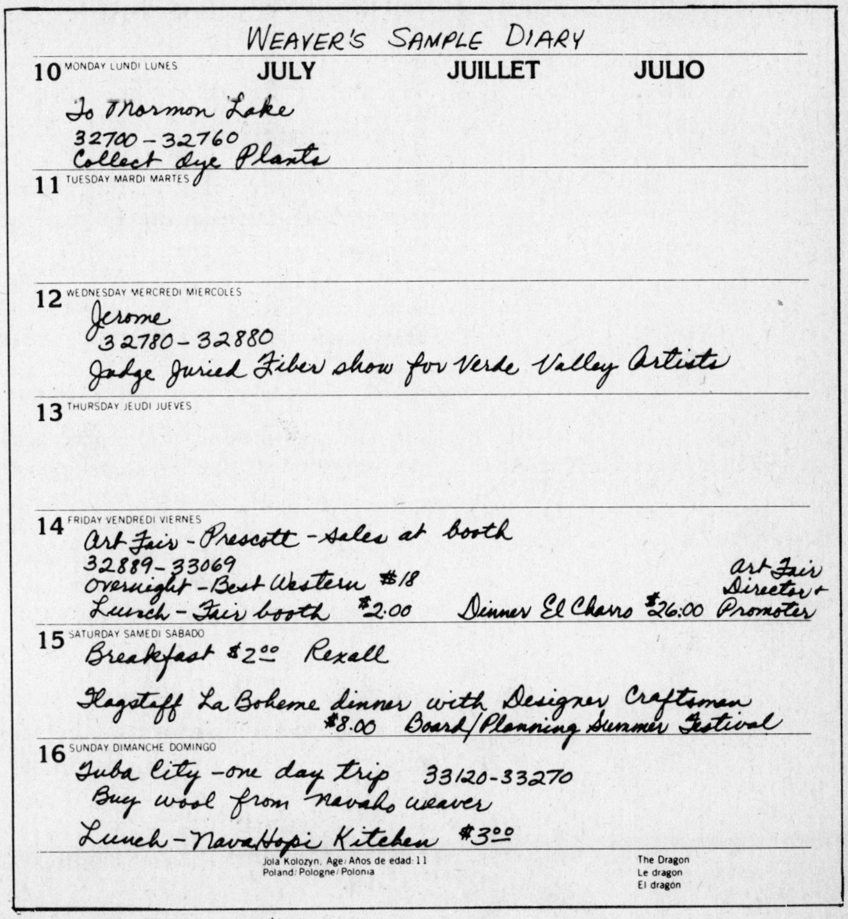

WEAVER'S SAMPLE DIARY

10 MONDAY LUNDI LUNES — JULY JUILLET JULIO

To Mormon Lake
32700 – 32760
Collect dye Plants

11 TUESDAY MARDI MARTES

12 WEDNESDAY MERCREDI MIERCOLES

Jerome
32780 – 32880
Judge Juried Fiber show for Verde Valley Artists

13 THURSDAY JEUDI JUEVES

14 FRIDAY VENDREDI VIERNES

Art Fair - Prescott - sales at booth
32889 – 33069
Overnight - Best Western #18
Lunch - Fair booth $2.00 Dinner El Charro $26.00 Art Fair Director + Promoter

15 SATURDAY SAMEDI SABADO

Breakfast $2.00 Rexall
Flagstaff La Boheme dinner with Designer Craftsman
$8.00 Board/Planning Summer Festival

16 SUNDAY DIMANCHE DOMINGO

Tuba City - one day trip 33120 – 33270
Buy wool from Navaho weaver
Lunch - NavaHopi Kitchen $3.00

Jola Kolozyn, Age/Años de edad: 11
Poland/Pologne/Polonia

The Dragon
Le dragon
El dragon

figure 5-3 Diary records

amount of information on the check. The government tax guide states that a canceled check standing alone is not by itself sufficient to support a business deduction. Accountants say *no*, for you can put whatever purpose you want on a check. However, canceled checks are better than nothing.

DIARY

Another important record-keeping method is a diary. A diary is a calendar, account book, or booklet where you can put down relevant expenditure information as it occurs regarding travel and entertainment expenses. It documents business trips and expenses not documented by receipt. If you are audited, the diary entries must show the purpose, business reason for the expense, the date, the place, business relationship, the cost and mileage if it involves travel. If the diary entries have insufficient information, the diary-based deduction may be disallowed.

In deducting your travel and entertainment expenses, follow these rules (check each year, for these rules are subject to change):

- travel—17 cents per mile for the first 15,000 miles, and 10 cents per mile over that for use of your personal automobile

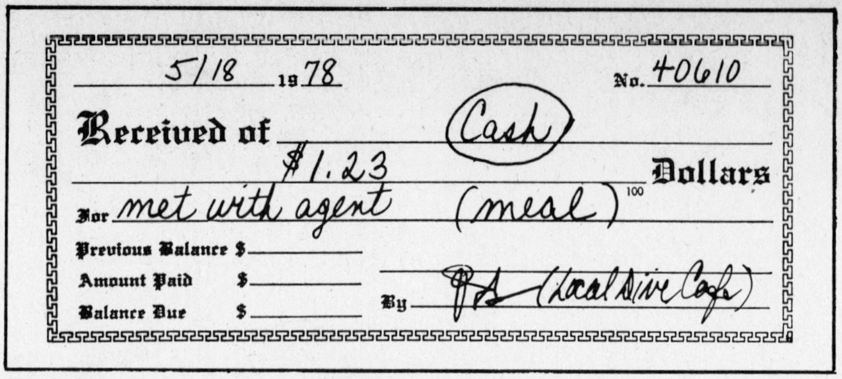

5/18 19 78 No. 40610

Received of (Cash)

$1.23 Dollars 100

For met with agent (meal)

Previous Balance $

Amount Paid $

Balance Due $

By PS (Local Dive Cafe)

figure 5-4 Receipt for breakfast on overnight business trip

RULES FOR TRAVEL AND ENTERTAINMENT EXPENSE

- lodging—receipts or itemized paid bills regardless of the amount
- other travel-entertainment expenses—need receipt if in excess of $25
- meals—the overnight-sleep test applies; this means you can only deduct meals if your business trips lasted longer than a regular working day and you had to take time off to sleep; naps in the car do not count
- business meals or entertainment—dining or entertainment with business associates for a business purpose

J. K. Lasser's *Your Income Tax* has lengthy discussions about these deductions. Some credit cards, such as American Express, already have a record expense form on the back of the cardholder's copy of the charge slip which you can complete.

Remember a receipted bill or voucher must show:

RECEIPTS

- cost
- date
- place
- nature of expense (business purpose, and business relationship to the taxpayer of each person entertained)

JOB WORK CARD

Another record-keeping method is a job work card. Have you ever asked yourself "What did I do last year? How many pieces did I do? What did I name that orange-white wall hanging?" You should keep a work record of each major piece, job lot, or series that you create. A job card can be used for this purpose. The cards should describe the work, date finished, materials (cost and amount), exhibit information, hours of labor, photograph information, and sale information. If possible, a slide of the work and sales receipt should be attached. Use a 4″ by 6″ card or make duplicate job cards. A sample card is shown below. You should modify the card to suit your needs. If you create small items, you may want to treat them as a series and use one card for the entire lot.

Refer to the copyright chapter for a discussion of the publication date and when you should file your copyright application. You should have the sales information for your mailing lists, but you will also need it in California to pursue resale royalties or if you have contractual provisions for resale royalties.

ADVANTAGES OF JOB WORK CARD

A job card serves many purposes:

- to provide evidence of professional attitude toward your work to meet IRS hobby challenge*
- to measure the number of your works produced
- to record information for insurance or proof of casualty loss
- to give you information you may need to fill out copyright forms and tell you the copyright status of the work
- to provide information for restoration
- to provide a track record of exhibition/sale
- to record your inspiration
- to provide a reference source after work leaves your possession
- to indicate labeling attached to work

```
                         JOB CARD
______________________________________________________

_____#   __________________  Title  ________  Size

Materials: _____________________
_______________________________
_______________________________

Label Info (attach)
Medium: _______________________
(technique, ___________________
 series)   ____________________
Theme: ________________________
Work for Hire: ___________________
Price: $ _____ Labor Hours ________
Compliation/Derivative Work ________
Publication Date ____/____/____   File Copyright By:
Copyright Reg. No.: ____________     ____/____/____
Photograph Info: ________________  Year completed _____
Exhibited: _____________________  How sold: _________
________________________________  ___________________
Sales Info: _____________________  Resold: ___________
Name & Address                     ___________________
     of Buyer: _______________________________________
______________________________________________________
______________________________________________________
Thoughts and inspiration on this work: _______________
______________________________________________________
```

figure 5-5

IN-OUT RECORD

Another handy record-keeping device is the in-out record. On this record your major works are listed in the order they are completed along with some identifying information. From this list you can tell at a glance where your work is located, what has sold, and whether the piece was damaged prior to return to you. If you keep job cards then you won't need to put so much identifying information regarding a piece on the in-out record. A simple in-out record is shown in Figure 5-6.

* See later discussion of business and hobby loss in this chapter.

IN-OUT RECORD 1978				
OUT	No.	TITLE	WHERE IN	PRICE
1 4	42	Noon (TPY)	Lame Duck Gallery	250 -
1 11	43	Desert (TPY)	Sale to FNB	100 -
1 22	44	April (B)	ADC (damaged-feathers 3/2 gone)	400 -
1 31	45	Moon (TPY)	Sale, my K to Ms. Lawyer	300 -
2 3	46	Lunch (TPY) series	Show at Univ.	2000 -
	K= Contract form & use B= Basketry TPY= Tapestry CST= Consignment			

figure 5-6

Job cards, in-out records (neither is required by IRS), and the income-expense file or journal will help you organize your daily art-craft work for your own information. These records help show you are in business to make money and not as a hobbyist. Also, they will help you plan and budget your business operation.

ACCOUNTING METHOD

The last basic choice that you must make when you start your business is which method of accounting to use—the "cash method" or the "accrual" method. With the cash method you include all income received during the year and deduct all expenses paid. With the accrual method you include all income *earned* whether received or not (e.g., bills sent) and deduct expenses when *incurred* (e.g., bills received). You may figure your business income on the accrual basis even if you report your nonbusiness income on a cash basis. If you have inventories, you generally must use the accrual basis in your business.* Once you choose a method, you must get the IRS's consent before changing to another.

ACCRUAL METHOD

CASH METHOD

The cash method records all income received** during the tax year and deducts all expenses actually paid during the tax year. A tax-saving device for the cash-basis taxpayer is to pay many expenses in December (assuming you are on the calendar year) and put off sales until January. Payment of those expenses at the end of the year would reduce your taxable income for that tax year. If you can use the cash basis, income and deductions can be shifted between years. Thus, you could structure your transactions to create

* See discussion which follows concerning inventories.

** This may include income not actually received if the income has been credited or set apart so as to be subject to your control. This is called *constructive receipt of income*, and would include a check received and not deposited, or royalties reported to you and credited to your account but not paid out to you.

income in two out of five years in order to help you meet a hobby-loss challenge by the IRS, because if you show a profit two out of five years, your activities are not usually considered a hobby and you can deduct your losses against any income received.* If you mail your check for expenses no later than December 31, then you can deduct the expense that year. Many businesses customarily send bills out in December reminding their clients that debts paid before the end of the year are deductible that year if they are on the cash basis.

CASH BASIS—PAY EXPENSES AT YEAR'S END

Under the accrual method you report income that has been earned whether or not received, and you deduct costs and expenses incurred whether or not you paid them,**—for example, Mr. Silk Screenprinter, who was on the accrual basis, sends a bill for $800 for a silk screen to Minby Co. and gets a bill for $200 from Exotic Paper Co. on December 30, 1979. Neither were actually paid until the next year. The income is reported and the expense deducted on the 1979 tax return because Mr. Screenprinter is on the accrual basis.

INVENTORIES

Many sales and manufacturing businesses must use inventory in calculating their taxes. So must a service business that stocks and sells parts.*** The Tax Law provides that "in any case in which it is necessary to use an inventory the accrual method of accounting must be used with regard to purchases and sales unless otherwise authorized. . . ." The phrase "necessary to use an inventory" may be interpreted to mean that it is necessary to use inventories to clearly reflect income. If you consistently use a method that accurately reflects income, then you probably wouldn't be required to use the accrual method. If you have a small number of handcrafted works on hand and low material costs, it is likely that the cash method of accounting would be acceptable. Potters who are using natural clay dug for free and creators of "found art" are obvious examples because the major cost of producing their work is their labor. On the other hand, if you are producing in volume, have a substantial number of works on hand, and high material costs, then the use of inventories would most clearly reflect income.

INVENTORIES AND THE ACCRUAL METHOD

What happens if you've used a cash basis and the IRS says you have to use the accrual method? If the cash basis reduced your income, then the IRS may find a tax liability.

But why all this fuss about inventories? Simply this: Cash expenditures won't reflect your true financial picture where inventories are involved. For example, if you spend $1,500 on wool your

* A discussion of the hobby loss challenge can be found at the end of this chapter.

** However, accrued interest, salaries, and other expenses paid to family members are deducted when accrued *only if* paid within two and one-half months after the close of tax year.

*** Service businesses usually do not involve inventories but businesses involving the production, purchase, or sale of merchandise or materials used for sale do.

first year and sell only three pieces at $100 each that year, the IRS would say that you haven't put several hundred dollars of weaving supplies into those three weavings; rather, you have put it into raw materials, works in progress, and unsold finished products. Thus, you must spread this supply cost over all the unsold and unfinished weavings and you cannot deduct the $1,500 from the $300, for you have really made a profit on the three weavings. To deduct the $1,500 would distort your real income from that work.

MATCHING COSTS AGAINST REVENUE

Inventories include:

DEFINITION OF INVENTORIES

- merchandise or stock in trade
- raw materials
- work in progress
- finished products
- supplies (which will become a part of sale items)

You do not include tools, equipment, office supplies, vehicles, or anything else purchased for reasons other than resale. Only the cost of those inventory items sold is deductible. This means that only a part of your inventory purchases can be deducted as yearly expenses. The cost of unsold inventory at year-end is an asset of the business and will not be a deduction until it is sold or becomes fully depreciated. So this inventory concept involves measuring the changes in quantity and value of your stock in trade from the beginning of the year to the end to get the costs of goods sold. The cost of goods sold goes on Schedule C-1 for a sole proprietorship.

UNSOLD INVENTORY IS ASSET

Schedule C (Form 1040) 1978 — Page 2

SCHEDULE C–1.—Cost of Goods Sold and/or Operations (See Schedule C Instructions for Part I, Line 2)

Item			Line	Amount
1 Inventory at beginning of year (if different from last year's closing inventory, attach explanation)			1	
2 a Purchases	2a			
b Cost of items withdrawn for personal use	2b			
c Balance (subtract line 2b from line 2a)			2c	
3 Cost of labor (do not include salary paid to yourself)			3	
4 Materials and supplies			4	
5 Other costs (attach schedule)			5	
6 Add lines 1, 2c, and 3 through 5			6	
7 Inventory at end of year			7	
8 Cost of goods sold and/or operations (subtract line 7 from line 6). Enter here and on Part I, line 2 ▶			8	

figure 5-7 Form 1040 Schedule C-1: Cost of Goods Sold

You can see from this that determining the ending inventory is a key step in establishing the cost of goods sold.*

cost of goods available for sale
− ending inventory
= cost of goods sold

The ending inventory must be determined by actually counting the merchandise on hand at the end of the year. You should do it when your business is closed, so that you can be accurate. It is common practice in counting inventory to have two persons do it. One

TAKING INVENTORY

* See IRS *Tax Guide for Small Businesses*, 1978 edition, p. 30 et seq.

person counts and calls the description and quantity of the item to another, who lists the information on an inventory sheet. When all the goods have been counted and listed, the items on the inventory sheet are priced at cost, then the unit prices are multiplied by quantities to get a dollar value, and these are added together to determine inventory value. Be sure to count all your inventory regardless of its location.* Or you could set up ongoing inventory cards. Perhaps you could use an envelope with cards by each item so "in" items could be marked on one card and "out" items on another.

PRICING THE INVENTORY

There are various methods of pricing inventory, and the method you choose will affect the amount of income tax you pay. Generally, the cost of an item to you is the basis for valuation. This cost includes transportation (to bring item to point of sale), materials, supplies, and *paid* labor but not the value of your labor. If you are a "manufacturer" then you must include overhead in your costs, which is called full absorption accounting.**

PRICE FLUCTUATION ON MATERIALS

Where identical materials are *purchased* at *different prices during the year*—for instance, truckloads of clay—what price shall be used as the cost of the merchandise remaining at the year-end inventory? In this situation, there are four valuation methods commonly used:

- specific identification
- average cost
- first-in, first-out (FIFO)
- last-in, first-out (LIFO)

Stop. If you will be involved with price fluctuation for materials and/or full-absorption accounting, then you should have the assistance of an accountant. In Appendix 5-2 there is a further discussion of valuation methods.

RECAP

Now let's recap. A few pages ago we were talking about using the cash or accrual method. Let's look at a simple example using the accrual method.***

Memorandum

TO: Weaver's Attorney
FROM: Mr. Figure
RE: Inventory of Ms. Weaver (Elected Accrual Basis for Accounting)

Ms. Weaver's inventory on December 31, 1978, consisted of ten tapestries which cost her, figuring all costs, $200 each to produce. Her cost of production for 1979 (including her overhead, labor, raw ma-

* Goods in transit are the inventory of the seller if the terms of shipment are FOB destination. Also includes goods on consignment.

** See Appendix 5:1 for a brief discussion of full absorption accounting and definition of manufacturers.

*** Assume all identical material was purchased at the same price throughout the year so methods of valuing materials with fluctuating costs is not a consideration.

terials, insurance, etc.) came to $7,500. Her total receipts for the year were $22,000. Her year-end inventory for 1979 was three tapestries which cost her, figuring all costs, $200 each to produce, and she had $300 worth of wool left.

total receipts		$22,000
beginning inventory 12/31/78	$2,000	
cost of production	7,500	
net cost	$9,500	
less year-end 12/31/79 inventory (three tapestries and wool)	−900	
cost of goods sold	$8,600	−8,600
profit		$13,400

INCOME—THINGS OF VALUE YOU GET

For visual artists, income results when you sell your works for cash or for a trade of property or for services. So most swaps are taxable.* The fair market value of the property or service is what is counted as income.

MOST TRADES ARE TAXABLE

Memorandum

TO: File of Ms. Queentrade
FROM: CPA
RE: Unreported Trade Income

Ms. Queentrade traded a walnut, circular end table with an epoxied, multicolor, beaded, sequined, feathered, tropical-rain-garden motif to her dentist for dental work for her much-neglected teeth. The dentist billed her $1,200 for the dental work, and the parties agreed that the fair market value of the table was $1,200. The dentist both counted the table's value as income and deducted it through depreciation as a business expense, since he kept the table in the waiting room of his office. He was audited, and the audit trail led to the flagstone walkway of Queentrade's two story dome, because she failed to report the income from the sale. Explained to client audit steps and worked out installment payment of delinquent taxes because the swap was income to her under these facts.

INCOME

You must report money, property, or receipt of anything of value as income. It is presumed that anything of value received is income unless it falls within a specific exception. Refer to the yearly edition of Lasser's *Your Income Tax* for a lengthy checklist of what must be counted as income. Listed below are some common examples of income:

- gross wages, salary, other employee compensations
- income from a business or farm

* See Appendix 5-3 for discussion of tax-free trades.

- tips
- installment payments
- pension, annuities, rents, royalties, trusts*
- net gain, from sale or exchange of capital assets
- interest and dividends (first $100 per person excluded)**
- grants, prizes, and awards (special rule discussed later)
- state and local tax refunds (if tax previously claimed as tax deduction)
- trades (most)
- illegal income***
- alimony received****
- per diem payments of more than $44 a day
- forgiveness of a debt

NOT CONSIDERED INCOME

The following are *not* considered *income:*

- alimony which is a lump-sum payment*****
- certain prizes and awards (special rule discussed later)
- child support
- federal tax refunds
- life insurance proceeds
- income earned abroad (up to $15,000)
- gifts
- return of capital (e.g., selling house for same price plus cost of improvements)******
- some scholarships and grants
- unemployment compensation, social security, workers' compensation, recoveries for personal injuries, and most government payments
- money received from an estate

PRIZES AND AWARDS

If prizes and awards are given in recognition of religious, charitable, scientific, educational, literary, or civic achievement, then they are not counted as income so long as recipient was selected without action on his or her part and does not have to perform services to receive it.

SCHOLARSHIPS

In order for scholarships to be nontaxable you must be a degree candidate at an educational institution and receive a scholarship from certain nonprofit organizations along with no obligation to teach or perform services. A degree candidate has no limits on what can be received.

* See Schedule E and instructions to Form 1040 if you have this income. It varies. There are fully taxable pensions and annuities not reported on Schedule E.

** Often income from municipal and state bonds is not taxed. See Lasser's *Your Income Tax* for a specific list.

*** Al Capone and other persons engaged in criminal activities were caught on this one.

**** Alimony must be periodic and contingent, e.g., "$100 per month alimony to my husband, an artist, for three years or until he receives a grant." Unlike alimony, child support is not considered income, and therefore is not deducted by the person who pays for it, *nor* must it be reported by the person who receives it.

***** Example: "I, Mary Rodaholler, will pay to my husband, Harry Hasbeen, the sum of $25,000." This is a special area—see your lawyer for the tax consequences of alimony, property settlements, and child support.

****** Record retention for home improvements should be from date of purchase to at least three years after the tax return is filed where the sole exchange of residence is reported.

Income			
Please attach Copy B of your Forms W-2 here.	8	Wages, salaries, tips, and other employee compensation	8
	9	Interest income (If over $400, attach Schedule B)	9
If you do not have a W-2, see page 5 of Instructions.	10a	Dividends (If over $400, attach Schedule B)..........., 10b Exclusion..........	
	10c	Subtract line 10b from line 10a	10c
	11	State and local income tax refunds (does not apply unless refund is for year you itemized deductions)	11
	12	Alimony received	12
	13	Business income or (loss) (attach Schedule C)	13
	14	Capital gain or (loss) (attach Schedule D)	14
	15	Taxable part of capital gain distributions not reported on Schedule D (see page 9 of Instructions) . .	15
	16	Net gain or (loss) from Supplemental Schedule of Gains and Losses (attach Form 4797)	16
Please attach check or money order here.	17	Fully taxable pensions and annuities not reported on Schedule E	17
	18	Pensions, annuities, rents, royalties, partnerships, estates or trusts, etc. (attach Schedule E)	18
	19	Farm income or (loss) (attach Schedule F)	19
	20	Other income (state nature and source—see page 10 of Instructions) ▶..................	20
	21	Total income. Add lines 8, 9, and 10c through 20 . . . . ▶	21

figure 5-8 Form 1040: Reporting Income

GRANTS

Nontaxable grants must be for study or research and not disguised compensation. You are allowed to receive tax free $300 a month in grants for up to thirty-six months in your lifetime. The grant must be received from the United States government, a state, or a nonprofit, tax-exempt organization. In addition to the $300 monthly exclusion, an allowance *specifically* designated for expenses incident to the grant, such as travel, clerical, and research, is not taxable if spent for such purposes. These amounts are limited to thirty-six months, even if less than $200 per month is received. The following examples illustrate these points:

> In 1979, Ms. Photographer, a nonstudent, received $3,500 from the state bicentennial commission for photographic study. An additional $1,000 was awarded for travel, clerical, and research expenses. She pocketed $200 of that amount and used $800 for travel expenses. She had used up thirty months of grant income exclusion before, so of the $3,500, she would be able to exclude six months at $300 a month or $1,800, but she would have to count $1,700 as income, as well as the $200 not used for travel expenses.
>
> In 1979, Ms. Camera received a $1,500 student research fellowship from the state university where she is a degree candidate so that she could study photography of insects. This is not counted as income.
>
> In 1979, Mr. Photographer is a degree candidate at the University of Pooh in moth photography and he receives a fellowship for $6,000, provided he teaches three hours a week. Normally he would be paid $2,000 a year for such work, so $2,000 of the fellowship is counted as income.

You report income on the front page of Form 1040. (See figure 5-8.)

MONEY YOU SPEND

"Over and over the courts have said
that there is nothing sinister
in so arranging one's affairs
as to keep taxes as low as possible.

Everybody does so, rich or poor,
and all do right,
for nobody owes a public duty
to pay more than the law demands.
Taxes are enforced exactions.
not voluntary contributions."
—Judge Learned Hand

Don't feel discouraged that every dollar you make is counted as income. Remember, it is only *net* income that is *taxed.*

income
− adjustments (moving expense, alimony, etc.)
= adjusted gross income
− itemized deductions
− dependent and other exemptions
= net income
× tax rate
= tax
− tax credits
= tax liability or refund due

Thus, to get to your net income you subtract all the legally allowable deductions and any adjustments to income.

In 1976, about 20 million Americans found themselves in the 25 percent or higher tax bracket. For those persons every dollar of deduction and adjustment that they are legally entitled to saves them at least 25 cents which would have gone to Uncle Sam.

ADJUSTMENTS TO INCOME

Following the gross income section of the 1040 form is a section called Adjustments to Income. After totaling your income, you can subtract certain items right off the top whether you itemize other deductions or not. These are adjustments to income: certain moving expenses, certain employee business expenses, payments to an in-

Section	Line	Item	Line no.	Amount	Line no.	Amount
Adjustments to Income	22	Moving expense *(attach Form 3903)*	22			
	23	Employee business expenses *(attach Form 2106)* . .	23			
	24	Payments to an IRA (see page 10 of Instructions)	24			
	25	Payments to a Keogh *(H.R. 10)* retirement plan . . .	25			
	26	Interest penalty due to early withdrawal of savings	26			
	27	Alimony paid (see page 10 of Instructions)	27			
	28	**Total adjustments.** Add lines 22 through 27 . . . . ▶			28	
Adjusted Gross Income	29	Subtract line 28 from line 21			29	
	30	Disability income exclusion *(attach Form 2440)*			30	
	31	**Adjusted gross income.** Subtract line 30 from line 29. *If this line is less than $8,000, see page 2 of Instructions.* **If you want IRS to figure your tax, see page 4 of Instructions** . . . . ▶			31	

Form 1040 (1978)

figure 5-9 Form 1040: Adjustments to Income

dividual retirement plan or Keogh plan, alimony paid, and sick pay. This information is put on the 1979 Form 1040 in the portion reproduced above and subtracted from your gross income.

MOVING EXPENSES

Some personal expenses from job-related moves may be deductible. If you move more than thirty-five miles to a new job you get an adjustment for moving costs, including personal expenses, provided you will work at the new job for thirty-nine weeks, or seventy-eight weeks if self-employed. The distance test and number of work-weeks test have special rules. Again check the yearly edition of Lasser's *Your Income Tax*. Use Form 3903, Moving Expense Adjustment, which shows you what items can be deducted. There are limitations on the deductions, but within those limitations you can deduct house-hunting expenses, meals, and many personal things. You do not need to meet the thirty-five mile test if you move your studio (workspace) from one place to another. The expenses of this move are deducted as an ordinary business expense, which is discussed later in this chapter.

EMPLOYEE BUSINESS EXPENSE

Employee business expenses are defined as those expenses ordinary and necessary to earn salary or wage income. These words *ordinary and necessary* are magic words to the IRS. For an employee, travel business expenses away from home, auto expenses, and certain entertainment expenses are deducted from gross income as adjustments to income.

You can use Form 2106, Employee Business Expenses, or you can write up your own employee-business-expense statement. This

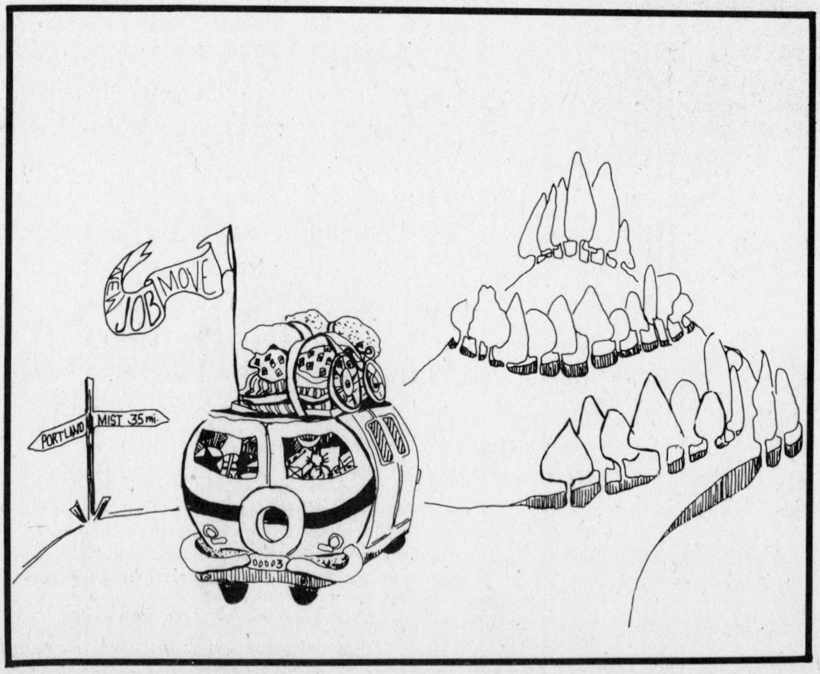

Moving expense deduction

means that even if you *don't* itemize, you can deduct these job costs. Other job expenses such as certain entertainment expenses, business gifts up to $25, union dues, uniform and work clothes (only if unacceptable for street attire) are deductible, if you itemize, under *miscellaneous itemized deductions,* Schedule A. Self-employed persons or independent contractors deduct those business expenses from business income on Schedule C.

BUSINESS AUTO EXPENSE

FIXED OPERATING COSTS

You can use one of two methods to figure the automobile expenses deduction—the fixed-operating-cost method or the optional standard-operating (or flat) mileage method. If you have an old car with lots of repairs, a gas guzzler, or a new car (three years for depreciation on car), it may be to your advantage to itemize your auto expenses. Under either method you need the number of business miles driven. Under the fixed-operating-cost method you keep receipts and report the cost of depreciation, gas, oil, insurance, repairs, taxes, and so on. The simpler flat-mileage method allows you to deduct 17 cents a mile (subject to change) for the first 15,000 miles of business use and 10 cents a mile thereafter. You don't need receipts for this method but you need to keep track of number of business miles driven and the business purpose of travel. Following is an example of an auto-expense computation at end of year:

FLAT-MILEAGE RATE

Business mileage total from diary—1,902
17 cents per mile × 1,902 miles is $323.34
Deduction for business auto expense 1979: $323.34

PRORATE BUSINESS AUTO EXPENSE

If an employee is reimbursed for auto expenses, then the employee may deduct only that portion of auto expenses for which he or she has not been reimbursed. For some persons it is more efficient to negotiate an auto rental and service package if that vehicle is used solely for business. However, most people don't use a vehicle solely for business purposes and the business auto expense then needs to be prorated against the nonbusiness use. See later discussion of prorating in this chapter.

A LITTLE LOOPHOLE: PAYMENTS TO RETIREMENT PLANS

By depositing income you don't need into a qualified retirement plan you avoid paying taxes on this money now. You pay taxes later when you draw these funds during retirement. Most people after retirement are in a lower tax bracket. This is another adjustment to income. You must be sure you don't need the money, for if you withdraw it before age fifty-nine and one-half, you pay tax plus 10 percent penalty.

Under a Keogh Plan for self-employed individuals, you contribute and get a tax deduction for up to 15 percent of your total earned income with a maximum tax deduction of $7,500 in one year. For employees without other retirement plans, you can have an individual retirement account (IRA).* You can put into an IRA account the lesser of 15 percent or $1,500 ($3,000 if married, both spouses working and filing a joint return) and adjust your gross income by that amount. The dividends and interest are tax free on all IRA accounts until retirement. In certain situations you can make contributions to an IRA account after the end of the tax year and the contribution is treated as made during the tax year! This is an especially complicated area and you should have assistance. See an accountant or your local bank or lawyer for more information.

ALIMONY PAID

Good news for ex's—if you are divorced, or separated under a written agreement, *periodic* payments made to your former spouse as alimony are deductible now *as an adjustment to income*. Previously, you had to itemize on Schedule A (Itemized Deductions) to get this deduction. Generally, then, whoever pays alimony gets to deduct and whoever receives alimony counts it as income. Legal fees paid to get alimony are deductible by the person who gets alimony, because it produces income.

You are finished now with the most common adjustments. Subtract the adjustments you have from your income and you get your adjusted gross income.

DEDUCTIONS—SCHEDULE A

The other place that you subtract employee expenses as well as your personal deductions is on Schedule A, Itemized Deductions. You get to take the itemized deductions which are in excess of the zero bracket amount (formerly called the standard deduction). So roughly figure your Schedule A itemized deductions to see if it is more than the zero bracket amount (standard deduction). You might review your financial situation toward the end of the tax year, and if your unpaid deductions won't help you top the standard deduction, wait, and pay those deductions the next year when they may help.

In 1979,** the zero bracket deduction is:

ZERO BRACKET (STANDARD) DEDUCTION

$3,400 married, filing joint return

$1,600 married, filing a separate return

$2,300 single or unmarried head of household

If you itemize your deductions, remember that the tax tables already have incorporated the standard deduction (zero bracket deduction), so you subtract the standard deduction from your total deductions on Schedule A and enter the excess amount on the return.

This area is subject to change, so check the Schedule A deductions each year.

* The Internal Revenue has approved for IRA investments government bonds (special retirement bonds), IRA savings accounts, certain insurance plans (retirement endowment plan and retirement annuity), and certain mutual funds.

** In 1978, it was $3,200 for marrieds filing a joint return and $2,200 for singles.

Schedules A&B—Itemized Deductions AND Interest and Dividend Income

(Form 1040)

Department of the Treasury
Internal Revenue Service

▶ Attach to Form 1040. ▶ See Instructions for Schedules A and B (Form 1040).

1978

Name(s) as shown on Form 1040 | Your social security number

Schedule A—Itemized Deductions (Schedule B is on back)

Medical and Dental Expenses (not paid by insurance or otherwise) (See page 15 of Instructions.)

1 One-half (but not more than $150) of insurance premiums you paid for medical care. (Be sure to include in line 10 below.) ▶

2 Medicine and drugs

3 Enter 1% of Form 1040, line 31

4 Subtract line 3 from line 2. If line 3 is more than line 2, enter zero

5 Balance of insurance premiums for medical care not entered on line 1

6 Other medical and dental expenses:

a Doctors, dentists, nurses, etc.

b Hospitals

c Other (itemize—include hearing aids, dentures, eyeglasses, transportation, etc.) ▶

7 Total (add lines 4 through 6c)

8 Enter 3% of Form 1040, line 31

9 Subtract line 8 from line 7. If line 8 is more than line 7, enter zero

10 **Total medical and dental expenses (add lines 1 and 9).** Enter here and on line 33 ▶

Taxes (See page 15 of Instructions.)

11 State and local income

12 Real estate

13 State and local gasoline (see gas tax tables)

14 General sales (see sales tax tables)

15 Personal property

16 Other (itemize) ▶

17 **Total taxes (add lines 11 through 16).** Enter here and on line 34 ▶

Interest Expense (See page 16 of Instructions.)

18 a Home mortgage

b Credit and charge cards

19 Other (itemize) ▶

Finance Charges
BAC
Master Charge
Interest

20 **Total interest expense (add lines 18a through 19).** Enter here and on line 35 ▶

Contributions (See page 17 of Instructions.)

21 a Cash contributions for which you have receipts, cancelled checks or other written evidence

b Other cash contributions (show who you gave to and how much you gave) ▶

22 Other than cash (see page 17 of instructions for required statement)

23 Carryover from prior years

24 **Total contributions (add lines 21a through 23).** Enter here and on line 36 ▶

Casualty or Theft Loss(es) (See page 17 of Instructions.)

25 Loss before insurance reimbursement

26 Insurance reimbursement

27 Subtract line 26 from line 25. If line 26 is more than line 25, enter zero

28 Enter $100 or amount on line 27, whichever is smaller

29 **Total casualty or theft loss(es) (subtract line 28 from line 27).** Enter here and on line 37 ▶

Miscellaneous Deductions (See page 17 of Instructions.)

30 Union dues

31 Other (itemize) ▶

Tax Preparation fee
Employee Business Expense

32 **Total miscellaneous deductions (add lines 30 and 31).** Enter here and on line 38 ▶

Summary of Itemized Deductions (See page 18 of Instructions.) **A**

33 Total medical and dental—from line 10

34 Total taxes—from line 17

35 Total interest—from line 20

36 Total contributions—from line 24

37 Total casualty or theft loss(es)—from line 29

38 Total miscellaneous—from line 32

39 **Total deductions (add lines 33 through 38)** ▶

40 If you checked Form 1040, Filing Status box:
2 or 5, enter $3,200
1 or 4, enter $2,200
3, enter $1,600

41 Subtract line 40 from line 39. Enter here and on Form 1040, line 33. (If line 40 is more than line 39, enter zero and see "You Must Itemize Deductions" on page 11 of the Instructions.) ▶

figure 5-10 Schedule A: Itemized Deductions

A thorough chart of deductible medical expenses is in the yearly edition of Lasser's *Your Income Tax.* Items such as medical equipment, prescribed hot tubs, swimming pools, air filters, and saunas have been deducted as medical expenses. Such equipment must be depreciated.

MEDICAL EXPENSES

The sales tax chart in the General Instructions *does not* include taxes on the purchase of an automobile, boat, or materials for building a house. So be sure to add the taxes paid on the purchase of those specific items. Contributions to churches, civic groups, and not-for-profit charities in the form of cash or merchandise is allowed. There is no deduction for contribution of services except for your out-of-pocket expenses related to services—for instance, gas for a car. Unfortunately for charitable institutions and creative persons, since 1969 artists and craftmakers who donate work they have created to charitable institutions can only deduct the cost of materials used in creating the work, while those noncreators who own such works can donate them to a charitable, educational, or cultural institution and receive an income tax deduction for the total value. Creative persons are trying to regain the charitable deduction for donor-created works through tax reform. See the Internal Revenue Service Publication 526, *Income Tax Reductions for Contributors.*

SALES TAX

CHARITABLE DONATIONS

If you have a loss due to fire, theft, storm, accident, or any act of God, you deduct the loss (less $100 per casualty) to the extent the loss is not covered by insurance. Unusual casualty losses can be the result of flooding, electrical blackouts, snow accumulation, freezing, et cetera. Be sure to report thefts to the appropriate authorities so that you have proof of the loss in case of an audit.

CASUALTY LOSSES

MISCELLANEOUS DEDUCTIONS ON SCHEDULE A

If you are an employee, you can claim the following as miscellaneous deductions on Schedule A *if* you have not been reimbursed and *if* they are ordinary and necessary for performing your job:

- unreimbursed entertainment expenses
- country club dues
- business gifts (not in excess of $25 per person)
- business association dues
- union dues
- special uniforms and work clothes (can't be adjustable to normal wear)
- expenses in looking for a new job
- educational costs
- investment expenses
- other ordinary and necessary expenses relating to your job not paid by employer (see Deductible Job Cost Chart in Lasser's *Your Income Tax*)

In order to deduct educational expenses you must be employed and already meet the minimum educational requisites for your job. Further, the educational activity must improve your job related skills—for example, Isabel Illustrator employed at *McDuck's* Magazine takes a class in calligraphy; it's deductible.

HOW DO YOUR SCHEDULE A DEDUCTIONS COMPARE WITH OTHERS?

In order to give you an idea of what other people deduct, the average 1975 tax deductions by persons in certain income categories is shown below.

Average Schedule A Tax Deductions

Adjusted Gross Income	Taxes	Interest	Contributions	Medical
9,000–10,000	873	1,164	382	833
10,000–15,000	1,068	1,274	405	570
15,000–20,000	1,446	1,540	469	506
20,000–25,000	1,793	1,679	534	439

EXEMPTIONS

EXEMPTIONS—YOU ALWAYS GET TO CLAIM YOURSELF

Available to all are the personal exemptions—one exemption as a taxpayer, one for a spouse, and one for each dependent. Starting in 1979, you were entitled to deduct $1,000 for each exemption claimed on your return. Dependents are persons to whose support you contributed 50 percent or more* and who earned less than $1,000 during the year.** In certain situations, children over nineteen, unrelated persons who live with you, and relatives who don't live with you can be claimed as dependent exemptions. Sometimes it is possible to arrange these situations so you can pick up an extra exemption, and a $1,000 deduction may be well worth the effort. Check with your accountant or Lasser's yearly tax publication, *Your Income Tax*. This is a common area of audit and you may well have to substantiate this deduction.

CHILDREN OF DIVORCED PARENTS

The divorce decree can give the children's exemptions to the parent without custody provided he or she pays at least $600 child support for each child. If there is no provision in the divorce decree and the parent *without* custody pays at least $1,200 per child per year, then the parent with custody must prove a larger contribution in order to take the exemption. Ask your lawyer to do your tax planning in the divorce. It should not be a surprise that audits occur often where both parents have claimed the children as exemptions, so it is best to state in your divorce papers who is entitled to the exemptions. The Tax Tables are charted to automatically cover exemptions up to

* If two or more persons pay in combined payments more than 50 percent of a dependent's support, then either may claim the person provided the person not claiming signs a Multiple Support Declaration, Form 2120. Example: Alice and Kate contribute together more than 50 percent of the support of their mother and they switch mother's dependent exemption from year to year and fill out proper forms.

** An exception to this rule is a child or stepchild under nineteen or a full-time student for five months during the year. This person can earn any amount and you can claim him or her as dependent as long as you provide 50 percent of his or her support. Such children can also claim themselves on their own return. Example: Charlie, age nine, did computer drawings which he framed and sold, netting $2,000 a year. His parents provide for his support. Both Charlie on his return and his parents on theirs can claim him as an exemption.

Exemptions

Always check the box labeled Yourself. Check other boxes if they apply.

6a ☐ Yourself	☐ 65 or over	☐ Blind	Enter number of boxes checked on 6a and b ▶	☐
b ☐ Spouse	☐ 65 or over	☐ Blind		
c First names of your dependent children who lived with you ▶			Enter number of children listed ▶	☐

d Other dependents: (1) Name	(2) Relationship	(3) Number of months lived in your home	(4) Did dependent have income of $750 or more?	(5) Did you provide more than one-half of dependent's support?	Enter number of other dependents ▶ ☐

7 Total number of exemptions claimed . . . . Add numbers entered in boxes above ▶ ☐

figure 5-11 Form 1040: Exemptions

a total of nine for married persons and eight for unmarried. If you have more exemptions than that, then you use Form TC, Tax Computation, first introduced in 1977.

*SELF-EMPLOYED BUSINESS EXPENSES**

The following expenses may be deductible if ordinary and necessary to your business. "Ordinary" means that the similar expenses are common or accepted in your particular business. A "necessary" expense is one that is appropriate and helpful in developing and maintaining your trade or business. Any expense incurred in the furtherance of your business and its economic goals should be deductible.

All cash payments are not necessarily counted as a business expense. For example, payments made for assets used in business (land, buildings, equipment, car, etc.) are not deducted all at once but rather over a period of time. The list that follows is not exhaustive for business expenses; rather common ordinary and necessary business expenses are listed to give you an idea of deductible expenses in your business. Check Lasser's *Your Income Tax*. Of course many of these payments must be prorated between business and personal use.

ALLOWABLE BUSINESS DEDUCTIONS

- *Accounting fees*—tax preparers' fees
- *Admissions*—to theater, films, or other events that relate to your work
- *Agency fees*—for jobs or commission work
- *Air fares*
- *Art and craft supplies*—for materials (check earlier inventory discussion)
- *Automobile expenses*—discussed in adjustments
- *Bad debts*—must have resulted from normal course of business. On cash accounting method you cannot claim uncollectible bills, fees, etc. as bad debts

DEDUCT THE PRICE OF THIS BOOK

- *Books, publications, professional journals*—fully deductible if in your field, or necessary to keep abreast or maintain skills for your job. If useful for more than one year, then it is a part of a professional library and must be depreciated

* This section discusses the expenses deductible by a self-employed person. Some of these expenses can also be deducted instead as an adjustment to income or as a miscellaneous deduction.

- *Business gifts*—deductible up to $25 per year per business associate or customer
- *Business machines and equipment*—having useful life of one year or less
- *Business meetings and entertainment*—cost of meals with actual or potential customers, clients, partners, professional advisers if it is in a clear business setting involving planning, discussion, negotiation, etc. of business. If entertainment for reasons directly involved with active conduct of your business or trade, then you can deduct meals, drinks, tickets, and home entertainment
- *Cleaning costs*
- *Commuting costs*—generally not deductible. If your business is at home, then you can deduct travel costs starting with your first call
- *Convention trips*—complicated, see Lasser's *Your Income Tax*
- *Depreciation*
- *Display samples, display space*
- *Driver's license*—remember to prorate
- *Dues*—membership, fees
- *Educational expenses*
- *Food and lodging*
- *Furniture*
- *Home studio/office expenses*—see later discussion
- *Insurance*
- *Interest*—deductible on business loans and mortgages
- *Legal and professional fees*—must be for business purposes, related to tax matters, or to protect income-producing assets
- *Magazines*
- *Meals*—overnight rule bars the deduction of the cost of meals on one-day business trips. Business lunch is allowable
- *Moving expenses*
- *Office supplies and postage*
- *Protective clothing*
- *Rent on separate studio/office*
- *Repairs*
- *Research for current projects or teaching your classes*

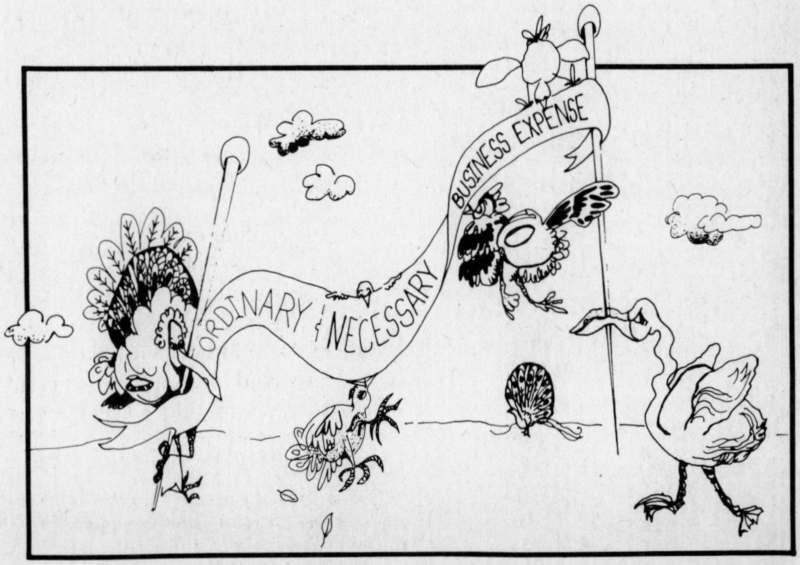

- *Retirement-plan payments*
- *Salaries, tips, and fees to performers and staff*
- *Taxi fares*
- *Tax-return-preparation books*
- *Telegrams*
- *Telephone and answering service*—a separate business phone—total deduction allowable; otherwise prorate basic service charge plus all long-distance business calls
- *Tips*
- *Toll charges*
- *Tools*
- *Training*—regular training such as cost of writing, drawing classes. Any classes that you need to maintain or improve your skills
- *Transportation and travel expenses*—if the reason for your trip is primarily business,* then you can deduct the ordinary and necessary travel costs including transportation—air, bus, train, your auto expenses, telephone, tips
- *Tuition*
- *Uniforms, costumes, protective or special clothing*—includes cleaning and repairing of same

Remember, there are many other ordinary and necessary business expenses not listed here which you may deduct—so you will have to analyze some of your transactions to see if they qualify.

HOME STUDIO
1. EXCLUSIVE-USE TEST
2. REGULAR-BASIS TEST

There are very strict new rules concerning the home studio/office expense which require that a home studio or office be used *exclusively* and on a *regular basis* as your principal place of business or place where you meet or deal with customers in the normal course of business. You can't take a home studio deduction if you use the guest room as a weaving studio.

One exception to this exclusive-use test is where you sell products and your home is the "sole fixed location" of your trade. Although you may have a mixed use, the deduction is allowable provided the space is identifiable. Example, you sell yarn and use part of your basement to store it.

There are two kinds of home studio/office expenses:

- *direct expenses* are work-related costs peculiar to your studio or office, such as painting your studio, repairing the studio ceiling.
- *indirect expenses* are those that apply to your whole house but have a relation to your work. These must be prorated on the basis of your business space to your house space using the number of rooms or percentage of space. Among indirect expenses are utilities, rent, taxes, and insurance.

OVERALL LIMIT ON HOME OFFICE/STUDIO DEDUCTIONS

Even if you meet all the tests, there is an overall limit on your home-office business expense deduction. These expenses cannot exceed the amount of gross income that is derived from the home studio.

BAD DEBTS

Worthless debts arising from sales, professional services, unpaid

* If your trip is primarily personal, then no traveling expenses are deductible, except for expenses incurred directly relating to business.

salary or rent are *not* deductible unless they were previously included in your gross income. Other business bad debts are deductible up to certain limits.

PRORATE CERTAIN DEDUCTIONS

If an item of expense is used for both personal and business use, then the expense must be prorated.

Examples:

- Ms. Weaver uses her basement to store all of her weaving fibers. The basement represents 20 percent of her house space, so she could deduct 20 percent of house-related expenses.
- Mr. Candlemaker residing in Phoenix attended a two-day arts and crafts fair in Tucson and stayed an extra two days (he transacted no business those two days) to visit friends near Tucson. He deducts his expenses during the fair plus his total mileage to and from Tucson.
- Mr. Candlemaker pays $200 a month rent for his house and studio. The studio is one-fifth of the total space. So he then deducts this as a business expense of $40 a month only for the studio.

CUTTING YOUR TAXES (WITHOUT CUTTING YOUR THROAT)

So far we have discussed several ways to legally cut your taxes—exemptions, deductions, and exclusions of certain income. There are other ways.

INCOME AVERAGING

When you finally make it, you will find that the receipt of more income has resulted in higher taxes. HiPrice Hilary earned minimal amounts for four years and in her fifth year sold a tapestry for $100,000. If she is eligible, it is probably worth her while to "income-average." If you are eligible to average your income, then you spread your income over a five-year period and thus you are taxed at a lower rate.* There are several calculations to make and limitations to consider before income-averaging on your return. The general rule is you may average if your taxable income for the past year exceeds by more than $3,000 an amount that is 20 percent greater than the average of your taxable income for the four preceding years.

GENERAL RULE

SHIFTING OF INCOME IN FAMILY

If you have a small business, you can shift some income to other members of the family by hiring your children, paying them up to $1,300 per year without the children paying tax on that income while you keep the dependent exemption of $1,000. Be sure to make all the proper withholdings and pay fair market value for the labor

CHILDREN MUST BE BONA FIDE EMPLOYEE

* See Lasser's *Your Income Tax* for general discussion and a step-by-step method to determine if you can income-average.

performed. Each child should have control over his or her earnings. You need to keep a complete worksheet on the hours worked. Also, child labor laws will apply. Tax dodgers using family members will often trigger an audit.

FAMILY PARTNERSHIP

If you form a family partnership, the family members must share the burdens of management and financing, for IRS will disallow shifts of income where tax avoidance is the sole motive and/or the partnership is a sham.

GIFTS TO MINORS

If you have interest-bearing bank accounts, you can disperse the interest to family members. Under the Uniform Gifts to Minors Act you can give up to $750* a year in interest from a savings account to a child without jeopardizing your claiming the child as a dependent and taking the dependent exemption. The account should be opened in the child's name with the parent as guardian/custodian. The bankbook should read "Mari Gold as guardian/custodian for Zoe Gold, under the Uniform Gifts to Minors Act."

INSTALLMENT SALES

INSTALLMENT SALES

If you are selling some fairly large works at hefty prices in one year, you may want to enter into an installment sales agreement with the buyers. This means that the payments would be made in different tax years. You would then have less gross income in one year and pay less taxes. Do not do this without a contract that secures your interest in the property. Tax laws provide that to qualify as an installment sale there must be two or more payments and the amount of cash received in the year of sale may not exceed 30 percent of the selling price. Personal property has to sell for more than $1,000. For example, if a piece sells for $1,100 and you get $350, you'll have to count the entire $1,100 as income in that year.**

BUYING A HOUSE AND OTHER TAX SHELTERS

HOMEOWNER'S TAX SHELTER

Buying a house can be a tax shelter. By spending your housing money on deductible mortgage interest and real estate taxes*** you shelter or remove some of your income from the tax collector's grasp.

Effective July 1978, taxpayers fifty-five years of age or older can exclude up to $100,000 in gains arising from the sale of their residence. In addition, a taxpayer who sells and buys more than one residence because of employment relocation within an eighteen-month period can defer gains under special rules.

* Amount may change after 1979 when the dependent exemption increases to $1,000.

** Where the work is a capital asset to the seller, the IRS can add or compute an interest amount on the sale which could bring the initial payment in IRS's eyes to over 30 percent. For the installment sale to qualify, the seller must not retain too much control. Consult an accountant in this special area.

*** Providing your other itemized deductions are in excess of the zero bracket amount.

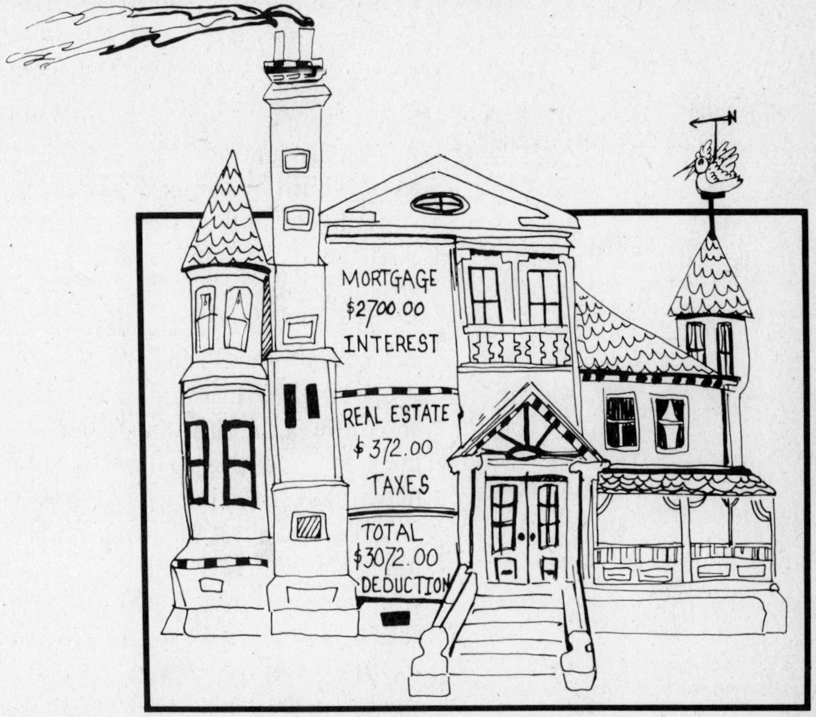

A tax credit for energy conservation (15 percent of expenses up to $2,000, not to exceed a $300 credit) and solar, wind, and geothermal expenditures (30 percent of first $2,000 spent plus 20 percent of expenditures between $2,000 to $10,000) spent on your principal residence after April 20, 1977, through December 31, 1985, is also allowed. Taxpayers may use credits for amounts spent in 1977 along with credits for 1978 to reduce their 1978 tax liability. If you had these expenditures in 1977 and 1978 and did not claim them on your 1978 return, then you should file an amended return on the short form 1040X.

"E" AND MUNICIPAL BONDS

There is also an "E Bond" tax shelter. Unlike savings account interest where the interest is taxed annually, you can delay your taxes on the interest earned until later when the bonds are cashed, that is, cash bonds in a period of lower income, such as a year when you travel a lot, when you retire, or when one of the spouses stops working.

There are also municipal bond mutual funds which have certain risks involved but also have tax-free income. See an investment counselor or broker for more information.

Sometimes the form in which you do business may save you money, that is, sole proprietorship, partnership, or corporation. If you are in the financial position that you have excess income, see a lawyer or an accountant for advice in this area.

CAPITAL ASSETS: DEPRECIATION AND INVESTMENT CREDIT

CAPITAL ASSETS—A TYPE OF BUSINESS PROPERTY

When business property has a useful life of over one year, it is considered a capital asset.* Depreciable capital assets include buildings, machines, equipment, furniture, and fixtures. For artists, capital assets could be cameras, kilns, looms, framing devices, pug wheels, spool racks, and so forth. These are more or less permanent equipment used in, but not consumed by, the process of creating the artist's work.

CAPITAL GAINS: TAXED AT A REDUCED RATE

The sale of a capital asset is usually granted preferential capital gains treatment. Form 4797 is used to report the sale or exchange of property used in trade or business; then the capital gains or losses shown on this form are transferred to Schedule D. The profit from the sale of your capital assets is known as a *capital gain*. This capital gain is part of your income for tax purposes. But, if you have held your capital asset for twelve months,** then you have a 50 percent long-term capital deduction, which means you pay tax on one-half of your gain. After November 31, 1978, the deduction for sales or exchanges is increased to 60 percent, which means that you only pay tax on 40 percent of the gain.

DEPRECIATION

As we stated above, a purchased asset which has a "useful life" of more than one year cannot be deducted as a business expense in the year you buy it. Instead you get an annual deduction based on the asset's total useful life. First you subtract the salvage value*** from the cost and then divide this figure by the useful years. This method of deduction is called *depreciation*. The theory is that equipment used in trade will not wear out in a year, thus it should for tax purposes be depreciated over its useful life.

PRORATED DEPRECIATION

Depreciation is an expense deduction for your capital investment in automobiles, buildings, machinery, and other property used for both business and personal use. The depreciation deduction is prorated.

cost of asset (easel)	$200
− salvage value	−50
net cost	$150
÷ useful life	÷ 5 years
Yearly Depreciation	$ 30

You have a choice of several different methods to use for depreciation. The straight-line depreciation method is the simplest to use. It distributes the depreciation expenses equally over the useful

* Small tools of low value are treated as ordinary and necessary business expenses even though they may last for more than one year.

** This used to be six months and has changed to twelve months. Watch for changes.

*** Salvage value may be ignored on personal property with a life of at least three years as long as it does not exceed 10 percent of the cost.

life of the asset. A potter buys a kiln for $3,000 and estimates the useful life at ten years and salvage value at $400. The kiln is calculated with the additional first-year depreciation, explained next.

cost of kiln	$3,000
first-year additional depreciation	600
estimated salvage value	400
useful life	10 years

2,000 ÷ 10 = 200

yearly depreciation for 10 years = $200

Don't worry if your asset outlives the tax "useful life." But don't take any more depreciation on it.

ADDITIONAL FIRST-YEAR DEPRECIATION

The year you get a capital asset you can deduct as an ordinary and necessary business expense 20 percent of the asset cost and then depreciate the remaining 80 percent over its useful life.* This is additional first-year depreciation. There are many limitations, so check with your accountant.

IRS ESTIMATES OF USEFUL LIFE

You have two methods to choose from in estimating the useful life of property bought in a taxable year—the class life system and your own estimate of the life. Under the class life system the useful life guidelines are set up by IRS. You can lengthen or shorten these useful life guidelines for a property by 20 percent. The class life system must apply to all depreciable property bought in that tax year. Asset life guidelines are available from IRS for specific items. A few class life guidelines are listed below:

	Asset Depreciation in Years		
Asset	***Lower Limit***	***Guideline***	***Upper Limit***
automobile	2.5	3	3.5
truck (light) (less than 3,000 lbs.)	3	4	5
truck (heavy)	5	6	7
farm buildings	20	25	30
office furniture and equipment (service business)	8	10	12

GUIDELINES FOR ESTABLISHING USEFUL LIFE

Or you can use your own estimate of useful life. When you list a useful life that is different from the class life system, if you are audited this difference is what you will have to prove valid. Example: You drive your van 100,000 miles per year because you attend all the regional arts and crafts fairs. Your vehicle would probably have a useful life of less than three years. Of course, the shorter the useful life of an item, the bigger the yearly deduction. Under this second method the test is the period of time the asset is expected to be *useful*

* Has to have at least six-year useful life.

to you, not its expected useful life. In calculating the useful life, you must consider the following:

- your past experience with similar property
- amount of use you give the property
- its age when you get it
- your upkeep and repair policy on the property
- climate

Form 1040, Schedule C: Depreciation is filled out with owner-estimated lives.

SCHEDULE C–2.—Depreciation (See Schedule C Instructions for line 13)
If you need more space, please use Form 4562.

Description of property (a)	Date acquired (b)	Cost or other basis (c)	Depreciation allowed or allowable in prior years (d)	Method of computing depreciation (e)	Life or rate (f)	Depreciation for this year (g)
1 Total additional first-year depreciation (do not include in items below) →						
2 Other depreciation:						
Buildings						
Furniture and fixtures						
Transportation equipment						
Machinery and other equipment						
Other (Specify)						
1. Kiln (Salvage value $300)	1/1/79	3,000	-0-	SL	10	270.00
2. pug mill (salvage $50)	6/1/79	1,000	-0-	SL	9	83.00
3. van (salvage value $500)	1/1/79	6,000	-0-	SL	1	5500.00
3 Totals					3	
4 Depreciation claimed in Schedule C–1					4	
5 Balance (subtract line 4 from line 3). Enter here and on Part II, line 13 ▶					5	

figure 5-12 Form 1040 Schedule C: Depreciation

INVESTMENT TAX CREDIT

Other tax advantages come from various tax credits which are subtracted from taxes owed. A tax discount for business equipment purchases, called an investment tax credit.* The investment credit applies to business machines, equipment, and livestock, but it does not apply to real estate investments. The purpose of the credit is to put dollars back in circulation in the economy by encouraging purchase of business equipment. You can claim a credit of 10 percent of the cost for purchases of business equipment, including real property, provided that:

- the equipment has a useful life of seven years or more
- *used* property acquired that does not exceed $100,000 a year

If the useful life is less than seven years but more than three, then only a percentage of the cost is used to calculate the credit.

This is not a business deduction but rather a dollar credit directly

* See Lasser's *Your Income Tax* for further details.

against your tax liability. Check special computations and limitations with your accountant.

Alice's Allegory # 19

or

A Tax-Reducing Plan for Everyone

One day Alice looked at the pot-shop yard and the collection of flowerpots from apple- to canoe-shaped containers and bemoaned losing income by selling through the local Funky Housewares Department Store. "I've got it," she said. "A potter bus with shelves lined with foam so no pots would break." She and Romero quickly purchased a new bus for $15,000 and converted it to the "Wild Potter from Timbuktu," a splendiforous rig. They spent the summer of 1978, after making pots all winter, traveling across the country selling pots from their bus. Buses have a nine-year class life rate. The basis for the investment tax credit is $15,000 and 10 percent of the basis is $1,500—the investment tax credit. This means the $1,500 would be divided between the two partners and each would get to deduct $750 from their respective tax liability. They also get to deduct additional first-year depreciation and regular depreciation on the bus from their income.

Warning: This section only alerts you to the availability of tax credits. This information shows you ways to reduce your final tax bill with specific exemptions, credits, adjustments, and deductions, but each has special rules which must be checked against your situation before it can be determined that you qualify. If it looks as though you can use one of these methods, check other sources or consult with your tax preparer for the specifics.

OTHER TAX CREDITS

TAX CREDITS ARE SUBTRACTED FROM YOUR TAX LIABILITY

There are several other tax credits available to individuals. With the exception of the earned income credit, these are entered in the credit section of the 1040 return. Please note the various credits on the tax return below, for we only will discuss a few.

Credits			
	38 Credit for contributions to candidates for public office . .	38	
	39 Credit for the elderly *(attach Schedules R&RP)*	39	
	40 Credit for child and dependent care expenses (attach Form 2441) .	40	
	41 Investment credit *(attach Form 3468)*	41	
	42 Foreign tax credit *(attach Form 1116)*	42	
	43 Work Incentive (WIN) Credit *(attach Form 4874)*	43	
	44 New jobs credit *(attach Form 5884)*	44	
	45 Residential energy credits (see page 12 of instructions. attach Form 5695) . . .	45	
	46 **Total credits.** Add lines 38 through 45		46
	47 **Balance.** Subtract line 46 from line 37 and enter difference (but not less than zero) . ▶		47

figure 5-13 Form 1040, page 2: Tax Credits

CHILD- AND DEPENDENT-CARE TAX CREDIT

To be eligible for a child and dependent* care credit, Form 2441, you must incur the sitter expenses to earn money, maintain a house-

* This can include a disabled dependent of any age or a spouse who because of a physical or mental condition cannot take care of him/herself. See Lasser's *Your Income Tax*.

hold for the dependent, and file a joint return if married. After 1979, child-care credit is allowed for payment to grandparents. The credit is 20 percent of child-care expenses up to $2,000 for one dependent (maximum of credit of $400 for one dependent). For more than one dependent there is a 20 percent maximum credit of $800. This credit is subtracted from your tax liability.

EARNED INCOME CREDIT—A BONUS FOR LOW-INCOME FAMILIES

The earned income credit or the "negative income tax" is very important, for you may get money even if you don't pay taxes. It is available to low-income workers with a dependent child or children (even if over eighteen) living with them in a household maintained in the United States. It is equal to 10 percent of the first $5,000 earned, but it is reduced by 10 percent of excess earnings over $5,000 so that the credit is gradually wiped out. The maximum credit is $500. Starting July 1979 the credit will be figured into the withholding tables to provide a gradual rebate instead of the lump sum previously available.

WIN AND NEW JOB CREDITS

You can get a WIN (Work Incentive Program) or a New Job tax credit of up to $3,000 for the first year of employment and up to $1,500 in the second year. The New Job credit is claimed for hiring new employees from eight target groups—for instance, certain welfare recipients, Vietnam veterans, handicapped persons, young people, and convicted felons. The credit is in force from 1979 through 1981 for employees hired after September 26, 1978. In certain situations, those hiring domestic help will be able to claim a maximum of $2,100 in the first year. These tax credits can be complicated, so please see your accountant.

Check each year to see if there are new tax credits, or if the old ones have been stopped or changed.

ENERGY/SOLAR TAX CREDIT

As discussed before, beginning in 1978 there are home energy credits. There is now a credit of 15 percent of the first $2,000 (maximum credit $300) of expenses for insulation, installation of storm doors, windows, and other energy-saving items. Installation of solar, wind, or geothermal energy devices after April 20, 1977 can result in a credit of 30 percent of the first $2,000 plus 20 percent after $8,000 (maximum credit $2,200). Consult with your accountant regarding these new credits.

MAXIMUM TAX ON PERSONAL SERVICE OR EARNED INCOME

A tax ceiling of 50 percent is applied to earned income which gives relief to salary earners and self-employed persons in top tax brackets, but your *taxable* personal service income must exceed $40,200 if you are single or a head of household or $55,200 if married and file jointly before the ceiling takes effect.

BUSINESS AND HOBBY LOSSES

Taxpayers who sustain a loss from a *business* can use the loss to offset income from other sources. If you have more than one source of income, your combined net profits and losses are reported as income (loss) on your return. A typical example of this situation would be the taxpayer who has a salaried job and a part-time craft business.

BUSINESS LOSS

If the business shows a loss, the taxpayer applies that loss against his income from the salary source—for instance, Mr. Potter substitute-teaches for $8,000 a year. He also incurs a $1,000 craft business loss, so his adjusted gross income is $7,000.

If your loss exceeds your income for the year, then it can be carried backward for three years and then forward for seven years. Carrying a loss back entitles you to a refund, and a loss forward reduces your taxes. This is another special area for which you should also see an accountant.

BUSINESS OR HOBBY?

When losses are incurred in an enterprise, then the IRS may raise the question of whether its activity is a legitimate business or a hobby. If an activity is ruled a hobby, the income is taxable *but* net losses (excess of expenses over income) are deductible only against hobby income. The IRS is concerned when a taxpayer has a salaried job and a part-time "business" which shows a loss or when a couple filing a joint return use a business loss to offset salaried income. In both cases the tax liability is reduced.

HOBBY LOSS CHALLENGE

If you consistently lose money in a sideline business, you are courting an IRS challenge that the activity is a hobby. Often artists and craftmakers face a hobby loss challenge, for even though they are dedicated to their work, they may show losses for many years.

TEST: PROFIT MOTIVE

The test distinguishing a business from a hobby is whether the activity engaged in is done with the bona fide intention and expectation of making a profit. The profit motive is checked by IRS when it applies the two-out-of-five-year test. If you show a profit two out of five consecutive years, the activity will be presumed to be a business with profit intent and expectation. Maybe plumbers, lawyers, and handymen can be judged by that test, but an artist, craftmaker, or writer usually does not achieve instant approval, recognition, and sales. Lesson: Arrange your affairs to show some profit some years. But even if you don't show profit in two out of the last five years, you can successfully beat an IRS challenge that you are a hobbyist, if you can show a profit motive. Some of the factors to consider in evaluating the profit motive are:

FACTORS TO EVALUATE PROFIT MOTIVE

- methods by which you record business activity—keeping receipts, journals, in-out records, job cards
- your expertise and experience—steady professional notice (gallery shows, prizes, mention in books)
- expectation that your work will increase in value
- your success in related and unrelated activities helps to show you can make a go of it
- profit/loss history—increasing income is helpful, but a continued large discrepancy between the activity income and expenses isn't

- your financial status—if you have independent income, this goes against finding of a profit motive*
- the extent to which you do the work for personal pleasure

Throughout this chapter we have made suggestions for doing your work in a businesslike fashion—if you have good record keeping, get into galleries, juried shows, win prizes, show an increase in income, study or achieve recognition, sell to people other than friends, then hopefully you can meet an IRS challenge.

One artist, Gloria Churchman, was engaged in painting, designing, sculpting, and drawing for twenty years, and her art-related income never exceeded her art-related expenses. The tax court held that she could deduct her art-related expenses because the facts showed that she engaged in the art activities with an intent to make a profit.** To obtain the 1970 and 1971 tax deductions for her art studio and studio office, Ms. Churchman argued that the Internal Revenue Code should allow her deduction because the activity was engaged in for profit. Even though she had a history of losses, she did not depend on the art income for her livelihood, and though there was a recreational element in her activities, there was still a profit motive. The profit motive was shown by her professional qualifications and commitment, her art training and experience at colleges and workshops, her effort to sell her work publicly, and her businesslike record keeping of art-related expenses and sales.

COMMON TAX RETURN ERRORS

COMMON ERRORS ON RETURNS

Some of the most common errors that crop up on returns completed by individuals are:

- entries placed on wrong lines
- failure to attach necessary schedules, a check for tax due, W-2 forms
- failure to have joint returns signed by both spouses
- incorrect computation of the zero bracket amount
- failure to claim tax credit such as the earned income credit
- confusion over the medical deductions and charitable gifts
- failure to include the previous year's deducted state and local tax refund as income
- putting casualty losses together and deducting the $100 exclusion only once
- failure to deduct sales tax paid on autos or expensive personal property
- failure to use income averaging
- failure to take 7 cents per mile for driving done for charitable or medical reasons
- taking a partnership loss as an itemized deduction rather than a reduction in income

* Several cases have held that where persons of independent wealth consistently had expenses in excess of income from their artwork, then the activity was a hobby and there was not the necessary profit motive.

** *Churchman v. Commissioner*, 68 T.C. 696 (1977).

AUDITS

His horse went dead, and his mule went lame,
And he lost six cows in a poker game;
Then a hurricane came on a Summer day,
And blew the house where he lived away;
An earthquake came when that was gone,
And swallowed the land the house stood on.
And then the tax collector came around,
And charged him up with the hole in the ground.

WHO GETS AUDITED

Much of this section on federal income taxes is in preparation for the time when your tax return is being questioned by the IRS. An audit is a review of your return by a revenue agent. About 2 percent of all returns are audited. The more money you make, the greater are your chances of being audited. Other factors making an audit more likely are if you are self-employed and could be paid in cash, if your alleged self-employment looks like a hobby, if your deductions are way out of line with the average itemized deductions, if you have high deductions for business and travel, and if it is unlikely that you can support the family on the income you state. Some returns are randomly picked for an audit. One family has been audited the past three years because of the wife's craft ventures and publishing efforts. She failed to separate these transactions from the general family business and failed to keep records.

COMPUTER CHECKS

Now in addition to audits, there are computers to match your tax return with computerized information on wages, interest, dividends, et cetera. A few months after filing your return you may receive a correction-to-arithmetic notice or a letter asking for fully completed related forms or other information which calls your attention to an obvious blunder. This is not an audit notice but rather is a notification of a glaring error that appeared on your return when it was checked. In this case, most people pay any tax liability or accept a refund as indicated on the correction notice because the goof is usually obvious.

MODERN-DAY BOUNTY HUNTERS

Even if you get a refund or if you pay an IRS demand for additional tax, the IRS has three years to audit a return, unless fraud is involved. Fraud leaves the door open longer for an audit (three years from the date the fraud is discovered). An audit can be triggered by an angry neighbor, ex-lover, ex-spouse, and employee turning you in—they can get a bounty of up to 10 percent of the taxes and penalties collected.

NOTICE LETTER

If you are to be audited, you will be notified by a letter setting up an appointment. The letter will also indicate what items are questioned and what supporting evidence you will need. *Don't ignore the letter.* See the Notice of Audit in Appendix 5-4. You can request a change of location or a postponement, but again, don't ignore the appointment. Usually a Form 5714, Confirmation of Appointment, is attached to your notice. On that form you indicate if you will keep the appointment or want another date. If someone prepared your return, ask him or her to go with you. If you did your own return and don't think you can handle an audit or if you have evaded taxes, then take a certified public accountant or attorney with you.* You will need to sign a 2848-D Authorization and Declaration form before information can be given to them. *Prepare yourself thoroughly for the meeting*—review your return, accumulate and organize your canceled checks, receipts, diary, and so on.** Don't overdress for the meeting. For example, if you have claimed $200 yearly income from your printmaking and you show up for the audit wearing a beaver-skin hat, alligator boots, and a genuine leopard vest, the auditor will be suspicious of your income. It won't help for you to be either hostile to the agent or overly friendly. Don't volunteer information. Let the agent set the pace and just answer questions asked. Be firm and positive if you know you are entitled to a deduction. You may have to talk to someone higher up.

PREPARE YOURSELF

APPEAL CASES

If you agree with the findings, the IRS agent will figure your additional taxes and ask you to sign an agreement form. After signing you lose your appeal rights, so wait until you get the Report of Individual Income Tax Examination Charges, Form 1902A. The report spells out amounts and reasons for the charges. In hardship situations you can make installment payments.

Remember in dealing with the agent that horse trading on issues is possible, for this avoids paperwork and litigation for all. The agent has authority to settle the questioned parts of your return. Occasionally, at the end of an audit people will even have a smaller tax bill.

If you and the agent disagree, you have several alternatives: an appeal within the IRS; litigation in the tax court; and/or a combination of these. You will be sent Publication 5, *Your Appeal Rights and Preparation of Protests for Unagreed Cases.* Generally, once you receive the written report you can submit additional information, discuss the findings with an examiner, or request a district conference. Or you could use the new small claims division of the tax court for amounts under $5,000. You file only one petition, the court usually is more lenient in accepting evidence than the IRS, and you can represent yourself. There is no appeal from the tax court small claims division if the IRS is upheld.

If you allegedly owe IRS a lot of money or it looks like a fraud situation, get professional help.

* There is an IRS manual that instructs agents on what to look for during an audit. You might look at it at a library. There is a summary of the manual called *How to Survive a Tax Audit* available from Reymont Associates, 29-S Reymont Ave., Rye, NY 10580 which may be worth getting.

** Keep all your notes and scribbles that go into making up your return. If audited, this will help piece together the basis for the deductions you claimed, i.e., if you claim $300 for professional books, then you keep the worksheet where you listed the books and totaled their price.

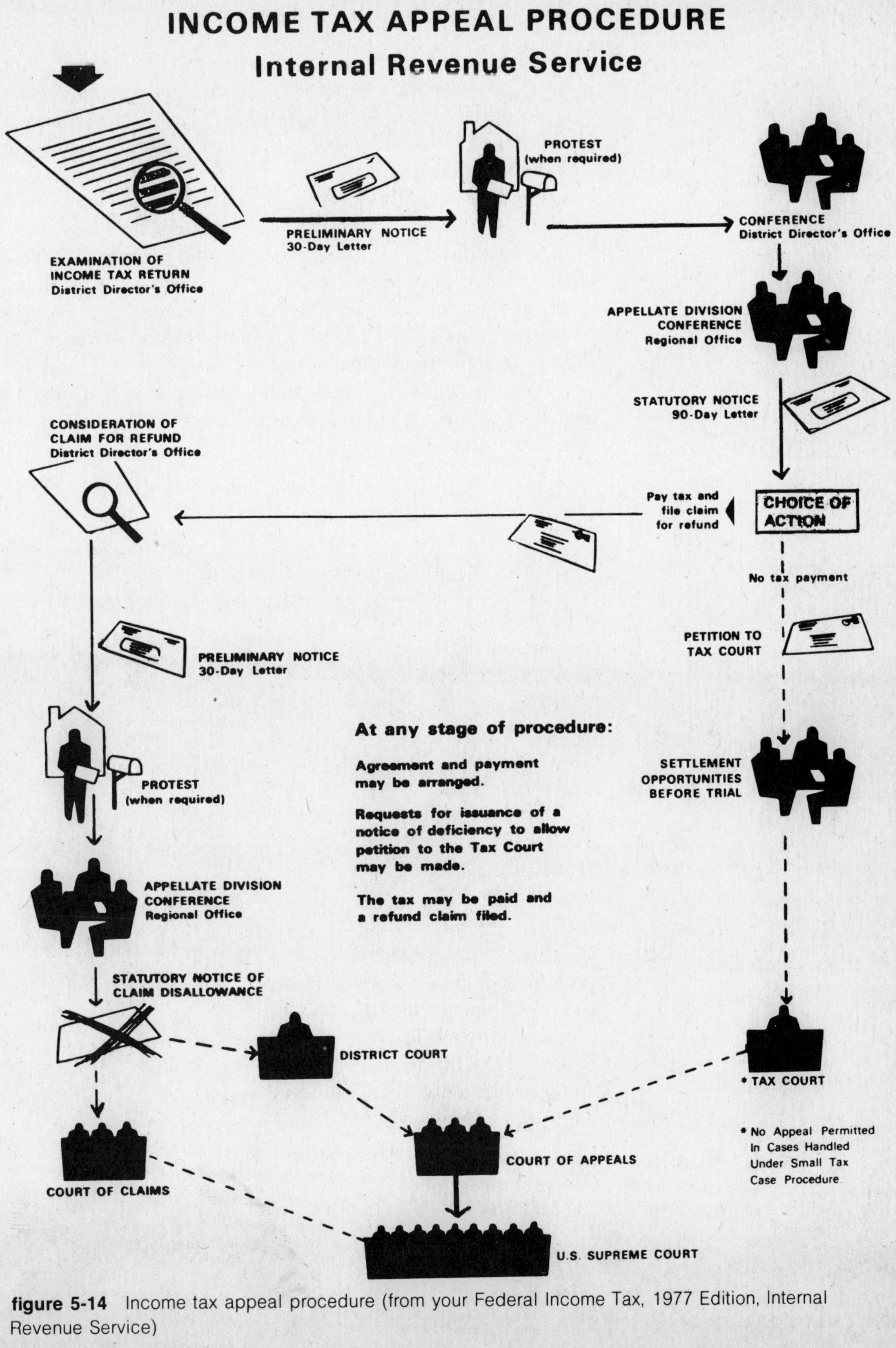

figure 5-14 Income tax appeal procedure (from your Federal Income Tax, 1977 Edition, Internal Revenue Service)

SUMMARY

You've had a pretty exhausting trip through the federal income tax maze. Maybe reform is around the corner and maybe it's not—but you've got the idea of keeping records so you can reconstruct your business and personal activities to determine the money you got, and the money you spent. Some friends, an English professor and his wife, filed recently not only for his salaried income, but for his sideline handyman business and her pottery business (they have built a beautiful double hexagon studio and huge kiln). With a very commendable doggedness our friends did their taxes themselves using mainly the IRS Business Tax Kit, Lasser's *Your Income Tax*, and calls to the IRS. It took them about thirty-five hours, *but now* they understand the forms, procedures, and computations, and next year they should spend considerably less time on their taxes. It can be done. But if you want to spend your time at other things, then see a good tax preparer.

Chapter 6 Other Taxes

INTRODUCTION

This chapter is a catchall for taxes not covered in the previous chapter—self-employment taxes, estimated taxes, sales tax, and various property taxes. Two of these, the self-employment and estimated taxes, are related to the previous chapter.

SELF-EMPLOYMENT TAX

You are liable for self-employment tax (your payment into the Social Security system), if you have an annual net income of $400 or more from operating a business(es) or profession(s). In 1978, you pay 8.10 percent on net self-employment income up to $17,700, with a $1,433.70 maximum. This is added to your income tax liability, and the two taxes are paid as one. The self-employment tax is computed

WHEN DUE

on Schedule SE, and is paid when you file your yearly tax return. Of course, in order to be self-employed you must be selling your work for a profit, that is, if you sell one pot or magazine article during the year you may not qualify as self-employed.

IF BOTH EMPLOYED AND SELF-EMPLOYED

If you work full or part time as an employee and are self-employed on the side, then you count your salary first and your net self-employment income second toward the $17,700 limit. You cannot receive Social Security benefits until you attain *insured status*, which you get by contributing tax for a certain number of quarters of work. You become fully insured for life when your credits consist of forty quarters of coverage or ten years of net earnings of $400 or more per year, though you may not stop making payments then. Social Security has all kinds of benefits (all with special qualifying rules). Generally, these are retirement benefits, Medicare, disability, and survivor benefits. See your local Social Security office for free copies of numerous Social Security information pamphlets.

ESTIMATED TAX

ESTIMATED TAX

Partially or totally self-employed persons, which would include artists, craftmakers, and writers, have to fill out and file quarterly a Form 1040-SE, Estimated Tax Declaration Voucher if there are earnings of more than $500 from which taxes will not be withheld or if the tax liability will be more than $100. This means you act as your

PAY-AS-YOU-GO PLAN

own employer and send in taxes quarterly on your income as you earn it.

To pay the estimated tax,* estimate your tax for the year, complete the voucher, and mail it by April 15 of that year. Other installments are due June 15, September 15, and January 15. The remaining estimated tax owed can be paid along with your regular 1040 form filed on or before April 15. If you overestimated your taxes, the excess can be deducted from next year's tax. If you underestimate your

* See IRS Publication 505, *Tax Withholding and Declaration of Estimated Tax*, for more detailed information.

tax but follow one of the four IRS safety zones,* then you won't be penalized. It's easiest to figure your estimated tax on the basis of your previous year's income tax and self-employment tax liability. For example, if your 1980 tax is $2,400, by fixing your 1981 estimated tax at $2,400 you will not be subject to a penalty as long as your quarterly payments are timely.** Of course, if you have reason to believe that your income will be over last year's, then you should pay additional estimated tax.

Alice's Allegory # 20

or

Enshrined for Eternity

Alice on filing her 1977 tax return had to pay a lot in taxes plus a penalty for failure to pay her estimated tax, which meant staying up nights throwing pots and selling her wares on the street to get the cash together for the local tax agent. She said, "Wow, I can't go through that again. Show me how to do it."

The local tax agent, who had been turned on to Alice's fantastic stoneware Oriental soup spoons in Maltese blue glazes said in March 1979, "This is it. Do you know how much you are making this year?" "I don't know but I paid $1,000 in taxes in 1978." He said, "You'll need the amount of your last year's tax liability to figure your estimated tax for this year. Take notes." She got a stylus and said, "I will enshrine this information for eternity." And on the slab she had just rolled she took dictation. "On the voucher form, figure you'll pay $1,000 in taxes. File the voucher form and your first quarterly installment of $250 by April 15, 1979. Then pay $250 on June 15, September 15, and January 15, 1980—or pay $1,000 before January 15, 1980, because that's what you paid last year."

"I got it," said Alice and she promptly popped the slab in her kiln, then bisqued, glazed, and fired it again for a beautiful wall hanging in her studio. One day the tax agent returned, and said, "I have an order for five hundred of those estimated tax slabs. By the way, you had better amend your estimated tax voucher or you'll be caught with a huge bill at the end of the year."

SALES TAX

SALES TAX A sales or gross receipts tax is a tax imposed by most states and some cities on retail sales to customers.*** As of 1976, New Hampshire, Delaware, Montana, Oregon, and Alaska did not have a sales tax. In some states sales tax is also placed on services. If the seller pays the tax, then it can be deducted as a business expense. For example, Mrs. Duffy wants to buy a flowerpot from you priced at $10. You add a 4 percent sales tax (the rate for your state) to the pot's price, selling it to her for $10.40. You report the $10.40 as income, send the

* Methods of computing your estimated taxes.

** Failure to make timely quarterly payments of your estimated tax can subject you to a penalty.

*** An individual not in business does not have to pay this. In California, the determination of whether or not you are in business depends on the number of sales you make. For example if you make fewer than five sales a year, then you probably are not in business.

$.40 to the state sales tax department, and deduct the $.40 on your tax return.

Check with other business people or your state tax department to see if your state has a sales tax. If it does, make an application for a sales permit, and you will get a resale number.* Some states require you to post a bond prior to the issuance of the permit. The reason for this is if you don't pay the sales tax either by pocketing the tax paid by your customer or by failing to charge the tax, recovery for the amount of the tax obligation can be made against the bond. If you don't collect or fail to forward the tax for whatever reason, you may be liable for not only the tax but also interest and a penalty.

Sometimes at fairs the management will get a sales tax permit, or the craftmaker (if the maker is from out-of-state or has no permit) will get a temporary permit. The person who makes the final sale (retailer) to the consumer collects and pays the tax. At art fairs usually you collect and pay, but at art exhibitions probably the sponsor pays. A person going to an art fair or other sale in another state should check to see if nonresidents have to collect sales taxes.

Some business people like to engage in mail-order business to avoid sales taxes. In that case, postal receipts regarding mail transactions should be kept.

Alice's Allegory # 21

or

Beware of Mellow Fellows

Alice was at the Third Annual Bread and Butter Crafts Fair in Marshmallow Beach, Nevada, when she discovered that she was the only craftmaker who had applied for and received a license to collect and remit sales tax by nonresidents. Barabella the Batikist, Lulu the Lithographer, and Qunito the Quilter all laughed at her, for they were charging the sales tax but had not applied for the license, had no intentions of remitting the sales tax, and were pocketing it instead. At the Fourth Annual Bread and Butter Crafts Fair she discovered that they had all had hassles with the state of Nevada. Some were assessed fines and penalties. Alice just smiled her quiet smile.

STATE AND LOCAL INCOME TAX

You should check with your state tax department, and county and city governments, to see what other taxes might be collected and to get copies of the necessary forms to pay these taxes. For instance, New York City, Chicago, and San Francisco have city taxes. As of 1976, Connecticut, Florida, Nevada, New Hampshire, South Dakota,

STATE INCOME TAX

Tennessee, Texas, Wyoming, and Washington did not have a state income tax. Usually states imposing a state income tax have rules

* If you have a resale number, then you do not have to pay taxes on your supplies (such as canvas, paint, fibers) for those goods are taxed as part of the final work you sell. Looms, easels, potter's wheels, etc. are not exempt, for they are not contained in the final product.

similar to the federal government, but some don't—so look carefully at your state tax package when you get it.

PROPERTY TAX

PROPERTY TAX

There are several kinds of property taxes—auto license tax, inventory tax, real property tax, and personal property tax. The imposition of these taxes as well as the rates vary from state to state. The latter two taxes, based on dollar values, are increased by a rise in the assessed value. Inventory taxes are locally imposed taxes on business inventory and equipment and are based on the market value of the property. If your state requires payment of an inventory tax, then reduce your inventory to the lowest workable minimum, by the assessment date.

ESTATE AND GIFT TAX

Under the 1976 Tax Reform Act a person's estate (after 1981) would only pay an estate tax if the total of the taxable gifts* and the taxable estate is greater than $175,625. It is beyond the scope of this primer to discuss this area in any detail.** You may need a will and an estate plan. See a competent lawyer for advice in this area.

* Gifts to persons during the deceased's life in excess of $3,000 per year.

** See Du Boff, *Deskbook of Art Law,* Federal Publications, Inc., 1977, pp. 652–670, for a further discussion.

Chapter 7
Especially for Writers

COPYING

- Copyright
- Other Protection from Copying

CONTRACTS

- Publishing Contracts
- Contracts with Literary Agents

BACK TO TAXES

- Record Keeping
- Business Deductions
- Hobby Loss Challenge
- Social Security
- Other Taxes

MISCELLANEOUS

- Freedom of Information Act and Sunshine Laws

■ LEGAL ADVICE, NOT ON YOUR LIFE

INTRODUCTION

Many earlier sections of this book apply to writers. The discussions of libel, obscenity, and invasion of privacy in the content section of Chapter 2, "Legal Limitations on Content and Materials," are certainly geared to writers as well as artists and craftmakers. This chapter will serve only as a supplement to the other chapters in this book and will probably be best understood after reading the chapters that appear before.

Legal matters arising from the writing business generally fall into three categories:

- protection of your work
  - copyright
  - sales contracts
  - unfair competition
  - misappropriation
- liability for the contents of your work
  - libel
  - obscenity
  - invasion of privacy
- governmental rights and obligations
  - taxes
  - freedom of information acts

This chapter will discuss the law of copyright as it pertains to writers, publishing and literary agency contracts, taxes for the writer, and the Freedom of Information Act. For further study on the subject of the writer and the law, see the other chapters of this book, the suggested readings indicated in various sections of this chapter as well as in the Further Readings section of this book.

COPYING

COPYRIGHT

HISTORY

The basics of copyright law are discussed in Chapter 3, "Copying." Here the aspects of copyright law that especially concern writers are covered. Historically, copyright laws evolved to protect literary works. Just as ancient poets and dramatists refused to sing unless they were paid in food and lodging, writers wanted to control the use of their work and to share in its profits. In the United States, Noah Webster, eager to protect his *Blue-backed Speller,* which was first published in 1783, journeyed to several Colonial state capitals to lobby successfully for the passage of state copyright acts. In 1790, the first federal copyright act was passed and a few days later the first copyright was issued for the *Philadelphia Spelling Book.* Nearly two hundred years later, in the year 1977, there were 122,080 registrations for books alone with the Copyright Office!

One question asked by writers is the term for their old unpublished works under the new law. If an unpublished work was created before 1978 and was still protected by the old common law copy-

PRE–JANUARY 1, 1978, UNPUBLISHED WORK

right on January 1, 1978 (that is, it had not been published), it automatically receives copyright protection for the usual term for all copyrighted works—the author's life plus fifty years. For anonymous or pseudonymous works or works for hire the term is seventy-five years from the date of first publication or one hundred years from the date of the creation, whichever is less. However, in no event can the copyright term for these unpublished works expire before December 31, 2002. For example if the author of an unpublished work entitled *The Colorado River Early Inhabitants* died in 1950, the copyright would not expire in 2000 (author's life plus fifty years) but 2002.

POST–JANUARY 1, 1978, UNPUBLISHED WORKS

Under the new law unpublished works can now be registered. This has advantages and disadvantages. When an unpublished work is infringed before it is registered, then no recovery of statutory damages and attorneys' fees is allowed after a lawsuit, though there still may be a monetary award, if the owner of the unpublished work wins the suit. Also, if you register the unpublished work, the copy that you deposit with the Copyright Office is a public record that *anyone can inspect.*

Some people may not wish to copyright their work. J. Frank Dobie declined to copyright his work *Guide to Life and Literature of the Southwest* with the following delightful non-notice:

Not copyright in 1942
Again not copyright in 1952
Anybody is welcome to help himself
to any of it in any way

CONTENTS OF COPYRIGHT NOTICE

If you *do* want to copyright your work, the same requirements concerning contents of the copyright notice as were discussed in Chapter 3, "Copying," apply here. Further, the notice must be affixed so as to give reasonable notice of the claim of copyright. The regulations describe what constitutes acceptable placement for the copyright notice:

LOCATION OF COPYRIGHT NOTICE

- title page
- page following title page
- either side of the front cover, and if none, either side of front page (same for back)
- first page of work's main body
- last page of work's main body
- between the front page and first page of main body as long as the pages between don't exceed ten and the notice is prominent and separated from other material (same for back)

In a collective work such as a magazine, any of the above are reasonable. In addition, the notice could be placed by the masthead or near the front of the issue alongside the issue number, date, and title. In order for a separate contribution to a collective work to bear its own notice of copyright, the notice must be positioned in one of the following ways:

POSITION OF AN INDIVIDUAL NOTICE IN A COLLECTIVE WORK

- for contribution of one page or less the notice must appear under the title, adjacent to the contribution, or somewhere else on the page as long as clear.
- for a contribution of more than one page the notice must appear under the title or near the beginning of the contribution, on the first page of the main body or at the immediate end of the contribution.
- or the notice could appear in a separate list of contributions by full titles and authors on a page, table of contents, or acknowledgments appearing in the front or back of the whole collective work.

GROUP REGISTRATION

Even if your contribution to a periodical does not have its own notice, you receive copyright protection based upon the magazine's copyright. However, you cannot use the registration form for group registrations unless each contribution bears your own notice. Use Form TX (for registering nondramatic literary works) if you are making a single registration for a group of contributions to various periodicals. This way you can register all your contributions printed in a twelve-month period together for a single fee of $10. At the same time, deposit two complete copies of each magazine, anthology, or periodical containing the works in question. Better yet, register these contributions quarterly so that no more than three months pass between publication and registration—the copyright annual fees would total $40 rather than $10, but you would not lose your statutory damages and attorneys' fees in the event of infringement. If it happens that your contributions are covered by a single copyright notice in the name of the publisher, then the publisher is the one to register the work and should register the work (make sure it is done in three months). It is better that you have the copyright in your name and you register it. Otherwise you may have to have the publisher assign it back to you.

REGISTER QUARTERLY

PUBLISHER REGISTRATION OF COLLECTIVE WORK

Whoever transfers and licenses a copyright can terminate the transfer at a later date. See Appendix 3-2. So if you want to save this right for your heirs or yourself, then you should get the copyright in your name. In this way you would be the grantor, the person giving the transfer, and could later terminate it. Note that the various applications have detailed instruction sheets which should be carefully read.

COPYRIGHT WITH CONTRIBUTOR TO COLLECTIVE WORK

The new copyright law provides for special treatment for contributions to collective works. Absent an agreement to the contrary, the copyright of each contribution remains with the author even though the only copyright notice appearing on the collective work is the publisher's. Further, unless otherwise agreed, the publisher receives not only the right to use the contribution in the collective work but also gets the right to use the contribution as part of any revision of the collective work or as part of a later collective work in

PUBLISHER'S RIGHTS TO USE OF CONTRIBUTION TO COLLECTIVE WORK the same series. So if you do not want your article "How to Make Fried Bread" which was contributed to the *Ole Cooking* magazine to be used again in their annual publication *100 Best Recipes of Ole Cooking* or to be run again three years later, then you need to state in your contract that you are giving one-time-use rights *only*, or the new copyright law will imply the two rights discussed above into your contract of sale.

RENEWAL OF FIRST-TERM COPYRIGHTS

For old copyrights (pre 1978) it is necessary to renew on or before December 31 of the year of the term's end any copyrights you originally registered between January 1, 1950,* and December 31, 1977, to obtain protection for a second term of forty-seven years. For example, a 1952 copyright must be registered for renewal during the 1980 calendar year. Use Form RE. The renewal fee is $6. The same form can be used to renew a group of works first published as contributions to periodicals in the same year—for example, in 1980 a renewal registration can be made for all the writer's contributions to collective works first published in 1952. If you are missing any important information that you need to complete the renewal form, the Copyright Office will do research for you for a minimum charge of $10.

RENEWAL OF PRE–1978 PERIODICAL CONTRIBUTIONS

For those pre-1978 situations where the contribution was copyrighted by the publisher, have the publisher assign in writing the copyright back to the author and record the assignment.

FAIR USE

In Chapter 3, "Copying," we discussed some of the fair-use provisions of the new copyright law. A report on the new law has added guidelines for the educational fair use of copyrighted works which set limits on the length of works that can be copied, requires that the copyright notice be placed on each copied work, and limits the number of times works can be copied. Since many writers also teach, these guidelines for educational fair use are important to summarize. Acceptable fair uses include:

EDUCATIONAL PURPOSES

- use of a single copy in teaching a class or in scholarly research of:
  - a book chapter.
  - an article from a periodical.
  - a short story, essay, poem.
  - a cartoon, chart, diagram drawing, graph, or picture from a periodical.
- use of multiple classroom copies (one copy per student in class) of:
  - a complete poem of less than 250 words and not longer than two pages.
  - a poem excerpt of less than 250 words.
  - a story, article, or essay of less than 2,500 words.
  - an excerpt from a prose work of the lesser of 1,000 words or 10 percent of the work.
  - one cartoon, chart, etc. per book or periodical.

* Any copyrights before that date have expired or are already in their second term.

A teacher *may not:*

- make multiple copies for classroom use if the work has been copied already for a class at the same institution.
- make multiple copies of a work from the same author more than once a term or more than three times a term from the same collective work or periodical.
- make multiple copies of works more than nine times in a term.
- make an overrun of copies for others.
- make a copy of works in place of an anthology.
- make a copy of materials such as workbooks that can be consumed.
- repeat copies from term to term.

LIBRARIES

For guidelines for fair use by libraries under the new law, obtain a copy of Circular R21, Reproduction of Copyrighted Works by Educators and Libraries, from the Copyright Office.

CRITICISM AND THE ADVANCE OF SCIENCE AND ART

There are other areas of concern under the fair-use section of the copyright act. Under the fair-use doctrine, you can quote directly from a work in dramatic or literary criticism. Also, those working in the fields of sciences and art can use existing copyrighted works to write new works, including comments, discussions, and long quotes from the earlier works. Since old work is a jumping-off place for the new work, this is an important fair use, and is considered necessary to the advancement of science and art.

PARODY AND BURLESQUE

Parody and burlesque necessarily involve the use of an original work, but the line between fair use and infringement is fine. Jack Benny performed a humorous sketch, "Autolight," which burlesqued a motion picture, *Gaslight*, and the court held that the use was unfair.

OBTAINING PERMISSION FOR THE USE OF COPYRIGHTED MATERIAL

How long should quotations be before you get permission? Different publishers have different word limits depending on the nature of the work: for scholarly works—fifty to two hundred words; poetry—three to four lines. If the use is for commercial purposes, don't use a line or the author's name without permission. See the Appendix 3-3 for a permission form. The notice printed in the front of some books stating that the "unauthorized use of [so many] words is forbidden" does not prevent the fair use of the work. A better practice is to authorize the use of up to a certain number of words without permission as long as it is not used for advertising or publicity, except for use in reviews. The Association of American Publishers (AAP) has designed a rapid and efficient permission system, and you should contact them to get a copy of their permission request form: AAP, 1707 L Street, NW, Suite 480, Washington, D.C. 20036. A Copyright Clearance Center (CCC), same address as above, is establishing a central royalty-paying clearinghouse where payment terms for photocopying magazine articles are set in advance and coded on each contribution's title page. An extra copy of the title page, indicating the number of copies made and the payment, would be sent to CCC, who would forward it to the publisher, and the publisher would forward it to the author.

CERTAIN PERFORMING AND DISPLAY RIGHTS

The new law grants another fair-use right for the performance or display of certain copyrighted works. This exception to the general rule of "no use without permission" is fairly specific. In summary, this fair-use exception applies to:

- works displayed in face-to-face teaching at a nonprofit educational institution
- performance or display of works at a religious function, assembly, or church
- performance of nondramatic literary works if there is no admission, no commercial advantage, and no one (promoter, organizer, or performer) receives a fee

Under the third exception, if an admission fee is charged, then all proceeds must go to an educational, religious, or charitable purpose. In this case, the copyright owner can prevent the performance under most circumstances. Otherwise copyright owners would be supporting causes that they may personally oppose.

LAWSUITS FOR INFRINGEMENT

The majority of legal actions for infringement have been brought by writers or publishers. The following are examples of successful infringement cases:

- *Adventures in Good Eating*, a guidebook for restaurants and hotels infringed another guide where there was similarity of expression and organization.
- Classified Geographic, Inc.'s compilation of cut-up copies of *National Geographic* magazine was an infringement.
- a fictional biography of Clara Barton in the form of a screenplay was found infringed by a so-called factual biographical book that used some of the fictionalized episodes.

The use of the same fundamental plot is not an infringement if there is a difference in the leading characters, action, dialogue, episodes, and locale. In a recent case involving *The Seven Per Cent Solution*, the court failed to find that a scholarly piece concerning cocaine addiction at the turn of the century was infringed upon by the movie. Even though plaintiff speculated in his scholarly work that Holmes' fear of Professor Moriarity was a drug-induced paranoid delusion cured by Freud—the basic plot of the movie *The Seven Per Cent Solution*—no infringement was found. On the other hand, the successful play *White Cargo* was held to infringe Ida Vera Simington's novel *Hell's Playground*, for the locales in both were the African tropics, the central character in both was a male who lives with a native woman, and both were full of similar incidents and episodes.

As advised previously, consult a competent lawyer if you think you have a copyright infringement on your hands.

OTHER PROTECTION FROM COPYING

Chapter 3, "Copying," listed several subjects that could not be protected under the copyright law, some of which are especially important to writers. Titles cannot be copyrighted but sometimes have protection through the theory of unfair competition,* fraud, or misappropriation. Hemingway prevented the use of one of his titles, *The Fifth Column,* from utilization as the title for a motion picture called *The Fifth Column Squad* using those legal theories. Other titles that have been protected are:

UNFAIR COMPETITION

TITLES

- *Sex and the Single Girl* as against *Sex and the Single Man*
- *Sesame Street*, against use on commercial goods unless a disclaimer indicated that the product was not connected with the television show
- the name *Frank Merribell,* which appeared in the title of a thousand stories
- *The Story of O* as against the *Journey of O*

But *Alice in Wonderland,* (the title) of an expensive Walt Disney motion picture was not protected from another movie with the same name, for the original work by Lewis Carroll was in the public domain. Also, the title *Test Pilot* was not given protection because it was purely descriptive and had not acquired a secondary meaning. In order for unfair competition to protect titles, the title must have acquired a secondary meaning, that is, use of the title for a sufficient length of time so the title becomes connected to the work in the public's mind.

"THERE IS NO PART OF THE LAW WHICH IS MORE PLASTIC THAN UNFAIR COMPETITION."
—JUDGE LEARNED HAND

Certain characters have been protected, but not under copyright laws. In one case a character was protected against misappropriation. Unfair competition protected the exclusive right of the cartoonists who created Mutt and Jeff to use the characters. Dashiell Hammett was ultimately successful in arguing that his rights to the character Sam Spade of the famous *The Maltese Falcon* were not lost with the sale of a right to publish a copyrighted story. Since the sale did not specifically include the character Sam Spade, which was his property, the character could be reused by him.

CHARACTERS

Since the new Copyright Act only covers original works fixed in a tangible medium, statutory copyright protection is not available for "unfixed" works such as an extemporaneous speech, broadcast, or performance. However, these works are probably protected under some of the legal theories discussed above.

CONTRACTS

INTRODUCTION

Writers make many contracts in the course of their business—with agents, magazines, book companies, newspapers, motion-picture studios, book clubs, record companies, and so on. In order to explore many of the basic issues found in most writers' contracts, this section will discuss two of the most common agreements made by writers—book publishing and literary agency contracts. Still, special issues arise from the peculiarities of each industry. Before dealing

* See discussion of unfair competition in Chapter 3, "Copying."

with a record company, for instance, it would be wise to consult a competent professional for advice and assistance as well as to read any literature on the subject.

PUBLISHING CONTRACTS

After fifteen rejection slips, who is going to quibble over the terms of an interested publisher's contract offer? After reading this section, perhaps *you* will. Since the contract basically determines the final form of your book, as well as how much you will receive for it, it does not make sense to close your eyes, cross your fingers, and sign.

Even before you read the proposed agreement, consider the company with whom you are contemplating a contract. The discussion that follows is based upon a typical, large, commercial publisher's contract. You may decide that the advantages of smaller regional presses, university presses, alternative presses, et cetera may better suit your needs and temperament. Richard Balkin has a chapter on alternatives to publishing with the large houses in his book *A Writer's Guide to Book Publishing* (Hawthorn Books, New York, 1978). If you do decide to choose a small press, check your prospective publisher very carefully to make sure that the press can and will handle your work the way you desire. Beware of deals where you have to pay a substantial sum of money to get your work published. Many times these arrangements result in losses to the writer.

TYPES OF PUBLISHERS

Next, sit down, open your eyes, and read the proposed contract from top to bottom. Mark any terms that you don't understand. Read the unclear sections over one by one. Do anything to dispel the confusion—read sections aloud, type them up, sing them in the shower. Go back and read the entire contract again until the basic terms are pretty clear. Most writers are good readers and most contracts are less than ten pages. Go to the library and get a book on publishing contracts. Hawthorn Books publishes Tad Crawford's book, *The Writer's Legal Guide,* which is informative. The Authors Guild, located in New York City, not only supplies their members with a model publishing contract and commentary but also takes important positions on various issues involving authors' rights and distributes an informative bulletin. Membership in the Authors Guild is only available to authors of published works or works in process.

OTHER RESOURCES

Next, put the contract down and list *all* the plans for your work, real and imaginary—magazine serialization, special format, emphasis on West Coast distribution, photographs, paperback version, whatever. Note any terms in the contract that might affect these plans and how you would wish to resolve any conflict.

THE NEGOTIATING PROCESS

If your agent or lawyer is negotiating your contract, have a meeting with him or her and discuss the contract, point by point, clarifying any puzzling terms. At each objectionable term, tell your representative *what* your objection is, *why* you object to the clause, and what your *alternative* term would be. Give your representative a memorandum clearly stating your thoughts. Your representative is not clairvoyant and cannot possibly know all the quirks of your particular work and your big plans for it. On the other hand, a good agent or attorney should know important items like the current percentage rates for royalties, the range for average advances, and when a publisher just won't budge. But in the final analysis, it is *your* work that is being bought, and who but you knows more of its needs and wants.

After all that work, you probably will receive a contract to sign that contains few of the agreed changes. Do not despair. Multinational conglomerates are not as efficient as one-man operations. (Testimony on the merger trend in book publishing was taken by the U.S. Senate's Subcommittee on Antitrust and Monopoly in May 1978.) Neatly indicate your changes right on the contract after you have photocopied a clean copy for posterity. Send this revision to your publisher, agent, or lawyer. This effort should bring a final contract for your signature that you can live with. In our contract negotiations, we exchanged three proposed drafts before a final contract was signed.

If you don't like the final contract, don't sign it simply because your editor says that this or that can be taken care of later. Your editor may not be there in six months, and you will be stuck with the terms of the contract.

In this section we will cover many of the issues that arise in negotiating a publishing contract. We will use standard terms from a contract of a major publisher as sample clauses throughout this section. Although publishing contracts greatly differ in form, the basic

AGENT

The Author hereby authorizes as agent:

of:

(1) to collect and receive all sums payable to the Author under this Agreement, the receipt of such sums by the agent being a full and valid discharge of the Publisher's obligation for the payment made, and (2) to act on behalf of the Author in all matters in any way arising out of this Agreement.

figure 7-1

contractual issues are pretty much the same whatever publisher you are dealing with. Be realistic about the terms you want changed. If you are negotiating about publication of an abstract scientific work, it will not be worthwhile to worry about the movie rights.

AGENTS

You had better trust your agent, because it is his or her address that usually will appear in the recital section of the contract. It is through your agent that you will receive important notifications from your publisher as well as advance and royalty payments. If you have an agent, your contract probably will contain an agency clause which authorizes the publisher to make all your payments to your agent. (See figure 7-1.)

RIGHTS CONVEYED

PRIMARY RIGHTS

SUBSIDIARY RIGHTS

The grant-of-rights clause, figure 7-2, spells out what rights you grant your publisher and concerns rights to publish and distribute, translate, and otherwise use your work in commercial ventures. These rights are usually divided into two areas—primary rights (to publish and sell the work in the United States, the Philippines, and Canada) and subsidiary rights (all other rights including paperback, book club, movie, record, commercial, foreign language version, issuance in the British Commonwealth, serialization, abridgement, etc.). Usually, if you have an agent, the publishing rights in the British Commonwealth and the first serialization (prepublication in a magazine) rights are retained by the author and marketed separately by the agent. Authors' advocate groups suggest that you do *not* grant performing rights to your publisher. Further, the sale of any subsidiary rights should require your consent. Request that the right to receive copies of any of these subsidiary sales agreements be included in your contract. Some contracts provide for a cut-off date before which the publisher has to exercise these subsidiary rights or they revert to the author. The Authors Guild suggests a maximum of twenty-four months during which time the publisher must exercise subsidiary rights. If possible, limit the grant-of-rights clause only to those expressly discussed in the contract and retain any other rights not granted to the publisher by the contract.

RESERVATION OF ALL RIGHTS NOT SPECIFICALLY TRANSFERRED

WARRANTY AND INDEMNITY CLAUSE

The author's warranty is an author's nightmare. First of all, you swear to the publisher that in no way is your work unlawful; it is neither libelous nor obscene; nor does it infringe on another's copyright; nor does it violate any other statutory or proprietary right. Yikes! Then, if that is not enough, you agree to pay any costs that your publisher may incur from any claims covered by the warranty term. Never mind that your publisher has a seventy-story office building and that you live in a teepee. The publisher wants a guarantee that all material in your book is lawful. If it's not, the entire financial burden is placed squarely on your shoulders. Furthermore, many publishing contracts allow the publisher to withhold all royalties in the event of a claim or lawsuit in this area. For obvious reasons, this particular term is the target of a major campaign of the

RIGHTS CONVEYED TO PUBLISHER AND PAYMENTS TO AUTHOR

a. Rights and Royalties. The Author grants and assigns exclusively to the Publisher the following rights, for which the Publisher shall pay to the Author the royalties indicated:

(1) *Sale by Publisher of the Work in the United States, Philippines, and Canada.* The right to reproduce and distribute the Work in the English language, and all revisions and future editions of it, in the United States of America and its territories and dependencies, the Philippines, and Canada.

(2) *Sale of the Work by the Publisher in the exclusive territory.* The right to reproduce and distribute copies of the Work in the English language, and all revisions and future editions of it, for use in the United Kingdom, the Republic of Ireland, the Republic of South Africa, Australia, and/or New Zealand (all such countries constituting the exclusive territory) through the Publisher's subsidiaries.

Royalty. On all copies sold, one-half the applicable royalty payable on sales of the Work in the United States.

(3) *Sale of the Work by the Publisher in the open market.* The right to reproduce and distribute copies of the Work in all parts of the world other than the United States of America, its territories and dependencies, the exclusive territory, Canada, and the Philippines.

Royalty. On all copies sold, one-half the applicable royalty payable on sales of the Work in the United States.

(4) *License to others to sell the Work in the exclusive territory.* The right to license others to reproduce and distribute the Work in book form either through separate manufacture and publication abroad or through exportation of sheets or bound books of the Publisher's edition.

Royalty. On all copies sold by such licensee: if sold from an edition separately manufactured and published abroad, 75 percent of the Publisher's receipts; if sold from exported Publisher's sheets or bound books, 10 percent of the Publisher's receipts.

(5) *Translations.* The right to translate, reproduce, and distribute and to license others to translate, reproduce, and distribute the Work in all foreign languages.

Royalty. On all copies sold: if sold by the Publisher or its subsidiaries, 5 percent of the translation's list price; if under license to others, 75 percent of the Publisher's receipts.

(6) *Reprint editions.* The right to license a reprint publisher to reprint and distribute the Work in a paperback edition and/or a hardbound edition.

Royalty. 50 percent of the Publisher's receipts.

(7) *License to book clubs.* The right to license recognized book clubs to reproduce and distribute the Work, either in whole or as a condensation.

Royalty. If from an edition manufactured by the book club through lease of the Publisher's reproductive materials, 50 percent of the Publisher's receipts, less one-half the cost of any additional reproductive materials ordered by the book club and furnished by the Publisher; if from a condensation of the Work manufactured by the book club, 50 percent of the Publisher's receipts; if from an edition supplied by the Publisher, one-half the royalty paid by the book club to the Publisher.

(8) *First serialization.* The right to license others to publish first serializations of the Work (which shall comprise all serializations published before publication of the Work).

Royalty. 90 percent of the Publisher's receipts.

(9) *Second serialization.* The right to license others to publish digests, abridgments, selections, and second serializations of the Work (which shall comprise all serializations published after publication of the Work).

Royalty. 50 percent of the Publisher's receipts.

(10) *Dramatization.* The right to license others to exercise dramatic, motion picture, television, and radio rights to the Work.

Royalty. 90 percent of the Publisher's receipts.

(11) *Audiovisual rights.* The right to exercise and to license others to exercise any or all of the other mechanical, visual, audiovisual, sound-reproducing, and recording rights to the Work.

Royalty. If such rights are exercised by the Publisher, 10 percent of the Publisher's net receipts; if such rights are licensed, 50 percent of the Publisher's receipts.

(12) *Commercial rights.* The right to exercise and to license others to exercise all commercial rights to the Work which shall mean the exploitation of the Work itself, all material contained in it, and all rights in connection with merchandise and/or use of the Author's name in connection with the merchandise.

Royalty. If such rights are exercised by the Publisher, 10 percent of the Publisher's net receipts; if such rights are licensed, 50 percent of the Publisher's receipts.

figure 7-2

Authors Guild, which feels that the indemnity clause is so onerous that it effectively denies the author important free speech rights.

There are several ways to lighten the impact of the author's warranty and indemnity clause. First, make sure that you do not agree to pay the publisher's costs arising from controversies caused by the publisher's changes or inserts. Further, publishers may agree to author indemnification only in the situation where a claim against the publisher is reduced to judgment. Otherwise the indemnity clause

AUTHOR'S WARRANTY

a. The Author represents and warrants to the Publisher that the Author has full power and authority to enter into this Agreement and to grant the rights granted in this Agreement; that the Work is original except for material in the public domain and those excerpts from other works as may be included with the written permission of the copyright owners; that the Work does not contain any libelous or obscene material or injurious formulas, recipes, or instructions; that it does not infringe any trade name, trademark, or copyright; and that it does not invade or violate any right of privacy, personal or proprietary right, or other common law or statutory right.

b. The Author agrees to indemnify the Publisher and its licensees and assignees under this Agreement and hold them harmless from any and all losses, damages, liabilities, costs, charges, and expenses, including reasonable attorneys' fees, arising out of any breach of any of the Author's representations and warranties contained in this Agreement or third-party claims relating to the matters covered by the representations and warranties in this Section 3 which are finally sustained in a court of original jurisdiction. If any action or proceeding is brought against the Publisher with respect to the matters covered by the representations and warranties in this Section 3, the Publisher shall have the right, in its sole discretion, to select counsel to defend against this action or proceeding. In addition to other remedies available to the Publisher, the Publisher may charge the amount of these losses, damages, liabilities, costs, charges, and expenses against any sums accruing to the Author under this Agreement or any other agreement currently existing between Author and Publisher.

c. If there is an infringement of any rights granted to the Publisher or rights which the Publisher is authorized to license or in which the Publisher is to share in the proceeds, the Publisher shall have the right, in its sole discretion, to select counsel to bring such action or proceeding, and the Author and the Publisher shall have the right to participate jointly in the action. If both participate, they shall share equally the expenses of and any sums recovered in the action, except that if the Author retains separate legal counsel, the Author shall be solely responsible for the legal expenses of the Author's counsel. If either party declines to participate in the action, the other may proceed, and the party maintaining the action shall bear all expenses and shall retain all sums recovered.
The provisions of this Section 3 shall survive any termination of this Agreement.

figure 7-3

requires the author to pay the publisher's costs no matter how frivolous the claim.

Since it is your money that will pay any settlement or judgment and other costs, include a term granting you the right to opt to participate in any proceedings through a lawyer of your choice. Also try to exclude the publisher's lawyers' fees from the author's indemnity coverage if you use your own attorney. You also might try to get your publisher to split any of these costs with you. Since, as indicated above, the indemnity clause gives the publisher the right to withhold royalties in the event of a controversy in this area, try to get this right deleted entirely from your contract or at least limited to only a percentage of your royalties.

NONCOMPETITION CLAUSE

Most publishing contracts include a noncompetition clause for the author (the publisher could publish and distribute a competing

COMPETING WORKS

While this Agreement is in effect, the Author shall not, without the prior written consent of the Publisher, write, edit, print, or publish, or cause to be written, edited, printed, or published, any other edition of the Work, whether revised, supplemented, corrected, enlarged, abridged, or otherwise, or any other work of a nature which might interfere with or injure the sales of the Work or any grant of rights or licenses permitted under this Agreement by the Publisher, or permit the use of the Author's name or likeness in connection with any such work.

figure 7-4

work). Attempt to have this clause deleted from the final contract, or limit its application by subject matter or time period as much as possible.

Many of the publishers' contract forms have not been revised since the enactment of the Copyright Revision Act of 1976, so many

COPYRIGHT

of these copyright terms are outdated. The copyright should be in the author's name, and the publisher should agree to properly register the copyright and to place the author's copyright notice on all versions of the author's work. For more information on copyright, see the section in this chapter on copyright as well as Chapter 3, "Copying."

Figure 7-5 refers to changes made by the author on galley or page proofs sent by the publisher for correction that are not correction of errors made by the printer. In the clause the author agrees

AUTHOR'S ALTERATIONS

to pay the cost of any changes, other than the correction of printer's errors, that exceed a certain percentage of the printer's initial bill. The sample contract provides for any costs over 15 percent of the initial bill; many contracts provide for any costs over 10 percent.

> If requested by the Publisher, the Author shall correct proof of the Work and return it promptly to the Publisher. If the Author makes or causes to be made any alterations in the type, illustrations, or film which are not typographical, drafting, or Publisher's errors and which exceed 15 percent of the original cost of composition and artwork independent of the cost of these Author's alterations, the cost of the excess alterations shall be charged against any sums accruing to the Author under this Agreement.

figure 7-5

PUBLICATION OF THE WORK

This clause spells out the general responsibility of the publisher to produce your work. If you want to make sure that the publisher will produce a paperback version of the work, for example, write in this requirement or other publisher production requirements here. Include deadlines as part of the added term.

> **PUBLICATION OF THE WORK**
>
> After giving written notice to the Author that it has accepted the Work for publication, the Publisher shall within 12 months of written acceptance of the manuscript publish the Work at its own expense and in such style and manner and with such trademarks, service marks, and imprints of Publisher, and sell the Work at such prices, as it shall deem suitable. The Publisher shall publish the Work with a copyright notice and register the Work in accordance with the United States copyright laws in the name of the Publisher or Author as the Author may elect.

figure 7-6

THE MANUSCRIPT

This term sets the all important delivery date, the grace period, and the penalties for late or unsatisfactory delivery of the work. The definition of a "satisfactory" or "acceptable" manuscript has posed problems to authors in the past. Apparently, publishers have found manuscripts unsatisfactory for reasons far afield of the manuscript itself—change in the political climate, simple marketing considerations, et cetera. A very informative article about an author who successfully represented himself after his publisher had both rejected his manuscript and demanded the return of his advance, was written by A. E. Hotchner and appeared in the April 1978 issue of *More* magazine. It is entitled "A Fool for a Client" and is well worth reading.

In an attempt to avoid wrongful rejection of your manuscript, request that the word *reasonably* be inserted before the word *satisfactory* to make the contract clear that the publisher cannot reject your manuscript on the basis of pure whim. Also change your contract to provide that the advance is only refundable if the author

MANUSCRIPT PREPARATION AND DELIVERY

a. The Author shall prepare and deliver to the Publisher on or before , 19 , two complete, clean copies of a manuscript for the Work in double-spaced typewritten form on $8\frac{1}{2}$- by 11-inch sheets (approximately 22 by 28 cm) or as may otherwise be specified by the Publisher. The manuscript for the Work must be acceptable to the Publisher in both form and content for publication. It shall be between and words in length and shall include such materials as the Publisher may reasonably specify for the Work, including but not limited to copy for the title page, table of contents, index, tables, and bibliographies, and copy for drawings, illustrations, and charts. The Author shall supply these in finished form to the Publisher within a reasonable time after the delivery of the completed manuscript; if the Author shall fail to do so, the Publisher may supply them and charge the expense to the Author.

b. The Author shall obtain, without expense to the Publisher, written permission to include in the Work any copyrighted material which is not in the public domain as well as any other material for which permission is necessary in connection with the Author's warranty in Section 3 of this Agreement. These permissions must be consistent with the rights granted to the Publisher in this Agreement so that they may cover all the uses to which the material may eventually be put. The Author shall deliver to the Publisher a copy of all these permissions with the complete manuscript.

c. If the Work or any subdivision of it contains a significant portion of material taken from documents prepared and published by the United States government and therefore not subject to copyright, the Author shall notify the Publisher in writing of the existence and location of all such material in the Work.

d. If the Author fails to deliver the complete manuscript within 90 days after the delivery date specified in this Agreement, or if the Author fails or refuses to perform any correction or revision of the manuscript within the time or as otherwise specified by the Publisher, the Publisher shall have the right in its discretion: (1) to give the Author written notice of its intention to terminate this Agreement, in which event the Author shall promptly reimburse the Publisher for all sums advanced to the Author against royalties under this Agreement, and upon such reimbursement this Agreement shall terminate; or (2) to make such other arrangements in connection with this Agreement as the Publisher deems advisable to complete, correct, or revise the manuscript, in which event the reasonable cost of such arrangements may be charged against any sums accruing to the Author under this Agreement.

figure 7-7

successfully peddles the manuscript to another publisher. Secondly, when negotiating this clause, tie down specifics concerning the form in which any artwork, photographs, and other exhibits must be delivered.

ADVANCES, ROYALTIES, AND OTHER PROCEEDS OF THE AUTHOR

A good agent or an experienced writer can tell you the going rates for advances and royalties in your area of concern. Also the Authors Guild makes results of its surveys on royalty and advance rates available to its members. An advance should be as high as possible since it could be the entire return for your work. An advance should be nonrefundable unless (as discussed in the paragraph above on manuscript) after being rejected as unsatisfactory by your first publisher, your manuscript is purchased by another publisher. Advances are many times split into at least two payments—the first made upon the

> *Royalty.* On all copies sold, a royalty of:
>
> of the Publisher's domestic list price, except:
>
> (i) On copies sold in Canada, one-half the applicable royalty payable on sales in the United States.
> (ii) On copies sold by mail direct to consumers by the Publisher, 5 percent of the Publisher's domestic list price.
> (iii) On copies sold to wholesale or retail distributors or booksellers, or to such groups as schools, reading circles, and newsdealers, when Publisher's net receipts are less than 50 percent of the Publisher's domestic list price, 1 percent less than the royalty percentage which would otherwise be applicable.
> (iv) On copies sold after two years from the date of first publication from a reprinting of 2000 copies or less where the regular sales in the six-month period preceding such reprinting did not exceed 500 copies, one-half the royalty percentage which would otherwise be applicable.
> (v) On copies sold through the Publisher's own book clubs, 5 percent of the club's member price.
> (vi) On paperback copies reproduced and sold by the Publisher, 5 percent of the Publisher's domestic list price.
> (vii) On copies of hardbound reprints of the Work which shall sell for no more than two-thirds of the Publisher's domestic list price of the original hardbound edition, 5 percent of the Publisher's domestic list price.
> (viii) On copies sold in bulk for premium or promotional use, 10 percent of the Publisher's net receipts.

figure 7-8

signing of the contract and the second upon the delivery of the satisfactory work or upon publication. Since advances are made against royalties, your publisher will take the amount of your advance out of the royalties.

After you discover the standard royalty for works like yours and hopefully reach a satisfactory rate and escalator clause, make sure that your contract provides for royalties based upon the *retail* sale (list) price. (Royalty rates based upon the wholesale price should be considerably higher.) Also read the list of exceptions to the standard royalty rates in your contract, which usually includes:

EXCEPTIONS

- mail-order sales
- large orders discounted more than 48 percent
- export sales
- sale of overstock
- copies of a small reprinting (to keep the book in circulation)

The royalty rate on the exceptions listed above should not be less than 50 percent of the regular rate.

RETURN FOR SALE OF SUBSIDIARY RIGHTS

The author's portion of the publisher's sale of subsidiary rights is sometimes glossed over in the excitement of the contract negotiations, usually to the author's disadvantage. Here again discover what authors are getting on the sale of each of the subsidiary rights that you contemplate selling to the publisher. Check to see that your percentage of the proceeds of the sale is not reduced by any of the publisher's sale costs such as an agent's fee.

STATEMENTS AND PAYMENTS

Many authors feel that waiting for six months for royalties is too long a time. Even more unfair, say authors' advocate groups, is the clause which allows the publisher to hang on to any proceeds from the sale of a subsidiary license for a full two months before the author sees a penny of it. The publisher W. W. Norton has broken rank with fellow publishers and issues the author's share of any book-club advance within two weeks of receipt of the advance. If Norton can . . . Figure 7-9 sets forth a standard settlement clause.

ROYALTIES WITHHELD FOR BOOK RETURNS

Another problem in this area is the percentage of royalties that is withheld by the publisher for returned books. Many publishers will automatically withhold up to 25 percent of the royalties for returns. For some books, where the return rate is small, the figure is greatly out of line.

Another area of dispute in this section of the contract is the form of the royalty statement. Many times statements will not contain such vital information as number of copies sold or a description of what subsidiary rights were sold to whom and for how much. Authors should check these statements as they have been known to be incorrect, especially with the advent of the computer. Also request a separate account for each publication to simplify the deciphering process. If your royalty statement still looks like Greek, ask your agent to assist in deciphering it.

Settlement. Within 90 days after June 30 and December 31 each year, the Publisher shall render a statement of the number of copies of the Work sold and the amount payable to the Author under this Agreement semiannually through June 30 and December 31 and make settlement for the amount due, except as follows: (i) For the first two semiannual accounting periods following the publication of the Work, the Publisher may withhold from payment to the Author a reasonable reserve for returned copies not to exceed 15 percent of the amount payable to the Author under this Section 1 as reflected on the statement. The balance of the reserve at the close of the second accounting period shall be paid to the Author with the payments for the following accounting period. (ii) Any sums due and owing from the Author to the Publisher, whether or not arising out of this Agreement, may be deducted from any sum due or to become due from the Publisher to the Author under this Agreement. For the purposes of this paragraph, a nonrecoverable unearned advance made to the Author under another agreement shall not be considered a sum due and owing unless the Author is in default under the other agreement.

figure 7-9

OPTION

You should have the option clause granting your publisher first refusal on your next book deleted from the contract. Many publishers today are agreeable to this. If your publisher will not delete the option term, then attempt to have it limited as to the period of time within which the publisher must decide to accept or reject your work. Thirty to sixty days has been suggested as a reasonable time, depending on the material. Also make sure that your option clause allows you to submit an outline to the publisher and does not require that you submit an entire manuscript in order to fulfill your responsibilities under the option clause.

DISCONTINUANCE OF PUBLICATION AND REVERSION

This clause in figure 7-10 allows the publisher to discontinue publication of the work at any time. The author has the right to be notified in such event and many times to purchase any plates, sheets, or bound stock of the book.

The reversion right returns all rights to the author in the event the work is out of print. Many times an author and a publisher will disagree over when a book is out of print, so define *out of print* as being when copies of a hard- or soft-cover version of the work are not available through normal trade channels. Also make sure that your reversion clause governs the return of *all* rights granted by the contract, not just publication rights.

AUTHOR'S CONTROL

Unfortunately, authors normally do not have control either over the form and content of the final product or over the style, format, cover, retail price, number of copies in the first printing, and marketing procedures. We were able to negotiate final approval over the manuscript because of the legal nature of our material. This is true with most technical books. We were also able to include a clause which requires our publisher to consult with us in advance concerning the format, graphics, and dust jacket. Decide which items in this area are critical to the proper presentation of your work and try to include the requirements that any textual changes be made by mutual consent and that you at least be consulted on format, style, graphics, and dust jacket.

Among other terms that you might consider including is one which bans the insertion of all advertisements in any version of your work, including those licensed by your publisher unless you consent to such insertion. Also request the return of all original materials, the right both to receive six to twelve free copies and to purchase an unlimited number of copies at least at a 40 percent discount.

CONTRACTS WITH LITERARY AGENTS

Many times contracting with your agent is quite a casual affair—a handshake and a few drinks. Although relations between authors and agents are usually quite pleasant and mutually beneficial, settle some basic issues at the outset so that you do not find yourself in a

DISCONTINUANCE OF PUBLICATION

a. When in the judgment of the Publisher the demand for the Work is no longer sufficient to warrant its continued publication, the Publisher shall have the right to discontinue the publication and declare the Work out of print, in which event the Author shall be so advised in writing.

b. If the Work is not for sale in at least one edition (including any revised edition or reprint edition) published by the Publisher or under license from the Publisher and, within eight months after written demand by the Author, the Publisher or its licensee fails to offer it again for sale, then this Agreement shall terminate and all rights granted to the Publisher in it shall revert to the Author (except for material prepared by or obtained at the expense of the Publisher which shall remain the property of the Publisher).

c. The termination of this Agreement under this Section 7 or otherwise shall be subject to (1) any license, contract, or option granted to third parties by the Publisher before the termination and the Publisher's right to its share of the proceeds from these agreements after the termination and (2) the Publisher's continuing right to sell all remaining bound copies and sheets of the Work and all derivative works which are on hand at the time of termination.

figure 7-10

later disagreement. Reduce your agreement to writing. A simple statement of the understanding reached by you and your agent signed by both parties is a perfectly good agreement.

SCOPE Most agents will want an exclusive right to market your work.* They are not going to expend the time and energy required to sell a manuscript only to discover that they have been scooped by another agent. An agent can be empowered to peddle all your works—plays, poems, and essays—or be limited to selling one line of work. Also an agent could be limited to selling all rights to a work or just one of the rights—for instance, performing rights.

POWER Since an agent can act on behalf of the principal (in this case, you the author), technically your agent could sign a binding publishing contract for you. Most agents, however, only negotiate the proposed draft to present to the author for signature. Your agency contract should make clear the extent of the agent's power in this area.

COMMISSIONS AND EXPENSES A literary agency agreement usually empowers the agent to collect all funds due the author, to deduct any commissions and expenses, and to remit the balance to the author. Because of the nature of the agency agreement, payment of the agent by the publisher satisfies any obligation that the publisher has to the author. So choose your agent wisely. Also clarify the manner in which your agent's expenses—photocopying, phone calls, and so forth—will be paid. Usually the agent will deduct these from the payments received on your behalf before remitting the balance to you.

CANCELLATION Any literary agency agreement should be easily terminated because of the nature of the beast. An unhappy agent will have a hard time peddling a work just as authors have a hard time mailing their freshly concocted masterpiece to an unappreciative agent. Most agency agreements provide for only thirty days notice to the other person in order to cancel. Certain matters cannot be terminated on such short notice, like the payment of the agent's commission or the conclusion of an ongoing negotiation for sale of work. Because of this, most agents' contracts provide that any sale of literary work within sixty days of cancellation of the contract should be treated as having occurred during the period of the contract.

Of course, your agent will have the right to receive commissions on the works he or she has sold after termination of the contract. Make sure, however, that the contract only grants your agent an interest in the commission earned and not an interest in the entire amount due the author from the publisher.

BACK TO TAXES

This special section on taxes for writers will not cover the basics of federal income and other taxes. Please read Chapter 5, "Federal In-

* Under certain agency agreements the author is still free to sell work without having to pay a commission to the agent.

come Tax," and Chapter 6, "Other Taxes," for the basic tax background. This section will only discuss the special tax problems of writers.

RECORD-KEEPING

METHOD OF ACCOUNTING

Most writers use the calendar year as their tax year, and most use the cash-basis method of accounting. Record-keeping for writers will vary depending on whether few or many works are sold each year.

If you sell numerous small works and/or do indexing, editing, et cetera, you probably will send bills for your work. Put the name of the job, the amount charged, and your name and address on the bill and address it to the publisher.

Some publishers may ask for your Social Security number, because the law requires one who pays another for services (payor) to fill out a Statement for Recipients of Miscellaneous Income, IRS Form 1099, when the recipient has done more than $600 worth of work during the year for the payor. Some payors do this regardless of the amount paid. You do not file Form 1099 with your return. Just remember that the IRS has a copy of it, and report this income.

A simple way of recording income and expenses is shown below:

INCOME

DATE BILLED/ OBLIGATED	TO WHOM/ FOR WHAT	AMOUNT	DATE RECEIVED
6-23-80	McGraw-Hill/Indexing "101 . . ."	$105	7-31-80
6-30-80	Smother Planet News, article on chicken feed	$ 50	7-28-80
	TOTAL FOR MONTH	$155	
	TOTAL YEAR TO DATE	$2,995	

EXPENSES July 1980

ITEM	THIS MONTH	BASIS	YEAR TO DATE
Rent	$50	(1 room of 5--$250)	$350
Electricity	8	($40 1/5)	70
Telephone	15	(1/2 of total)	150
Office Supplies	22	PBSW	80
Promotion	32	(dinner 7/1/78) for agent B.B.	150
Capital Expenses (Depreciation)	--	Office furniture	200
		Equipment	150

figure 7-11 Sample writer ledger

RECORD KEEPING

If you are a novelist, your record-keeping needs would differ from a contributor to periodicals. A job work card could be very helpful to the writer who does a lot of small pieces by giving the writer a bird's-eye view of his or her work, by totaling the amount of time required and respective amounts of earnings from specific assignments, and by providing information for copyright registration. Reproduced below is a sample job work card that could be adapted to your individual needs:

WORK CARD

Subject: ______________________ Word length: ________
Title: ____
Labor Hours (weeks, days, hours): ___________________
Queries ____
____
Date Begun _____ Date completed _____ Date Published ____
Copyright Reg. No. ________ Copyright Reg.: _________
Sold to: ____
Price: ______________ Payments Due/Terms ____________
Other Sales Information. __________________________
Rights Reserved: _________________________________

figure 7-12 Sample work card

If you are a free-lancer, you might want to keep a running tally of your works in progress. A sample format for a tally sheet is reproduced for you.

WORKS IN PROGRESS

IDEAS TO QUERY	OUT	IN RESEARCH	IN WRITING	MS OUT	ACCEPTED	PMT. DUE
Home Remedies of Indians	1-10-80 McCalls	2-80	3-80	6-80	11-80	1-5-81
Fairy Clothing	Sesame St. Magazine					
Homemade Puppets	Sesame St. Magazine	3-80	5-80			

figure 7-13 Writer's tally sheet

Income levels for most writers vary greatly from year to year. Consequently, the methods of spreading income are of great importance here so that the lowest tax can be paid. See the discussion in Chapter 5, "Federal Income Tax," on cutting your taxes, and remember, if you are on the cash basis, to give special consideration to year-end transactions to manipulate year-end income levels, in order to show a two-out-of-five-year profit or to level out a particularly profitable year. Remember that even under the cash method of accounting, money received by your agent is taxable to you unless there are restrictions on how or when your agent makes payment. If you have hit the jackpot with a best seller, you should try to spread this income over the lean years through income averaging or contracting for payments of royalties over a longer period of time. If you find yourself in this enviable situation, it would be worth your while to consult a tax attorney or accountant for some tax-planning assistance.

SPREADING INCOME

BUSINESS DEDUCTIONS

Some business-expense deductions that writers should not forget are:

BUSINESS DEDUCTIONS

- printing—letterheads, cards, etc.
- stationery
- postage—express, telegrams, messenger service
- commissions
- clipping-service charges
- courses in writing instruction
- typewriter repair and depreciation
- membership fees in writers' associations
- payments for publication
- insurance on manuscripts
- copyright registration and renewal fees or searches
- photocopying
- promotion

RESEARCH, TRAVEL, AND SIMILAR EXPENSES

There is not a clear answer as to whether research, travel, and similar expenses of professional authors can be deducted in the year incurred or whether those expenses must be capitalized. The current deduction of such expenses was allowed in a district court case, but the IRS would not follow that rule where publishers tried to deduct similar publication costs as current expenses. The Authors Guild has taken the position that *authors* engaged in the business of writing are entitled to currently deduct travel, research, and similar expenses. They argue that although the taxpayer is required to capitalize the costs of producing books, records, and motion pictures and to deduct the costs over the life stream of income generated by the work, the legislative report on the Tax Reform Act implies that this capitalization requirement applies only where the work is acquired as a result of the taxpayer's *investment*. For this reason the

Authors Guild takes the position that capitalization of travel and related expenses covers publisher and producer costs but not the author's expenses, since the author's income is earned by personal effort and not through investment of money.

COPYRIGHTS HELD BY CREATOR IS NOT A CAPITAL ASSET

A copyright held by the creator or the creator's heir or donee is not treated as a capital asset by the tax law. Thus the proceeds of a sale or exchange of a copyright by the author (donee or heir) is ordinary income to them. On the other hand, income from the sale or licensing of a copyright by persons not authors of a work is entitled to capital gains treatment if the copyright has been held the minimum required period of time.

FORMS TO USE IN REPORTING INCOME

Generally, royalty payments are entered on Schedule E, Supplemental Income, but this form is meant as a catchall for those persons whose major income is reported on other forms—for example, a circus clown who writes a book reports his or her book income (including advances) on Schedule E. A full-time writer would enter both royalty and flat-fee income on Schedule C.

HOBBY LOSS CHALLENGE

HOBBY LOSS CHALLENGE

Writers may face a hobby loss challenge. You should keep records showing the profit motive in your writing including query letters, replies, rejection slips, sales, costs, manuscript mailing dates, proof of other submissions, contracts, deadline letters, and so forth. Refer to Chapter 5, "Federal Income Tax," for a discussion of the hobby loss challenges. One writer who was a full-time pilot had gross receipts from his writing of $2,500 in the fifties but nothing after that time. Although he wrote and submitted at least fourteen short stories and had two novels in process between 1958 and 1965, his deduction for expenses in 1964 and 1965 were disallowed because the court did not think he wrote for financial gain. Try to arrange sales so you show income from your writing in at least two years out of every five. This showing will beat most hobby loss challenges.

SOCIAL SECURITY

SOCIAL SECURITY

When employees retire, they cannot earn more than $3,000 a year or $250 in a single month without reduction of their Social Security benefits. However, self-employed writers are allowed to receive Social Security benefits at the age of retirement provided they do not perform "substantial services." Income in excess of $250 a month may not be sufficient to show substantial services. So if you retire as an employee and turn to writing, you should change your status from employee to self-employed with Social Security so any income will be considered under the more lenient substantial-services test. Usually less than forty-five hours a month work (research, writing, editing) is not considered substantial services, but if your writing

SUBSTANTIAL-SERVICES TEST

ROYALTIES FROM PRERETIREMENT SALES NOT COUNTED

brings in a lot of money with a few hours of effort, then you may have your check reduced. An important plus for writers is that royalties from any preretirement sales do not count toward the substantial-services test.

OTHER TAXES

Some states or cities may have other taxes* such as an occupation license, which may affect a writer. An occupation license may require payment of a tax on your gross receipts but there may be certain nontaxable transactions such as out-of-state sales, which are excepted. Some states collect personal-property or intangible taxes on a writer's royalties.

MISCELLANEOUS

FREEDOM OF INFORMATION ACT AND SUNSHINE LAWS

STATE LAWS

Facts are a basic stock-in-trade for many writers. The federal and state Freedom of Information Acts and Sunshine Acts are relatively new tools with which writers can pry information out of federal and some state governments. Not all states have enacted laws concerning the public's access to information. Check with your local chapter of the American Civil Liberties Union to see if your state has a Freedom of Information Act and a Sunshine Act.

The federal Freedom of Information Act (FOIA) was initially passed in 1966. The 1975 amendments closed some of the loopholes through which various federal agencies had previously denied citizens' requests for information.

The FOIA rules apply only to information held by administrative agencies of the federal government. It does not cover documents belonging to the legislative or judicial branches of government.* Also, the act exempts nine separate categories of documents to which agencies can deny public access:

DOCUMENTS NOT AVAILABLE UNDER FOIA

- classified documents concerning national defense and foreign policy
- internal personnel rules and practices
- information exempt from disclosure under other laws
- confidential business information
- internal communications
- protection of individual privacy
- investigatory files
- information concerning federal financial institutions
- information concerning wells

Your local congressman or senator's office may be helpful in determining whether your request for information falls within one of the nine categories above.

* See discussion in the *Law and the Writer*, edited by Keith Polking and Leonard S. Meranus, Writer's Digest, pp. 120–122, for a discussion of one writer's local tax dilemmas.

* Much of this is public information.

The steps involved in obtaining government documents under the Freedom of Information Act are:

- locate the agency that has the records
- make a request for specific records
- send the requested search fee
- appeal to the head of the agency if the request is denied

LOCATE AGENCY

The first step in getting the information that you want is to determine which federal agency has the information that you are looking for. If you are not sure which agency has the information, call the U.S. Government Federal Information Center listed in your phone book or consult the *United States Government Organization Manual* for a list of all the federal agencies and their functions.

REQUEST LETTER

A sample FOIA request letter is reproduced in the illustration below. Be as specific as you can in your description of the documents. The better your description of the desired information,

Agency Head or FOIA Officer
Title
Name of Agency
Address of Agency
City, State, zip

Re: Freedom of Information Act Request.

Dear __________:

Under the provisions of the Freedom of Information Act, 5 U.S.C. 552, I am requesting access to (identify the records as clearly and specifically as possible).

If there are any fees for searching for, or copying, the records I have requested, please inform me before you fill the request. (Or: . . . please supply the records without informing me if the fees do not exceed $——.)

[Optional] I am requesting this information (state the reason for your request if you think it will assist you in obtaining the information.)

[Optional] As you know, the act permits you to reduce or waive fees when the release of the information is considered as "primarily benefiting the public". I believe that this request fits that category and I therefore ask that you waive any fees.

If all or any part of this request is denied, please cite the specific exemption(s) which you think justifies your refusal to release the information, and inform me of the appeal procedures available to me under the law.

I would appreciate your handling this request as quickly as possible, and I look forward to hearing from you within 10 days, as the law stipulates.

Sincerely,

Signature
Name
Address
City, State, zip

figure 7-14 Sample FOIA request letter

Name of Agency Official
Title
Name of Agency
Address of Agency
City, State, zip
Re: Freedom of Information Act Appeal.

Dear __________:

This is to appeal the denial of my request for information pursuant to the Freedom of Information Act, 5 U.S.C. 522.

On __________ (date), I received a letter from ____________________ (individual's name) of your agency denying my request for access to ____________________ (description of the information sought). I am enclosing a copy of this denial along with a copy of my original request. I trust that upon examination of these communications you will conclude that the information I am seeking should be disclosed.

As provided for in the Act, I will expect to receive a reply within 20 working days.

[Optional] If you decide not to release the requested information, I plan to take this matter to court.

Sincerely,

Signature
Name
Address
City, State, zip

figure 7-15 Sample FOIA appeal letter

the smaller the search fee will be because of the savings in the search time.

FEES

Search fees run at around $5 an hour and $.10 a page for copies of standard-size pages. The law provides that these fees can be waived if the agency determines that "furnishing the information can be considered as primarily benefiting the general public."

DENIAL

Federal agencies are supposed to reply to all requests for information within ten working days from the date of receipt of the request. If the agency denies your request for information, it must tell you the reason for the denial and to whom you can appeal within the agency. Most appeals must be filed within thirty days of your receipt of the denial. See Figure 7-15 for a sample appeal letter.

The agency must act upon your appeal within thirty working days of the agency's receipt of your appeal. If this appeal is unsuccessful, you can take your case to court.

FEDERAL SUNSHINE LAW

The federal government Sunshine Act became law on March 12, 1977. The policy behind the Act was that "the public is entitled to the fullest practicable information regarding the decision making processes of the Federal Government." To implement this policy, the Act declares a presumption in favor of open meetings and requires publication of notices of meetings. Some states have also passed similar laws.

SOURCES:

pg. 173 Copyright with author of contribution to collective work: Title 17, U.S.Code Annotated, Section 201(c).

pg. 176 Fair-use exception for certain performances and displays: Title 17, U.S.Code Annotated, Section 110.

pg. 176 *Hemingway v. Film Alliance of the U. S.*, 174 Misc. 725, 21 N.Y.S.2d 827 (Sup. Ct. N.Y. 1940).

pg. 177 *Seven Per cent Solution: Musto v. Meyer*, 2 Med. L. Reporter 2222 (S.D.N.Y. June 24, 1977).

pg. 194 Hobby loss challenge of pilot/writer: *Nemish v. Commissioner*, 29 T.C.M.1249 (1970), affirmed 452 F.2d 611 (1971).

pg. 195 Freedom of Information Act: Title 5, U.S.Code Annotated, Section 552.

pg. 197 Government in Sunshine Act: Title 5, U.S.Code Annotated, Section 552b.

Chapter 8

Obtaining Legal Assistance

WHAT DO I DO NOW?

WHAT CAN YOU DO YOURSELF?

SO WHEN DO I NEED A LAWYER?

FINDING A LAWYER

CHOOSING YOUR FAMILY LAWYER

WORKING WITH YOUR LAWYER

YOU AND YOUR LAWYER

■ LEGAL ADVICE, NOT ON YOUR LIFE

WHAT DO I DO NOW?

Alice's Last Allegory

On Friday the thirteenth Alice was nearly swept away by a tide of unfortunate events.

Her new landlord sent her a special-delivery letter demanding a 300 percent rent increase. A Little Old Grandmother had borrowed her grandson's souped-up, four-wheel-drive pickup to visit Rainbow Hill and purchase some of Alice's ceramic heart planters. She ran over one hundred heart planters and hit Alice's cat, Goldy. Goldy was rushed to Vera the Vet for treatment. Then Careless Contractor told Alice that he had finished building her storage shed but instead of the plan's double doors he had installed a single door. Romero called from jail. He had been picked up for driving while intoxicated and speeding when returning from his friend Big Boozer's bachelor party. That afternoon the Sheriff had come by Rainbow Hill to serve Romero with a paternity complaint.

At the end of the day Goldy died. Vera the Vet said they would bury the cat for a $25 charge, and Alice agreed; the Little Old Grandmother's insurance company, Not-Too-Fast Service, told Alice that a check was in the mail for $550 for the damage; Careless Contractor refused to put double doors on the shed; Romero was still in jail and the Sheriff served the paternity papers on him there. Alice called her family lawyer, Sam Violet, and told him all. He said for Alice to come in next week to discuss the other problems and he'd call the judge now to get Romero out. On her way to get Romero she went down the alley bordering Vera the Vet's and saw a pile of dead animals by the trash with Goldy on top. In tears she retrieved Goldy and picked up a grateful Romero at the jail. The check never came the following week from Not-Too-Fast Service, and the company refused to issue another check.

When Alice and Romero saw Sam Violet, he told her to write letters of complaint to the state regulatory agencies for contractors, insurance companies, and veterinarians. He agreed to handle the criminal charges against Romero, the paternity complaint (which Romero claimed was a case of mistaken identity), and the rent-increase problem.

Alice wrote the letters of complaint to the state regulatory boards. Sometime later she received a new check from the insurance company, a refund of the $25 cat-burial charge and a Siamese cat from Vera the Vet, and Careless Contractor sent his brother out to put a double door on the storage shed. Violet arranged to have the driving-while-intoxicated charges dropped in exchange for a plea of guilty to the speeding ticket because the arresting officer had lost the blood-alcohol test. The paternity action had named Romero as a defendant instead of his brother Romeo, and the complaint was dismissed. Violet got a copy of Alice's lease from the old owner's lawyer and told the new owners that no increase was allowed, for the lease was still in effect. To top it all off, Alice's bachelor lawyer accepted in trade several ceramic valentine planters as gifts for his ladies and a ceramic sculptured fountain for his office.

Some of these situations Alice handled herself, and others were handled by her lawyer. This chapter will explore those two alternatives to solving legal problems. Besides suggesting what problems you might handle yourself and recommending when you should see a lawyer, we will also discuss the range and variety of available legal services, advise you on how to work with a lawyer, and outline steps for you to properly document potential legal problems.

SAVE IMPORTANT PAPERS

In your business and personal life, you should make a habit of record keeping. Keep track of important documents and papers such as loans, mortgages, marriage licenses, juried-show brochures, leases, canceled checks and deposit slips, birth certificates, diplomas, court papers, copies of wills, disputed bills, tax returns, and warranties and guarantees on goods purchased. Keep those documents and papers which concern business and personal matters that could develop into legal difficulties. For example, save a letter from your ex-husband which says that he has been busted again but wants custody of his kids when he gets out. Keep them in a drawer, file cabinet, or metal box. At the beginning of any possible legal problem, keep notes of conversations and telephone calls, and write up a description of the events while your memory is fresh.

REMEMBER THE CHINESE PROVERB: "THE BEST MEMORY IS NOT SO FIRM AS FADED INK."

WHAT CAN YOU DO YOURSELF?

COMPLAINTS TO STATE AGENCIES

If you have been wronged, try a telephone call first and then a polite complaint letter to the wrongdoer.* If after contacting the wrongdoer there is still no relief, consider a complaint letter to the appropriate agency or filing in a small claims court.** Since states regulate many professions and occupations, a state could deny, suspend, or limit the use of a license of a wrongdoer. Those whose occupations are regulated in some states are (check with your Consumer Fraud Department):

- collection agents
- attorneys
- veterinarians
- insurance agencies
- contractors
- architects
- accountants
- cosmetologists
- doctors
- dentists
- real estate salesmen
- undertakers
- photographers

STATE CONSUMER FRAUD DIVISION

There are also Consumer Fraud Departments in the Attorney General's Office of all states except Alabama. If the wrongdoer lives in your state, write to the Attorney General's Office in your state's capital and mark your correspondence "Attention Consumer Fraud Division." Otherwise, contact the Attorney General in the state in

* You may want to have a lawyer review a rough draft of your complaint letter if it concerns a lot of money or a complex problem.

** See the section on enforcing your contracts in Chapter 4, "Making Contracts," for more information on filing complaint letters and using small claims court.

which the company is located, because that investigating office will have jurisdiction over the offender. Be sure to include copies of your correspondence with the offending company as well as any proofs of purchase and payment in your letter to the Consumer Fraud Department.

BETTER BUSINESS BUREAUS

Some cities have a Better Business Bureau* to handle complaints against businesses. The BBB has established arbitration systems to handle complaints in most areas. Check your phone book. Another private agency you can contact regarding mail-order matters is the Mail Order Action Line Service, Direct/Mail Marketing Association, 6 East Forty-third Street, New York, NY 10007. This organization has a phone reference service (212/689-4977).

Keep these points in mind when writing a complaint letter:

- use correct address.
- direct letter to specific person (keep copies).
- state complaint clearly.
- state your demand.
- give an action deadline (if letter to wrongdoer).
- indicate where copies were sent.
- attach copies of documents (keep originals).

For a sample complaint letter see the section on enforcing your contracts in Chapter 4, "Making Contracts."

FEDERAL AGENCIES

At the federal level there is the Federal Trade Commission (FTC), which deals with a variety of unfair business practices.** The Post Office Department*** handles mail fraud or mail-order problems. The Equal Employment Opportunities Commission (EEOC), 1800 G Street, NW, Washington, D.C. 20506 handles complaints on job discrimination by reason of age, sex, color, religion, and national origin. Write the EEOC for a discrimination charge form. Remember, some states have nondiscrimination laws. Check with the Attorney General's Office of your state for this information. The Department of Labor will investigate charges involving minimum wages, equal pay, and age discrimination. You also can complain to the Wage and Hour Division, Employment Standards Administration, U.S. Department of Labor, Washington, D.C. 20210. Besides the local federal information number for your state, there is a network of toll-free hotlines. Some of these are:

HOTLINES

Consumer Product Safety Commission Hotline (800/638-8326): Handles complaints or questions about safety of toys and other products. See Chapter 2: "Legal Restrictions on Content and Materials."

* Contact the Council of Better Business Bureaus, 1150 Seventeenth Street, NW, Washington, D.C. 20036 for more information.

** Bureau of Consumer Protection, FTC, Washington, D.C. 20580. Usually the FTC does not get involved in individual cases but looks for a pattern of wrongdoing.

*** Contact the U.S. Postal Service, Washington, D.C. 20260 or the postal inspector in the city nearest the area in which the wrongdoer is located. Your local post office will supply the address.

Housing Discrimination Hotline (800/424-8590): Call if you think you've been denied accommodation because of sex, race, religion, age, or national origin. Also advice on renting or buying a home.

National Highway Traffic Safety Administration Hotline (800/424-9393): Answers questions on automobile safety and gives advice about car recalls and where to complain about auto defects.

Moving Hotline (800/424-9312): Call if complaints or problems involve interstate moving companies, buses, trains.

LEGAL MATTERS YOU DO YOURSELF

Other legal matters you may already handle include arranging small loans from credit institutions, negotiation of routine small contracts with galleries and publishers, registering your copyright, registering your business name with the state, obtaining business licenses and permits, handling minor traffic complaints, and handling small insurance claims. In more serious or complicated matters, remember the old saying: The person who is his/her own lawyer has a fool for a client.

SO WHEN DO I NEED A LAWYER?

Sometimes a lawyer just gives advice (consultation); other times a lawyer will do more work for you. You need a lawyer, and sometimes a specialist, in the following situations:

YOU SHOULD HAVE A LAWYER FOR THESE

- before signing an agreement or legal document that you do not understand; for example, a waiver of appearance in court on a domestic matter.
- in adoptions, regardless of whether you are the adopting party or the natural parent of the child
- in matters involving juvenile delinquency as well as temporary custody of your children and guardianships
- in preparing a will and in estate planning
- in a divorce, annulment, or separation involving property and/or children
- when you purchase real estate, if the transaction involves a large sum of money
- when you have a dispute with someone represented by a lawyer
- in criminal cases when you are accused of a crime that involves jail time, heavy fines, or penalties (loss of driver's license)
- if a claim for money damages is made against you or if you have a claim for money damages against someone which involves a serious amount of money
- if you form a business organization
- if you want to obtain a patent or sue for patent infringement
- if you are involved in a legal transaction that is important to your business, profession, or personal life, e.g., a long-term business lease, an exclusive gallery contract, a book contract
- if you are considering bankruptcy or other debtors' remedies
- if you want to register your trade name or trademark with the patent office
- if you want to pursue a copyright infringement
- if you have landlord-tenant problems

- if you have received personal injuries, lost income, or had property destroyed
- if you are denied benefits to which you believe you are entitled, e.g., Social Security, unemployment benefits, or workers' compensation
- if you cannot resolve a consumer complaint, and the money involved is significant
- if you have discriminatory employment problems
- if you are being audited by IRS for a large amount of money or if the audit may show fraud
- if a government agency takes or proposes to take action against you that you don't agree with such as a zoning change, eminent domain, construction of a government nuclear installation
- other problems or situations of a legal nature that are complex or very important to you

There are about four hundred thousand lawyers in the United States. Lawyers represent their clients on legal problems by providing information, giving advice, writing letters, preparing legal documents, making telephone calls, doing legal research, and appearing in court. You need to locate the right lawyer for your problem. There are many kinds of lawyers. A general practitioner is just that—one who practices law in most areas. Some lawyers specialize in one area—domestic relations law, estate planning, corporate law, patent work, trials, tax work, and criminal law. The state or local bar association or your family lawyer should be able to refer you to a specialist if the need arises. Until recently, only admiralty, trademark, and patent lawyers were allowed to advertise their specialty. There is now a broadening of the rules concerning lawyers advertising.

WHO ARE LAWYERS

FINDING A LAWYER

Studies have shown that 70 percent of people with legal problems do *without* legal advice because they don't know how to locate the right lawyer. This section will assist you in finding a helpful lawyer, whether free or paid.

CRIMINAL MATTERS

Free legal services usually are divided into two categories, civil and criminal. In criminal matters where you may go to jail, you have a *right* to a free lawyer if you are too poor to hire one. If you cannot afford a private lawyer, insist that a lawyer be appointed to represent you without charge or request to see the public defender. The public defender program handles criminal cases for poor persons in some courts.

CIVIL MATTERS

LEGAL AID PROGRAMS

For free legal assistance in noncriminal areas there are two kinds of programs—government-supported legal aid and privately funded organizations. Over five hundred Legal Aid Programs operate in this country, servicing eligible people with civil legal problems. Eligibility for these services is limited by income level, residence, and type of problem. Organizations like State Education Associations, the American Civil Liberties Union, the National Association for the

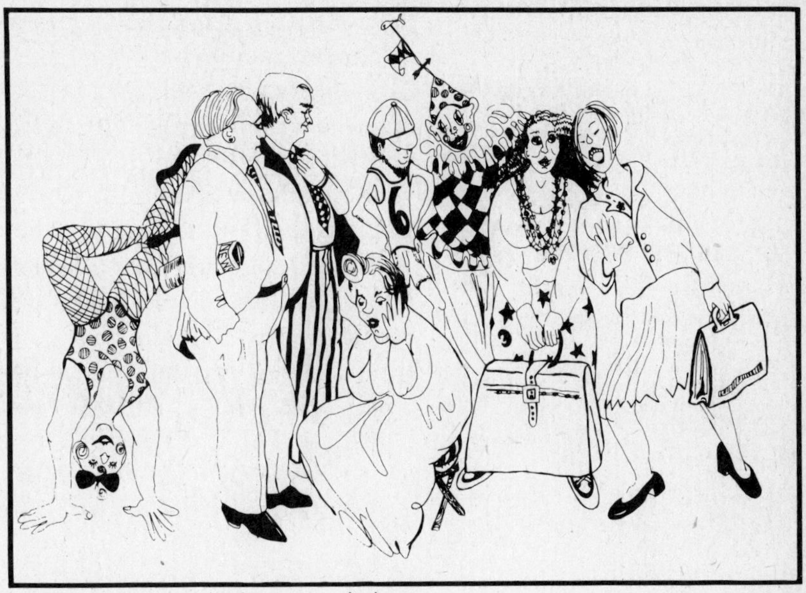

Lawyers come in all shapes and sizes

Advancement of Colored People, and the National Organization for Women Legal Defense Fund may help with problems that relate to their special interest.

VOLUNTEER LAWYERS FOR THE ARTS (VLA)

Volunteer Lawyers for the Arts, a relatively new legal assistance program for the creative person, has been organized the past few years and has offices in some major cities. Write to VLA, 36 West Forty-fourth Street, Suite 1110, New York, NY 10036 for information on where to contact a VLA group in your state. Also, your State Bar Association may have an Art Law Committee that will refer you to lawyers interested in representing creative persons. If you can't find any of the legal assistance programs described by checking with an attorney's office, the courthouse, or the phone book, then contact the State Bar Association, which would be located in your state's capital.

LAWYER ADVERTISING

Between free legal services and traditional law firms are law firms and clinics that provide routine legal services for a set, advertised fee. Of course, your problem may not fall within the category of a simple, routine problem, so the prices quoted may be misleading. The standardization of their service may mean less personal attention on your problem, and perhaps there will not be expertise in other areas of interest to you—for instance, a name change might be easily handled by them but not a gallery contract.

PREPAID LEGAL SERVICES

There are also prepaid legal services available to people affiliated with special groups such as credit unions, teachers, labor unions, and so forth. For a set premium (the average in 1975 was $60 per year), you gain access to legal assistance that is covered by the plan. Sometimes consultations are free. Usually the fees for routine work are set in advance. Write the National Consumer Center for Legal

Services, 1302 Eighteenth Street NW, Washington, D.C. 20036 for information on prepaid legal services.

CHOOSING A LAWYER

If your choice, for whatever reason, is to use a private lawyer, then the search begins with talking to people you trust for suggestions. Be sure to find out why the lawyer is recommended—were your friends satisfied with the work, what sort of work was done, and was the bill reasonable. There are lawyer referral panels sponsored by local county bar associations which have lists of attorneys interested in receiving referrals who have agreed to charge a flat rate for a consultation. The disadvantage is that the luck of draw applies; Ms. X may be the next lawyer on the list and she has never done a will, which may be the service you want. For the address of the nearest Lawyers Referral Service, write to the Standing Committee on Lawyers Referral Service, American Bar Association, 1155 East Sixtieth Street, Chicago, IL 60637 or check your phone directory.

LAWYER REFERRAL SERVICES (SEE THE YELLOW PAGES)

Another aid in your search for a lawyer is a directory known as the *Martindale-Hubbell Legal Directory*, which can be found in many law and other libraries. This "establishment" directory lists lawyers in most communities, sometimes their specialty, and often rates the lawyers on the basis of number of years of practice and other factors.

CHOOSING YOUR FAMILY LAWYER

At this point you should know what lawyers or legal services are available in your community, and you are ready to make a choice. As you can see, the selection process may be lengthy, so don't wait until the eleventh hour to choose your lawyer.

In our opinion, it makes sense for many in the art, craft, or writing fields (as well as others) to have their own lawyers. Most lawyers will not give legal advice to a stranger over the phone, because often the advice must be based on an examination of papers and documents, a personal interview, and of course the establishment of a paying relationship. If you are evicted, involved in an accident, land in jail, or have some other legal emergency, you can call your lawyer immediately for assistance. Aside from the benefits of an immediate telephone or personal consultation, the lawyer has knowledge about your particular circumstances, and you have, hopefully, established credit with the lawyer by paying your bill. In your search for a family lawyer, shop around.

ADVANTAGES OF HAVING A FAMILY LAWYER

A consultation with a prospective lawyer will be helpful in making a selection. Most offices have an initial fee for consultation on a legal problem. Sometimes a consultation may be all you need to help you with your problem. If the lawyer is lukewarm about your problem, then try another.

After a consultation with a lawyer, you might consider these additional factors in selecting your lawyer:

SELECTION FACTORS

- ability to explain things simply to you
- attention and interest in your problem
- kinds of clients represented by the lawyer
- the size of the firm
- specialization within the firm
- experience of the lawyer
- if you feel comfortable in the office (remember, all that glitters is not gold)
- specialization in your problem area
- fees charged for services
- age of lawyer

Keep in mind that the selection of an attorney is quite personal. Some people say you should like your attorney in order to confide in and trust him or her. Others say they would not want to pay someone they didn't like. All these considerations are valid, for a comfortable attorney-client relationship is quite valuable to you.

WORKING WITH YOUR LAWYER

PREPARE TO SEE YOUR LAWYER

"A LAWYER'S TIME AND ADVICE ARE HIS STOCK IN TRADE."
—ABRAHAM LINCOLN

Prepare yourself before seeing your lawyer. Go over your papers and be sure *to bring them with you*. Read up on your problem if you have access to any information about it. Prepare a list of questions.

Discuss fees before you hire the lawyer for anything more than a consultation. Often a lawyer won't be able to give you an exact fee for handling your case, because the cost of the case will be dictated by which of the several solutions to your legal problem is chosen. There are several basic fee arrangements:

FEE ARRANGEMENTS

- hourly rate: Tax experts may charge $75 an hour but have the information at their fingertips. The average charge for a lawyer's time is $40 to $60 hourly.
- flat rates for routine cases: Such cases include wills, adoptions, or divorces.
- contingent fee: Under this arrangement the lawyer takes a percentage of the amount won in a lawsuit, and gets nothing if the case is lost. The contingent fee is used in cases involving personal injuries, property damage, bill collections, Social Security, etc. Nevertheless, you have to pay the out-of-pocket costs of such cases, i.e., phone, photocopying, filing fees, depositions, and court costs.
- percentage of an estate can serve as the fee.
- statutory attorneys' fees: Examples would be discrimination complaints, certain consumer actions, and in some states complaints based on writings, for these laws permit the recovery of attorneys' fees.

Try to get the best deal and consider other possible fee arrangements. Bargain a little bit or suggest a lower percentage on a contingent-fee case or discuss payment of the hourly rate if you have a simple, routine case rather than the flat fee. Offer to trade for your work or services. For example, jewelry, repairs, prints, rugs, pottery, tables, carpentry work, and typing services have all been traded for legal services. Lawyers seem to be more amenable to half-cash, half-trade proposals.

TRADES

RETAINER

Sometimes the lawyer will expect a down payment (a retainer) on the case. The amount depends on the type of legal problem, the amount of work that may be involved, and whether you are an old or new client. If it is your family lawyer, then you may just be billed for the work.

After these discussions, you and your lawyer will make a contract concerning the specifics of his or her representation of you. Make sure that you are clear concerning the terms of the contract and that you sign and keep a copy of it. For more information on contracts, see Chapter 4, "Making Contracts."

SAVING FEES

There are many ways to save on fees:

- Drop off your papers before your appointment so your lawyer can review them.
- Completely fill out any forms or interview sheets your lawyer may use, and read carefully any information papers your lawyer may give you.
- Write up a detailed narrative of the facts of your problem.
- Have names, addresses, and telephone numbers of witnesses and opponents.
- Don't repeat yourself.
- Keep brief notes on a calendar of the sequence of events.

One client who had been harassed by creditors had noted on his calendar the frequency and times a collection agent had called over one week. This was helpful in settling the case. Another client kept an extensive journal concerning events about his children, who were in his ex-wife's custody. This helped in preparing the case for trial.

YOU AND YOUR LAWYER

FEE DISAGREEMENTS

Even after you get your bill, if you believe the fee is wrong or too much, discuss it first with your lawyer. The lawyer should be able to show the amount of work done on the problem. Usually, time is kept by the tenths of an hour. The lawyer may have spent a lot of time on research or investigation that you don't realize. Don't forget that in a fee dispute the unpaid lawyer may exert a lien on the client's papers, documents, and file until the dispute is settled. If you still are not satisfied, some Bar Associations have a special committee to arbitrate fee disagreements.

Before you leave the lawyer's office, determine if the lawyer needs more documents or facts, whom you should or should not talk to, what work the lawyer will do on the case, when he or she will contact you, and how you will be kept informed of developments. Be sure the lawyer explains all the alternative solutions available to you on your particular problem. Listen to the lawyer's recommendation on what solution you should use *but* remember that some options may be too expensive for you. Paying a lawyer to file a suit for an unpaid account of $50 just doesn't make sense.

BE INFORMED

Your lawyer should inform you of developments as they occur on your case. If the lawyer doesn't, then request copies of correspondence, most court papers, and information on developments on your case. If you are involved in a lawsuit, you must be told of offers of settlement.

RIGHT TO CONFIDENTIALITY

You have a right to confidentiality. The law regards your conversations with your lawyer as confidential. Even if you reveal your involvement with a past crime or misconduct, your lawyer cannot release this information. Remember that your lawyer cannot give you advice unless he or she has all the facts. Do not lie or hide the facts. Lawyers are pretty hard to shock. Despite warnings about this, it is not uncommon for clients to hide or not admit certain facts that make them look bad and then decide in court to tell those facts. Disastrous.

MONEY AND YOUR LAWYER

A lawyer must keep clients' funds (cost deposit money and recoveries for clients) in a separate account. If you win money, then you should receive a statement from your lawyer indicating the costs involved, your share of the recovery, and the lawyer's share of the recovery. The lawyer may not mix clients' moneys with his or her business account. If your lawyer has misspent your funds, report this immediately to the State Bar.

DISSATISFACTION WITH YOUR LAWYER

Sometimes clients have problems with their lawyer. Maybe the lawyer is too slow to work on your case, misses a deadline on your problem, gives you inaccurate advice, or represents you poorly. Discuss with your lawyer openly and frankly your dissatisfaction and try to resolve the matter.

If you are still dissatisfied after talking to your lawyer, then consult with another lawyer. Be sure to tell the consulting lawyer about your legal problem first, then relate your complaint about your lawyer and ask the consulting lawyer's advice.

DISCHARGING YOUR ATTORNEY

Discharge your attorney if necessary. In a court case you may need the judge's permission to do that (as would the lawyer if he or she did not want to represent you further). Sometimes attorneys are reluctant to take over a case from another lawyer.

You should complain to your State Bar Association if you think your attorney has engaged in wrongdoing. As a last and final resort, consider making a malpractice claim if the lawyer made some serious mistake. Of course you should see a lawyer for assistance with this.

Dear Chatty Lawyer Syndicated Column:

I am so happy. After tripping through the Yellow Pages, seeing my friends' lawyers, trying the hectic legal clinics, I have finally found me a lawyer. It's actually two lawyers, Saphronia Green and Sam Violet, who consult together. I am a sculptress, and my work is rather controversial because I sculpt phallic symbols. My business is small and I've just started out on my own. My new lawyer's office is in a house and not a stuffy, tall office building. It is full of artworks. The waiting room has unusual reading material, such as *Sunset, Mother Earth News,* and *Art and the Law.* Best of all they are interested in me and my problems. They have told me things I can do myself if I want to save on my fee. I understand my papers after they explain them. I called them on the phone last week when my brother was in jail, and they got him out. Sure sometimes they're pretty busy and aren't there when I call, but they get back to me.

They have also accepted a half-cash, half-fee arrangement. Last year I deducted what I paid them as a business expense, but their services saved more money than the fees! They renegotiated my studio lease for a longer term with a fixed rent, got a refund on some defective merchandise, made the Annual City Art Festival accept my work in a recent show even though it shocked the city council, and negotiated my exclusive gallery contract with terms more favorable to me.

So tell your readers to keep looking for their family lawyer, for somewhere out there is the right lawyer for them.

Love ya,

The Sensuella Sculptress

Appendixes

CHAPTER ONE

Appendix 1-1 SAMPLE PARTNERSHIP AGREEMENT

____

This agreement is made between ___________________________ of __________________, __________, __________ of __________, __________, and __________ of ________________, ___________ intending to be legally bound and to form a partnership and do business as __________________ which shall be located principally in ____________, ____________ and other locations that the parties may agree upon.

1. *Purpose:* The purpose of this partnership is to engage in a ______________ business and in such other businesses as may be agreed upon by the partners.

2. *Duration of the Partnership:* This partnership shall begin on __________________, 19____ and will continue until terminated by agreement of the partners or by the retirement, death or insanity of any one of the partners.

3. *Capital Contribution:* The original capital of the partnership shall consist of the amount of ____________ cash, goods or services contributed by each partner in the following fashion:

Name	*Contribution*	*Percentage*

This capital and any future capital contribution cannot be withdrawn except by the unanimous agreement of all the partners or upon dissolution.

4. *Profits and Losses:* The net profits and losses shall be apportioned to each individual partner in proportion to his/her percentage of the capital contribution and paid as the partners see fit.

5. *Fiscal Year and Accounting Method:* The fiscal year shall be the calendar year and the accounting method for income tax purposes shall be the __________________ method.

6. *Duties and Authority of Partners:* Each partner shall apply all of his experience, training and ability to his/her partnership tasks. No partner shall enter into a business that in some way competes with the partnership except with the unanimous agreement of the other partners. No partner shall buy any goods or articles or enter into any contract exceeding the value of __________________ dollars ($__________) without the prior consent in writing of the other partners. Each partner shall pay his/her separate debts on time and shall indemnify and repay the partnership for any liability of the partnership for his separate debts.

7. *Decision Making and Arbitration:* Partnership decisions shall be made by majority vote except for any decision that is contrary to this agreement which shall require the consent of each partner. In the event of a disagreement as to the rights or liabilities of any partner, the difference shall be determined by ____________________________, acting as arbitrator.

8. *Record Keeping:* In addition to the normal business books, the partnership shall maintain records of all contributions, withdrawals and profit shares for each partner. These books shall be available for inspection by any partner.

9. *Involuntary Dissolution:* Any partner can leave the partnership after giving _________ days notice to the other partners. Retirement, death or insanity of any of the partners shall result in an immediate dissolution of the partnership. Upon dissolution, an accounting shall be made of the capital shares of each partner, the profits received by each partner and the net profit or loss of the partnership from the date of the previous accounting.

If one partner retires, dies or becomes insane, the other partners may continue the partnership with themselves or with others that they might choose but they shall pay the retiring partner or his/her representative the value of his/her interest in the partnership. The value of the existing partner's interest is, as of the date of dissolution:

1. partner's share of capital
2. partner's share of profit or loss

10. *Dissolution by Agreement:* Upon the agreement of the partners to dissolve, the assets of the partnership shall be liquidated and the proceeds shall be paid in the following order:

a. creditors of the partnership
b. profits *owed* to the partners
c. repayment of the capital investment to each partner.
d. payment of proportionate share of any remaining profits.

11. *Boilerplate:* This agreement is the entire agreement made between the partners and can be modified by agreement of the parties placed in writing. The laws of the state of _________________________ governs this agreement.

____

Subscribed and sworn to before me this ____ day of ________, 19______.

____

Notary Public
My Commission Expires: _______

____

Subscribed and sworn to before me this ____ day of ________, 19______.

____

Notary Public
My Commission Expires _______

____

Subscribed and sworn to before me this ____ day of ________, 19 ______.

____

Notary Public
My Commission Expires _______

CHAPTER TWO

Appendix 2-1 CODE OF FEDERAL REGULATIONS ON FUR PROCESSING

§ 301.19 Pointing, dyeing, bleaching or otherwise artifically coloring.

(a) Where a fur or fur product is pointed or contains or is composed of bleached, dyed or otherwise artificially colored fur, such facts shall be disclosed as a part of the required information in labeling, invoicing and advertising.

(b) The term "pointing" means the process of inserting separate hairs into furs or fur products for the purpose of adding guard hairs, either to repair damaged areas or to simulate other furs.

(c) The term "bleaching" means the process for producing a lighter shade of a fur, or removing off-color spots and stains by a bleaching agent.

(d) The term "dyeing" (which includes the processes known in the trade of tipping the hair or fur, feathering, and beautifying) means the process of applying dyestuffs to the hair or fur, either by immersion in a dye bath or by application of the dye by brush, feather, spray, or otherwise, for the purpose of changing the color of the fur or hair, or to accentuate its natural color. When dyestuff is applied by immersion in a dye bath or by application of the dye by brush, feather, or spray, it may respectively be described as "vat dyed", "brush dyed", "feather dyed", or "spray dyed", as the case may be. When dyestuff is applied only to the ends of the hair or fur, by feather or otherwise, it may also be described as "tip-dyed". The application of dyestuff to the leather or the skin (known in the trade as "tipping", as distinguished from tip-dyeing the hair or fur as above described) and which does not affect a change of, nor accentuate the natural color of the hair or fur, shall not be considered as "dyeing". When fluorescent dye is applied to a fur or fur product it may be described as "brightener added".

(e) The term "artificial coloring" means any change or improvement in color of a fur or fur product in any manner other than by pointing, bleaching, dyeing, or tip-dyeing, and shall be described in labeling, invoicing and advertising as "color altered" or "color added".

(f) The term "blended" shall not be used as a part of the required information to describe the pointing, bleaching, dyeing, tip-dyeing, or otherwise artificially coloring of furs.

(g) Where a fur or fur product is not pointed, bleached, dyed, tip-dyed, or otherwise artificially colored it shall be described as "natural".

(h) (*1*) Where any fur or fur product is dressed, processed or treated with a solution or compound containing any metal and such compound or solution effects any change or improvement in the color of the hair, fleece or fur fiber, such fur or fur product shall be described in labeling, invoicing and advertising as "color altered" or "color added".

(*2*) When any fur or fur product is dressed, processed or treated with a solution or compound containing iron or copper and after processing any of the hair, fleece or fur fiber contains more than 300 parts per million of iron or more than 75 parts per million of copper, such fur or fur product shall be described in labeling, invoicing and advertising as "color altered" or "color added".

(i) (*1*) Any person dressing, processing or treating a fur pelt in such a manner that it is required under paragraph (e) or (h) of this section to be described as "color altered" or "color added" shall place a black stripe at least one half inch in width across the leather side of the skin immediately above the rump or place a stamp with a solid black center in the form of either a two inch square or a circle at least two inches in diameter on the leather side of the pelt and shall use black ink for all other stamps or markings on the leather side of the pelt.

(*2*) Any person dressing, processing or treating a fur pelt which after processing is considered natural under paragraph (g) of this section shall place a white stripe at least one-half inch in width across the leather side of the skin immediately above the rump or place a stamp with a solid white center in the form of either a 2-inch square or a circle at least 2 inches in diameter on the leather side of the pelt and shall use white ink for all other stamps or markings on the leather side of the pelt.

(3) Any person dressing, processing or treating a fur pelt in such a manner that it is considered dyed under paragraph (d) of this section shall place a yellow stripe at least one-half inch in width across the leather side immediately above the rump or place a stamp with a solid yellow center in the form of either a 2-inch square or a circle at least 2 inches in diameter on the leather side of the pelt and shall use yellow ink for all other stamps or markings on the leather side of the pelt.

(4) In lieu of the marking or stamping otherwise required by subparagraphs (*1*), (*2*), and (*3*) of this paragraph, any person dressing, processing or treating a fur pelt so as to be subject to the stamping or marking requirements of this paragraph may stamp the leather side of the pelt with the appropriate truthful designation "dyed", "color altered", "color added", or "natural", as the case may be, in such manner that the stamp will not be obliterated or mutilated by further processing and will remain clearly legible until the finished fur product reaches the ultimate consumer.

(5) Where, after assembling, fur garment shells, mats, plates or other assembled furs are processed or treated in such a manner as to fall within the stamping or marking provisions of this paragraph, such assembled furs, in lieu of the stamping or marking of each individual pelt or piece, may be appropriately stamped on the leather side as provided in this paragraph in such a manner that the stamp will remain on the finished fur product and clearly legible until it reaches the ultimate consumer and will not be mutilated or obliterated by further processing.

(j) Any person who shall process a fur pelt in such a manner that after such processing it is no longer considered as natural shall clearly, conspicuously and legibly stamp on the leather side of the pelt and on required invoices relating thereto a lot number or other identifying number which relates to such records of the processor as will show the source and disposition of the pelts and the details of the processing performed. Such person shall also stamp his name or registered identification number on the leather side of the pelt.

(k) Any person who processes fur pelts of a type which are always considered as dyed under paragraph (d) of this section after processing or any person who processes fur pelts which are always natural at the time of sale to the ultimate consumer, which pelts for a valid reason cannot be marked or stamped as provided in this section, may file an affidavit with the Federal Trade Commission's Bureau of Textiles and Furs setting forth such facts as will show that the pelts are always dyed or natural as the case may be and that the stamping of such pelts cannot be reasonably accomplished. If the Bureau of Textiles and Furs is satisfied that the public interest will be protected by the filing of the affidavit it may accept such affidavit and advise the affiant that marking of the fur pelts themselves as provided in this section will be unnecessary until further notice. Any person filing such an affidavit shall promptly notify the Commission of any change in circumstances with respect to its operations.

(l) Any person subject to this section who incorrectly marks or fails to mark fur pelts as provided in paragraphs (i) and (j) of this section shall be deemed to have misbranded such products under section 4(l) of the Act. Any person subject to this section who furnishes a false or misleading affidavit under paragraph (k) of this section or fails to give the notice required by paragraph (k) of this section shall be deemed to have neglected and refused to maintain the records required by section 8(d) of the Act.

[17 F.R. 6075, July 8, 1952, as amended at 26 F.R. 3186, Apr. 14, 1961; 34 F.R. 381, Jan. 10, 1969; 36 F.R. 5689, Mar. 26, 1971]

CHAPTER THREE

Appendix 3-1 COPYRIGHT FORMS

For applications for registration of copyright write to:

United States Copyright Office
Library of Congress
Washington, D.C.

Form TX. This is the appropriate application to use for © registration covering nondramatic literary works, whether published or unpublished.

Form VA. This is the appropriate form to use for copyright registration covering works of the visual arts. Both published and unpublished works can be registered on Form VA.

Form GR/CP. This is the appropriate adjunct application form to use when you are submitting a basic application on Form TX, Form PA, or Form VA, for a group of works that qualify for a single registration under section 408(c) of the Copyright statute.

Appendix 3-2 TERMINATION OF COPYRIGHT TRANSFER AND LICENSES

During the revision of the old law a hot issue was a provision for protecting authors against unfair copyright transfers. The problem stems from the unequal bargaining positions of authors and the difficulty of determining a work's value until it has been exploited. Under Section 203 of the new law, grants of right by authors, excepting work for hire, may be terminated by the author, or if he or she is deceased, by a majority of the owners of the author's termination interest.

Termination can be accomplished at the end of thirty-five years from the date of the grant.* A written termination notice** must be served between the two and ten years before the effective date of the termination. You cannot contract away these rights of termination.

Appendix 3-3 SAMPLE PERMISSION FORM AND LOCATING THE COPYRIGHT OWNER

Dear ________________________:

I would like to use the following material in a book entitled
_______(title)_______ that I am preparing to be published by
_______(publisher)_______.

(Describe the material to be used.)

My book will be published in _______(date)_______ at a list price of _________. It will be distributed _______(territory)_______.

The material would be used in future revision and editions of the work. Should you not have sole control over these rights, would you let me know whom else I should contact.

Unless you object, I will use the following credit line _____________ _________________________ and copyright notice _____________.

* If the grant covers the right of publication, then the shorter period of thirty-five years from the publication date or forty years from the grant date.

** There are specific Copyright Office regulations for the form of the notice, and the notice must be recorded before the termination date.

Thank you for your assistance. Enclosed for your convenience is a release form and copy of this letter for your files.

Sincerely yours,

____

Writer

I (we) grant the permission for use as requested above.

Date ______________ ______________________________

Appendix 3-4 APPLICATION FOR REGISTRATION OF TRADE NAMES

STATE OF ARIZONA

SECRETARY OF STATE

APPLICATION FOR REGISTRATION OF TRADE NAMES

(Title 44, Chapter 10, Article 3.1, Arizona Revised Statutes)

No. ....

Approved ....

Date ....

Fee ....

...., a person, partnership,
(Name of Applicant)
corporation, firm, association, society, foundation, federation or organization (strike words inapplicable) or foreign corporation licensed to do business in this state, hereby makes application for registration of the name, title or designation under which such applicant is operating by filing the following statements with the Secretary of State of Arizona:

1. a. Name of Applicant(s) ....

   b. Business Address ....

2. If incorporated, state of incorporation ....
3. Name, Title or Designation to be registered ....
4. General nature of business conducted ....
5. The length of time during which the name, title or designation has been used by applicant in operations within this state is ....

....
(SIGN HERE)

By ....

STATE OF ARIZONA

COUNTY OF .... ss.

...., being first duly sworn says that
(Applicant or Agent of Applicant)

he is the applicant, agent of applicant (strike words inapplicable), and that all statements made in the above written application are true.

....
(SIGN HERE)

Sworn to before me and subscribed in my presence this .... day of ....

A.D. 19..........

....
Notary Public

Filing Fee: $3.25

CHAPTER FOUR

Appendix 4-1 SAMPLE DIRECT SALE AGREEMENT BETWEEN ARTIST AND PURCHASER

Names

Name: ______________________ ______________________

Address: ______________________ ______________________

______________________ ______________________

Phone: ______________________ ______________________

Artist agrees to sell and Purchaser agrees to buy the Work described in paragraph 2 below. Artist and Purchaser further agree to the following terms as part of the sale and purchase of artist's Work:

PRICE

1. The price of the Work will be ______________. Payment shall be made in the following fashion ______________________. Title to the Work will be transferred upon Artist's receipt of the full payment price. In the event of any default by Purchaser, Artist will have the rights of a secured party under the Uniform Commercial Code.

DESCRIPTION

2. The Work which is transferred by this agreement is:

Title: ______________________________

Medium: ______________________________

Date: ______________________________

Dimensions: ______________________________

WARRANTIES

3. Artist states that she/he owns the work and that it is an original work created by him/her. If purchaser requests, Artist will provide a written statement of authenticity and a history of the work. Purchaser warrants that any display of the Work will include Artist's name.

CARE OF WORK

4. Purchaser will not permit destruction, modification or damage to the Work. If the Work is damaged, Purchaser shall give Artist the opportunity to repair the Work, if possible.

EXHIBITION RIGHTS

5. Artist reserves the right to borrow the work from Purchaser for the purpose of public exhibition, for ________ days every ________ year(s). Artist will insure the work during the period of the loan and purchaser shall incur no expense as a result of this loan.

COPYRIGHT

6. As provided by the Copyright Revision Act of 1976, Artist reserves all the rights of copyright.

RISK OF LOSS AND DELIVERY

7. Responsibility for delivery of work upon:

________ Artist ________ Purchaser

Insurance of work prior to delivery shall be provided by:

________ Artist ________ Purchaser

Any damage or loss to work prior to receipt by Purchaser shall be at the expense of:

________ Artist ________ Purchaser

RESALE OF WORK

8. If the Purchaser sells, trades, or otherwise transfers the work, she/he must:

________ pay the Artist ________% of the resale profits resulting from the transfer.

________ get the new owner to ratify this contract by signing the attached Ratification Agreement.

________ give the Ratification Agreement to Artist.

BOILERPLATE 9. This agreement represents the entire contract made by the parties. Its terms cannot be modified except by a written document signed by the parties. A waiver of any breach of any form will not be construed as a continuing waiver of other breaches of the same or other provisions of the contract. If any part of this agreement is held to be illegal, void or unenforceable, this shall not effect the validity of any other part of the contract.

ARTIST: ______________________ PURCHASER: ______________________

Date: ______________________

Appendix 4-2 THE ARTIST'S RESERVED RIGHTS TRANSFER AND SALE AGREEMENT (Second Edition)

fill in names, addresses of parties

Artist: ______________ address: ______________

Purchaser: ______________ address: ______________

WHEREAS Artist has created that certain Work of Art ("the Work"):

fill in data identifying the Work

Title: ______________ dimensions: ______________

media: ______________ year: ______________ and

WHEREAS the parties want the Artist to have certain rights in the future economics and integrity of the Work. The parties mutually agree as follows:

fill in agreed value

1. **SALE**: Artist hereby sells the Work to Purchaser at the agreed value of $ ______________
2. **RETRANSFER**: If Purchaser in any way whatsoever sells, gives or trades the Work, or if it is inherited from Purchaser, or if a third party pays compensation for its destruction, Purchaser (or the representative of his estate) must within 30 days

(a) Pay Artist 15% of the "gross art profit", if any, on the transfer; and

(b) Get the new owner to ratify this contract by signing a properly filled-out "Transfer Agreement and Record" (TAR); and

(c) Deliver the signed TAR to the Artist.

(d) "Gross art profit" for this contract means only: "Agreed value" on a TAR less the "agreed value" on the last prior TAR, or (if there hasn't been a prior resale) less the agreed value in Paragraph 1 of this contract.

(e) "Agreed value" to be filled in on each TAR shall be the actual sale price if the Work is sold for money or the fair market value at the time if transferred any other way.

3. **NON-DELIVERY**: If the TAR isn't delivered in 30 days, Artist may compute "gross art profit" and Artist's 15% as if it had, using the fair market value at the time of the transfer or at the time Artist discovers the transfer.
4. **NOTICE OF EXHIBITION**: Before committing the Work to a show, Purchaser must give Artist notice of intent to do so, telling Artist all the details of the show that Purchaser then knows.
5. **PROVENANCE**: Upon request Artist will furnish Purchaser and his successors a written history and provenance of the Work, based on TAR's and Artist's best information as to shows.
6. **ARTISTS EXHIBITION**: Artist may show the Work for up to 60 days once every 5 years at a non-profit institution at no expense to Purchaser, upon written notice no later than 120 days before opening and upon satisfactory proof of insurance and prepaid transportation.
7. **NON-DESTRUCTION**: Purchaser will not permit any intentional destruction, damage or modification of the Work.
8. **RESTORATION**: If the Work is damaged, Purchaser will consult Artist before any restoration and must give Artist first opportunity to restore it, if practicable.
9. **RENTS**: If the Work is rented, Purchaser must pay Artist 50% of the rents within 30 days of receipt.
10. **REPRODUCTION**: Artist reserves all rights to reproduce the Work.
11. **NOTICE**: A Notice, in the form below, must be permanently affixed to the Work, warning that ownership, etc., are subject to this contract. If, however, a document represents the Work or is part of the Work, the Notice must instead be a permanent part of that document.
12. **TRANSFEREES BOUND:** If anyone becomes the owner of the Work with notice of this contract, that person shall be bound to all its terms as if he had signed a TAR when he acquired the Work.
13. **EXPIRATION**: This contract binds the parties, their heirs and all their successors in interest, and all Purchaser's obligations are attached to the Work and go with ownership of the Work, all for the life of the Artist and Artist's surviving spouse plus 21 years, except the obligations of Paragraphs 4, 6 and 8 shall last only for Artist's lifetime.
14. **ATTORNEYS' FEES**: In any proceeding to enforce any part of this contract, the aggrieved party shall be entitled to reasonable attorneys' fees in addition to any available remedy.

fill in date both sign

Date: ______________

______________ Artist

______________ Purchaser

TRANSFER AGREEMENT AND RECORD

fill in data identifying the Work

Title: ______________ dimensions: ______________

media: ______________ year: ______________

fill in date

Ownership of the above Work of Art has been transferred between the undersigned persons, and the new owner hereby expressly ratifies, assumes and agrees to be bound by the terms of the Contract dated ______________ between:

fill in names, addresses of parties

Artist: ______________ address: ______________ and

Purchaser: ______________ address: ______________

Agreed value (as defined in said contract) at the time of this transfer: $ ______________

do not FILL in anything between these lines

Old owner: ______________ address: ______________

New owner: ______________ address: ______________

Date of this transfer: ______________

fill in date fill in names of parties and Artist's address on both Notices

SPECIMEN NOTICE

Ownership, transfer, exhibition and reproduction of this Work of Art are subject to a certain Contract dated ______________ between:

Artist: ______________

Address: ______________ and

Purchaser: ______________

Artist has a copy.

cut out, affix to Work

NOTICE

Ownership, transfer, exhibition and reproduction of this Work of Art are subject to a certain Contract dated ______________ between:

Artist: ______________

Address: ______________ and

Purchaser: ______________

Artist has a copy.

Appendix 4-3 SAMPLE AGREEMENT BETWEEN ARTIST AND GALLERY

Artist and Gallery agree to make a contract effective ______________, 19______. The terms of the agreement between Artist and Gallery are:

		ARTIST	GALLERY
NAMES	Name:	______________	______________
	Address:	______________	______________
		______________	______________
	Phone:	______________	______________

AGENCY 1. Artist appoints Gallery to act as his/her agent in the exhibition and sale of Artist's ______________ (*medium*) work in ______________ (*geographic*) area.

ARTWORKS COVERED 2. The Artist will deliver to the Gallery:

______ all works produced.

______ all works except for gifts, commissions, studio sales, trades, juried shows.

______ those works selected by Gallery.

______ those works agreed to by Artist and Gallery.

DELIVERY AND RETURN 3. ______________ will be responsible for delivery including costs and complete insurance coverage.

______________ will be responsible for return of works including costs and complete insurance coverage.

ARTIST'S WARRANTIES 4. Artist states that s/he created and owns all the works delivered to Gallery.

GALLERY RECEIPT 5. Gallery acknowledges receipt of the works described in the List of Art Works. A supplemental List of Art Works concerning any additional Works delivered to Gallery shall be provided by artist and acknowledged by gallery.

SALE PRICE 6. Gallery will sell the Works at the price listed on the attached List of Works. Gallery may discount ____% in sales to museums, galleries, decorators and architects.

COMMISSION 7. Gallery will receive ____% commission on the sale price of:

______ all sales by Artist.

______ all sales by Artist arising from Gallery contact.

______ Gallery sales only.

PAYMENT 8. Payment of each party's percentage share will be made within 30 days of the date of receipt of payment from the customer. All proceeds from installment payments will be made to Artist until his or her share is paid in full. The Gallery agrees to guarantee the credit of its customers, and to bear all losses due to the failure of the customer's credit.

PROMOTION AND EXHIBITION 9. ______________ will pay for the cost of framing or other expenses necessary in preparation for display and sale of work. The Gallery will make a reasonable effort to promote the Artist and to sell his/her work. The Gallery will hold at least ______ exhibition(s) of Artist's work of at least ______ weeks in length every ______ year. Artist will be consulted concerning the details of the exhibition including any promotional materials, other exhibitors and arrangements. Responsibility for the costs of the exhibition shall be agreed upon in advance. Neither party may obtain reimbursement for these costs from the other without prior approval.

STATEMENT 10. Gallery will give Artist a statement every ____________________, beginning with ____________________, 19______. This statement shall include:

______ works sold.

______ date, price and terms of sale.

______ commission due to the Gallery.

______ name and address of each Purchaser.

______ location of all unsold works not at Gallery.

Artist and Gallery will have the right to inspect the other's financial records concerning transactions covered by this agreement.

SALE CONTRACT 11. The Gallery will use the sale contract which is attached to this agreement for all sales of Artist's work governed by this contract.

COPYRIGHT 12. As provided by the Copyright Revision Act of 1976, the Artist retains all copyrights in the works delivered to Gallery. Gallery will prohibit the public from copying Artist's Works. All reproductions of Artist's Work in Gallery publications will be accompanied by a complete notice of copyright including the copyright symbol, the Artist's first and last names, the year of first publication.

LOSS OR DAMAGE 13. Gallery is responsible for providing insurance coverage from date of delivery to date of receipt by customer or Artist. Works will be insured at ______% of the retail sale price. Insurance shall cover fire, theft, loss, damage from negligence in Gallery and outside Gallery premises when under Gallery control.

TERMINATION 14. Unless already terminated this agreement will terminate one year from its effective date. Artist or Gallery may terminate the agreement by giving the other party written notice 30 days prior to the date upon which the party wishes to terminate. The agreement may not be terminated for 90 days following a solo exhibition of Artist's work by Gallery.

BOILERPLATE 15. This agreement represents the entire contract made by the parties. Its terms cannot be modified except by a written document signed by the parties. Neither party may assign any of the rights or responsibilities contained in the contract without the consent of the other party. If any part of this agreement is held to be illegal, void or unenforceable, this shall not effect the validity of any other part of the contract.

GOVERNING LAW 16. This agreement shall be governed by the laws of the State of

____________________________.

ARTIST	GALLERY
____________________________	By ____________________________
	(Signature of Authorized Representative)

LIST OF ART WORKS

	Name	*Size*	*Retail Price*	*Medium (if contract covers more than one)*
1.				
2.				
3.				
4.				
5.				
6.				
7.				
8.				
9.				
10.				

Pursuant to contract between Artist and Gallery dated ______________,

19______.

Artist submits this list of Art Works for gallery acknowledgement.

______________________________ ______________________________

Artist date

Gallery acknowledges receipt of the above art works.

______________________________ ______________________________

Gallery date

FINANCING STATEMENT

Name of Gallery (*debtor*) ______________________________

Address: ______________________________

____

Name of Artist (*secured party*) ______________________________

Address: ______________________________

____

This financing statement covers the following types of property whenever acquired by Gallery: ______________________________

____

____

____

Signature of Authorized Gallery Representative

____

Signature of Artist

____

date

Appendix 4-4a COMMISSION AGREEMENT FOR DESIGN OF ART WORK

Reprinted with permission from *Art Workers News*

Commission Agreement for Design of Art Work

The Collector .... residing at ...., acknowledges sufficient familiarity with the style and quality of the work of the Artist ...., residing at .... The parties have made and entered into this agreement on this ....day of ...., 19.........

1. DESCRIPTION. The Artist in consideration of the covenants and agreements herein contained, agrees to design .... (hereinafter "Work") as preparation for its creation by the Artist for an approximate production budget of between $...... and $......

a. Approximate size of finished Work:

b. Material & construction:

c. Scope of the Artist's work:

d. Collector is responsible for:

2. DESIGN AGREEMENT. The receipt of good and valuable consideration of $....... on this day for the design work to be provided by Artist after signing of this agreement is hereby mutually acknowledged.

a. Artist agrees to provide reasonable study, sketch or mockette of the Work to the Collector on or about ....(date). Upon receipt of design, the Collector shall notify Artist within ten (10) days of any proposed changes in design.

b. Artist will provide a maximum of .... designs or revisions for this Work. Additional designs or revisions shall cost an additional design fee of $..... per hour.

c. If Collector decides not to proceed with creation of the Work, all designs must be returned to Artist, Artist shall retain the design fee, and this agreement shall be terminated.

d. If Collector determines to proceed with creation of the Work pursuant to a selected design, the WORK OF ART COMMISSION AGREEMENT must be completed and signed by both parties, and the first one-third progress payment will be paid at that time.

3. COPYRIGHT. It is agreed that all designs are instruments of service and shall remain in the possession of and the property of the Artist, and thereby Artist retains the exclusive right to use and create Works according to the designs. Collector agrees to make no public display or commercial use of the designs, or any copy or facsimile thereof, without the Artist's consent. It is agreed that if consent is granted for commercial use, the Artist shall be entitled to a minimim of ten percent (10%) of any and all consideration paid or exchanged for such commercial use.

IN WITNESS WHEREOF the parties have hereunto set their hands.

By............................... By.................................
Artist Collector

Appendix 4-4b WORK OF ART COMMISSION AGREEMENT

Reprinted with permission from *Art Workers News*

Work of Art Commission Agreement

On this.....day of ...., 19..., ...(Collector) has selected the design and given the final approval for .... (Artist) to proceed with the creation of this Work of Art:

Title:

Materials:

Approximate size upon completion:

Price:

Description of the Art Work:

Scope of the Artist's work:

Collector is responsible for:

1. **PROGRESS SCHEDULE AND PAYMENTS.** Collector agrees to pay to Artist one-third (⅓) of the price of the Work ($.......) at this time or within ten (10) days.

Collector agrees to pay an additional one-third (⅓) of the cost of the Work ($.....) when the Work is approximately two-thirds (⅔) completed. Documentation of the progress of the Work may be made by photographs of the Work or by the personal inspection of the Collector at the discretion of the Artist.

Upon nearing completion of the Work the Artist will give the Collector five (5) days advance notice of specific date of delivery so that Collector will be ready to receive the Work, make the final payment ($........), and sign the AGREEMENT OF ORIGINAL TRANSFER OF WORK OF ART. Any Sales Tax that may be required by law will be paid at this time ($........).

a. It is hereby understood and agreed that it may not be possible to create the Work exactly as depicted in the design, and the Artist shall only be bound to use his best aesthetic judgement to create the Work according to the style and intent of the design. The Artist is hereby free to make design modifications as the Work progresses.

2. **FINAL DELIVERY.** The parties agree that final delivery of the Work will be made on or about .... The Artist will make every effort to honor and meet this deadline. It is agreed, however, that this delivery date is an estimate only and that Artist shall not be responsible for any general, special or consequential damages for failing to deliver by this date. The Artist will immediately notify Collector of any delay occurring or anticipated.

a. In the event the Artist is unable to finish the Work within sixty (60) days of the estimated delivery date, or is unable to produce the Work for any reason, the Artist shall be liable for no special, general or consequential damages, but the Artist shall return all payments received. The Artist shall retain all rights to the concept, design, and the Work itself.

3. **DELAYED PAYMENTS.** In the event Collector fails to make the progress payments when due, interest at the rate of three-fourths percent (¾%) per month shall be assessed against the unpaid balance due. In addition, the Artist has the right to retain all previous payments plus all rights to the Work until full payment is made. It is understood that delay of any payment may proportionately extend the time required to complete the Work.

4. **TERMINATION OF AGREEMENT.** If Collector does not find the Work as it progresses fulfilling his expectations or needs and therefore wishes to terminate the agreement, Collector shall immediately notify the Artist of the termination. The Artist shall thereupon be entitled to retain all payments which Artist has received or was entitled to receive pursuant to this agreement prior to such notification. Further, the Artist shall retain all rights to the concept, design and Work itself, including the right to complete, exhibit and sell the Work.

5. **TRANSFER OF WORK OF ART.** It is hereby stated and acknowledged that Artist retains all rights and title to the Work until final payment has been received and the AGREEMENT OF ORIGINAL TRANSFER OF WORK OF ART has been duly completed and signed by the parties.

6. **ATTORNEYS' FEES.** In any proceeding to enforce any part of this contract, the aggrieved party shall be entitled to reasonable attorneys' fees in addition to any available remedy.

INWITNESS WHEREOF the parties have hereunto set their hands.

By..............................
Artist

By..............................
Collector

Appendix 4-5 SAMPLE MUSEUM LOAN AGREEMENT

ART DEPARTMENT
The Oakland Museum
1000 Oak Street
Oakland, California 94607
415/273-3005

Loan Agreement

PLEASE COMPLETE, READ, SIGN AND RETURN ORIGINAL TO THE OAKLAND MUSEUM. RETAIN COPY FOR YOUR RECORDS.

EXHIBITION: ______

EXHIBITION DATES: ______

Lender: ______ Telephone: ______

Address: ______

Attention: ______

Exact form in which lender's name should appear on exhibition label and catalog: ______

Artist: ______

Exact title of work: ______

Date of work: ______ Medium and support: ______

Acc. no.: ______ Dimensions unframed: H______ W______ (D ______

Dimensions framed: ______

Signed or inscribed as follows: ______

Is the painting securely framed? ______ Please list any scratches, chips, cracks, etc., found on painting, frame, or sculpture. Enclose separate condition report if necessary. ______

Insurance evaluation: $ ______ *See Reverse

SHIPPING ARRANGEMENTS: ______

Case already available ______ case needs to be built ______ case unnecessary ______

To be packed/crated by: ______

(Unless notified to the contrary, the loan will be returned to the address listed under "Lender".)

Date required for receiving loan: ______

Pick up and return dates will be as agreed upon with the lender, not to begin before ______ and to be concluded by ______.

The Oakland Museum requests permission to photograph this loan, and to reproduce it in its publications for publicity and/or educational purposes in connection with this exhibition. YES ______ NO ______. May this loan also be photographed by the public for non-commercial purposes? YES ______ NO ______. If there is a photograph available, may we borrow? ______.

COMMENTS (Provenance, Special Handling Requirements)

Borrower:

______
Signature

______
Title

______
Date

Lender:

______
Signature

______
Title (If institution)

______
Date

In the event of a claim, the amount indicated as to value may need to be substantiated. Unless the lender expressly elects to maintain his own insurance, The Oakland Museum will insure the loan under its own standard fine arts policy, for the amount indicated above, against all risks of loss or damage while in transit and on location during the period of the loan. The policy referred to contains the usual exclusions for loss or damage due to acts of God, wear and tear, gradual deterioration, warlike action, moths, vermin or inherent vice.

If the lender elects to maintain his own insurance, The Oakland Museum must be supplied with either a Certificate of Insurance naming it as additional insured with respect to the loaned object, or a Waiver of Subrogation against The Oakland Museum from any liability in connection with the loaned property. The Museum can accept no responsibility for any error or deficiency in information furnished to the lender's insurers or for lapses in their coverage.

The Oakland Museum agrees to pay all crating, shipping, and transportation costs of the loan, as long as such arrangements are authorized by the Museum in advance. It is understood that the object covered on this form shall remain in the condition in which it was received. It shall not be cleaned, repaired, retouched or altered in any way whatsoever, except with written permission of the lender. Damages, whether in transit or on the borrowing institution's premises and regardless of who may be responsible therefore, shall be reported to the lender immediately.

This will constitute an official loan agreement. Signature of the Director, Curator or authorized agent of the lending party will acknowledge acceptance of the above conditions, and confirmation that the loan arrangements may proceed.

Appendix 4-6 PRINT DISCLOSURE FORM

1. Artist: ______________________
2. Title: ______________________
3. Type of Print: ______________________
4. Date of Print: ______________________
5. Name of Printer: ______________________
6. Status of Plate: ______________________
   ____
   ____
7. If a Limited Edition:
   Total Number in Edition: __________
   Number Signed or Numbered: __________
   Number Unsigned or Unnumbered: __________
   Number of Artist's or Other Proofs: __________
8. If Prior State of Same Impression: yes [ ] no [ ]
   Number of Prior states: __________
9. If Prior Editions of the Current Edition: yes [ ]
   no [ ]
   Series Number of the Current Edition: __________
10. If the Edition is a Posthumous or a restrike: yes [ ]
    no [ ]
    Has the Plate Been Reworked: yes [ ]
    no [ ]

Appendix 4-7 DESIGN AND ART PURCHASE ORDER FORM

Design and Art Purchase Order

Vendor ______ Date ______ Order Number **14738**

Refer to above Order Number in all correspondence.

Address ______ Author ______

______ Title ______

Deliver To ______ Product Code ______

Data within shaded area MUST appear on invoice.

Division ______

Accounting Code ______ Major ______ Stat Sponsor ______

TYPE OF PURCHASE
(SEE COMMENTS FOR DETAILS)

- ☐ Design
- ☐ Cover-Endsheet, Inserts
- ☐ Composition
- ☐ Art
- ☐ Author Alterations
- ☐ Office Alterations
- ☐ Jackets-Promotion
- ☐ Dummy
- ☐ New Media
- ☐ Photography
- ☐ Other (Explain): ______

ART PREPARATION

Color ______ B/W ______

- ☐ Hot Type
- ☐ Cold Type
- ☐ Type Stamp
- ☐ Leroy
- ☐ Freehand
- ☐ Illustration Proofs
- ☐ Zipatone
- ☐ Stipple
- ☐ Tints
- ☐ Airbrush
- ☐ Ink
- ☐ Wash
- ☐ Pickup Art
- ☐ Halftone Labels
- ☐ Halftone Cropping and Sizing
- ☐ Domestic Standard Format
- ☐ Overseas Standard Format
- ☐ Touch-up
- ☐ Other (Explain below)

ILLUSTRATIONS (Include number of figures and total number of parts on invoice.)

Number of Figures ______ Date Required ______

Total Number of Parts ______ Price per Part ______

Total Number of Halftones ______ TOTAL COST ▶ $ ______

COPY TO CONTRACT FILE ☐ Yes ☐ No

See Reverse Side for Terms and Conditions

COMMENTS:

Vendor Acceptance ______ Date ______ Art Director Approval ______ Date ______

FORM 9444-034 (Rev. 11/77)

VENDOR

GENERAL TERMS AND CONDITIONS OF PURCHASE

1. Terms and Conditions:

(a) Seller agrees to be bound by, and to comply with all the terms and conditions of this order, including any supplements, and all specifications and other documents referred to in this order.

(b) This order does not constitute an acceptance by the publisher of any offer to sell, quotation, or any proposal. Reference in this order to any offer to sell, quotation, or proposal shall in no way constitute a modification of any of the terms and conditions of this order to any degree whatsoever. An attempted acknowledgment of this order containing terms and conditions inconsistent with or in addition to the terms and conditions of this order constitutes a counteroffer by Seller to the publisher, whether or not such terms "materially alter" this order, and is not binding upon the publisher unless specifically accepted by the publisher in writing.

(c) In absence of a written acknowledgement hereof, the delivery of any portion of the merchandise ordered hereunder shall, at the publisher's option, constitute full acceptance by Seller of all the terms and conditions of this order with respect to the merchandise delivered.

2. Taxes:
Except as may be otherwise provided in this order, the price includes all applicable Federal, State or local taxes and duties except those for which exemption may be claimed.

3. Delivery Schedule:
Time shall be of the essence with respect to any delivery or work schedule hereunder.

4. Termination and Rejections:
In the event that Seller is unable or unwilling to complete the work specified under this contract, does not comply with the delivery schedule, or does not complete it to the satisfaction of the publisher, then the publisher, at its sole discretion and in addition to any other rights which it may have, shall have the right to terminate this order and/or to reject all or any part of said work, all without liability to the publisher except for goods delivered and accepted by the publisher or services performed to its satisfaction prior to the date on which notice of termination was given to Seller.

5. Unauthorized Changes in Approved Designs, Parts or Processes:
Seller specifically agrees to make no changes in any design, material, part or manufacturing process which has been approved by the publisher and/or which is applicable to this order without the prior written approval of the publisher.

6. Changes:
(a) The publisher may at any time, by written order, make changes within the general scope of this order, in any one or more of the following:

(b) If any such change order causes an increase or decrease in the cost of, or the time required for, performance of this order, or otherwise affects any other provision of this order whether changed or not changed by such a change order, an equitable adjustment shall be negotiated in the price of delivery schedule, or both, and in such provisions of this order as may be so affected. Such adjustment shall be accomplished by a written amendment to this order signed by the publisher. Any claim by Seller for such adjustment must be made within ***thirty*** days from the date of receipt of such change, although the publisher in its sole discretion may receive and act upon any such claim at any time prior to final payment.

(c) Information such as technical and/or other direction or guidance provided to Seller by the publisher in connection with Seller's performance of this order shall not be construed either as a change within the meaning of this provision or as direction to proceed outside the scope of this order. Should Seller consider that accomplishment of or compliance with any element of such information received requires action on its part which would entitle Seller to have any provisions of this order modified; Seller shall not take such action, but shall advise the publisher as soon as possible, but no later than twenty-four (24) hours, weekends and legal holidays excluded, after receipt of such information, of the modifications Seller deems necessary in order for such action to be taken.

(d) Nothing in this clause, including any disagreement with the publisher as to the equitable adjustment to be made, shall excuse Seller from proceeding with the order as changed.

7. Seller's Representations and Warranties:
(a) Unless specifically agreed upon in writing, information which Seller discloses to the publisher shall not be deemed to be confidential or proprietary information and shall be acquired free from any restriction as part of the consideration for this order.

(b) Except as may be specifically provided to the contrary on the reverse hereof, Seller hereby acknowledges that the publisher, as the proprietor of work for hire, will possess all right, title and interest in the aforesaid sketch(es) and finished art, including the right of copyright thereto and the right to use and reuse the same in any medium or manner it desires.

(c) Seller hereby warrants that work will be original with the Seller, that the publisher will be the sole owner of all the rights therein, that the work will not be libelous and does not violate or infringe upon the copyright or the literary, artistic, dramatic, property, patent, privacy, or statutory or common-law rights of others, and that Seller will indemnify and hold harmless the publisher, Inc., against any costs, expenses and damages arising from any breach or alleged breach of the foregoing.

8. Purchaser's Property:
Unless otherwise agreed in writing, all material of every description, including but not limited to, drawings, layouts, artwork, reproducible copy and photolithographic negatives, furnished to Seller by the publisher or specifically commissioned or paid for by the publisher and any replacement thereof, or any materials affixed or attached thereto, shall be and remain the exclusive personal property of the publisher. Such property, and whenever practical, each individual item thereof, shall be plainly marked or otherwise adequately identified by Seller as property of the publisher and shall be safely stored separate and apart from Seller's property. Seller shall not substitute any property for the publisher's property and shall not use such property except in filling the publisher's orders. Such property, with the exception of drawings, layouts, artwork, reproducible copy and photolithographic negatives, shall be held at Seller's risk, shall be kept insured by Seller at Seller's expenses in an amount equal to the replacement cost with loss payable to the publisher and shall be subject to removal at the publisher's written request, in which event Seller shall prepare for shipment and shall redeliver such property to the publisher in the same condition as original received by Seller, reasonable wear and tear excepted. All drawings, layouts, artwork, reproducible copy and photolithographic negatives shall be returned to the publisher.

9. Non-Assignment:
No assignment of this order or any interest herein or any payment due or to become due hereunder shall be valid without the prior written consent of the publisher.

10. Equal Employment Opportunity Compliance:
Pursuant to Executive Order 11246, as amended by Executive Order 11375 and regulations thereunder, Seller, by returning a copy of this document to the publisher has recorded Seller's concurrence that during the performance of any contract or orders for the publisher amounting to $10,000 or more per year, the following shall apply: (a) the equal employment opportunity clause of the Orders is incorporated by reference in the contract and each order to Seller; (b) Seller certifies to the publisher that Seller does not maintain facilities of a segregated nature contrary to the regulations under the Orders.

11. Bankruptcy:
If Seller ceases to conduct its operations in the normal course of business (including liability to meet its obligations as they mature) or if any proceedings under the bankruptcy or insolvency laws is brought by or against Seller or receiver for Seller is appointed or applied for, or an assignment for the benefit of creditors is made by Seller, the publisher may terminate this order without liability except for deliveries previously made or for goods then completed and subsequently delivered in accordance with the terms of this order.

12. General:

(a) ***Nonwaiver***—Failure by the publisher to enforce at any time or for any period of time any of the provisions hereof shall not be construed to be a waiver of such provisions nor of the right of the publisher thereafter to enforce each and every, such provision.

(b) ***Entire Agreement***—This order constitutes the entire understanding between the parties with respect to the purchase and sales of the goods and services hereunder and supersedes all previous negotiations, commitments and writings with respect thereto. No alteration, modification or amendment of any of the provisions hereof shall be binding unless in writing and signed by the duly authorized representatives of both parties.

(c) ***Construction***—This order will be governed by and construed in accordance with the laws of the State of New York.

CHAPTER FIVE

Appendix 5-1 FEDERAL INCOME TAX: FULL-ABSORPTION ACCOUNTING

In Chapter Five, references are made to full-absorption accounting, which is a method used by manufacturers to compute costs. An artist or craftmaker who produces a number of *like* items for sale *may* be said to be in the art or craft manufacturing business.

Absorption costing and variable costing:

Full Absorption—Artists who produce a number of like items for sale may be said to be in the art manufacturing business. The cost of manufactured products consists of three costs: (1) direct cost, that is, the cost of raw materials that become part of the finished product; (2) direct labor, that is, the cost of labor performed on the product; and (3) all other costs of manufacturing the product. All three costs are included in the cost of the finished product and remain as part of the finished-goods inventory until sold.

Absorption costing absorbs all cost related to manufacturing a product into the finished good. Therefore, the depreciation on items used in the manufacturing process becomes part of the overhead cost and part of the cost of finished goods. These costs do not become an expense until the product is sold.

Obviously, if you need to use this method or have questions as to whether you should use it, see an accountant.*

Appendix 5-2 VALUATION OF INVENTORIES

If you have to use inventories, there are four methods of valuing materials that have price fluctuations during the year:

1. Specific identification may be used if the units in the ending inventory can be identified as coming from specific purchases.
2. Average cost method is computed by dividing the total costs of the units available for sale by the number of the units available for sale.
3. FIFO First-in, first-out method values the ending inventory at prices paid for end-of-the-year purchases.
4. LIFO Last-in, first-out method assumes that recent purchases go out first, and the ending inventory consists of the oldest materials.

You can choose any of the above methods to value your inventories without regard to the actual order in which your materials are consumed in your product, but once you choose a method, you cannot change it without permission from the IRS. Many people during a period of inflation choose the LIFO method because it will yield the smallest inventory value, the lowest net income, and the lowest income tax. Why? Because the higher, more recent costs are included in the cost of the sold items, and the earlier, lower purchase price reduces the value of the ending inventory.

Appendix 5-3 TAX-FREE TRADES

While most swaps are taxable, there can be tax-free trades where the exchange involves "like-kind" property, that is, real estate for real estate, business equipment for business equipment, or investment property for investment property, or trades of business property held for sale. Artists or craftmakers' wares are not considered business property. However, the trade of antique spinning wheels between two spinners would probably have no tax consequences. See Lasser's *Your Income Tax* or your accountant for further information.

* See also Scott, *The Craft Report*, pp. 120–123 and Kamoroff, *The Smalltime Operator*, Bell Springs, California, 1978. pp. 95–97.

Appendix 5-4 NOTICE TO AUDIT

Internal Revenue Service
District Director

Department of the Treasury

Date:

Tax Year(s):

Day and Date of Appointment:

Time:

Place of Appointment:

Room Number:

Contact Telephone Number:

Appointment Clerk:

We are examining your Federal income tax return for the above year(s) and find we need additional information to verify your correct tax. We have, therefore, scheduled the above appointment for you. If you filed a joint return, either husband or wife may keep the appointment, or you may have someone represent you or accompany you. An attorney, a certified public accountant, an individual enrolled to practice before the Internal Revenue Service, or the person who prepared the return and signed it as the preparer, may represent or accompany you.

We would appreciate your bringing to our office the records you used as a basis for the items checked at the end of this letter so we can discuss them with you.

The enclosed Information Guides will help you decide what records to bring. It will save you time if you keep together the records related to each item. Please bring this letter also.

Taxpayers are required by law to substantiate all information reported on their returns when requested. If you do not keep this appointment and do not arrange another, we will have to proceed on the basis of the information we have.

About the examination and your appeal rights--

We realize some taxpayers may be concerned about an examination of their tax returns. We hope we can relieve any concern you may have by briefly explaining why we examine, what our procedures are, and what your appeal rights are if you do not agree with the results.

We examine returns to verify the correctness of income, exemptions, and deductions. We find that the vast majority of taxpayers are honest and have nothing to fear from an examination of their tax returns. An examination of such a taxpayer's return does not suggest a suspicion of dishonesty or criminal liability. In many cases, the taxpayer's return is either closed without change in reported tax liability or the taxpayer receives a refund. However, if taxpayers do not substantiate items when requested, we have to act on available information that may be incomplete. That is why your cooperation is so important.

We will go over your return and records and then explain any proposals to change your tax liability. We want you to understand fully any recommended increase or decrease in your tax, so please don't hesitate to ask questions about anything not clear to you.

(over)

Federal Bldg., Phoenix, Ariz. 85025

Form L–14 (Rev. 10–75)

If changes are recommended and you agree with the proposals, we will ask you to sign an agreement form. By signing, you will indicate your agreement to the amount shown on the form as additional tax you owe or as a refund due you and simplify closing your case.

Most people agree with our proposals, and we believe this is because they find our examiners to be fair. But you don't have to agree. If you choose, we can easily arrange for you to have your case given further consideration. You need only tell the examiner you want to discuss the issue informally with a supervisor, and a conference will be arranged immediately. If this discussion does not result in agreement, you may take your case to a conferee for still further consideration.

In addition to these District office appeal rights, you may request the Service's Appellate Division, which is separate from the District office, to consider your case. We will be glad to explain this procedure and also how to appeal outside the Service to the courts.

We will also be happy to furnish you a copy of our Publication 556, Audit of Returns, Appeal Rights and Claims for Refund, which explains in detail our procedures covering examinations of tax returns and appeal rights. You can get a copy of this publication by writing us for it or by asking for it when you come to our office.

Your appointment is the next step. We will consider the appointment confirmed if we do not hear from you at least seven days before the scheduled date. We will make our examination as pleasant and brief as possible and will welcome any questions you raise.

Please contact us if you have any questions. Thank you for your cooperation.

Sincerely yours,

District Director

Enclosures:
Information Guides

Please bring the records to support the following items reported on your tax return:

- ☐ Alimony Payments
- ☐ Automobile Expenses
- ☐ Bad Debts
- ☐ Capital Gains and Losses
- ☐ Casualty Losses
- ☐ Child and Dependent Care Expenses
- ☐ Contributions
- ☐ Education Expenses
- ☐ Employee Business Expenses
- ☐ Exemptions
- ☐ Interest Expenses
- ☐ Medical and Dental Expenses
- ☐ Moving Expenses
- ☐ Rental Income and Expenses
- ☐ Sale or Exchange of Residence
- ☐ Sick Pay Exclusion
- ☐ Taxes
- ☐ Uniforms, Equipment, and Tools
- ☐ ____________ ☐ ____________ ☐ ____________
- ☐ ________________________________

Form L–14 (Rev. 10–75)

☐ Alimony Payments	☐ Contributions	☐ Moving Expenses
☐ Automobile Expenses	☐ Education Expenses	☐ Rental Income and Expenses
☐ Bad Debts	☒ Employee Business Expenses	☐ Sale or Exchange of Residence
☐ Capital Gains and Losses	☐ Exemptions	☐ Sick Pay Exclusion
☒ Casualty Losses	☐ Interest Expenses	☐ Taxes
☐ Child and Dependent Care Expenses	☐ Medical and Dental Expenses	☐ Uniforms, Equipment, and Tools
☐ ______________	☐ ______________	☐ ______________

☐ ____

Please bring evidence such as accounting ledgers and journals, bank statements, and canceled checks to support the following items shown on Schedule C:

☐ All Business Expenses	☐ Insurance	☐ Salaries and Wages
☐ Bad Debts	☐ Interest	☐ Taxes
☐ Cost of Goods Sold	☐ Losses of Business Property	☐ Travel and Entertainment
☐ Depreciation	☐ Rents	☐ ______________
☐ Gross Receipts	☐ Repairs	☐ ______________

Please bring evidence such as accounting ledgers and journals, bank statements, and canceled checks to support the following items shown on Schedule F:

☐ All Farm Expenses	☐ Insurance	☐ Repairs and Maintenance
☐ Depreciation	☐ Inventories	☐ Supplies Purchased
☐ Feed and Seed Purchased	☐ Labor Hired	☐ Taxes
☐ Fertilizers, Lime	☐ Machine Hire	☐ ______________
☐ Gross Receipts	☐ Other Farm Income	☐ ______________

Form L–14A (Rev. 10–75)

Further Readings

GENERAL LEGAL BOOKS—ARTS AND CRAFT

Association Councils on the Arts et al.: *Visual Artist and the Law*, rev. ed., Praeger Publishers, New York, 1974, $3.95, available from Volunteer Lawyers for the Arts, Suite 1110, 36 West Forty-fourth Street, New York, NY 10036. (Masterful succinct treatment of the subject and full of useful citations. For lawyer or sophisticated reader.)

Cochrane, Diane: *This Business of Art*, Watson-Guptill Publications, New York, 1978, $12.50. (Lively, down-to-earth discussion of the actual legal issues confronting the visual artist in a question and answer style. Index.)

Crawford, Tad: *Legal Guide for the Visual Artist*, Hawthorn Books, New York, 1977, $9.95. (Covers most aspects of art law. Style geared for lawyer or sophisticated layperson.)

Duboff, Leonard: *The Deskbook of Art Law*, Federal Publications, Washington D.C., 1977, around $90. (*The* work on art law. A must for any lawyer practicing art law.)

Leavens, T. R., ed.: *Law and the Arts*, 1976, $2. Available from Lawyers for the Creative Arts, Suite 610, 111 North Wabash, Chicago, IL 60602. (Excellent compilation of articles on the various aspects of art law, and it's cheap, too!)

Lindey, Alexander: *Entertainment, Publishing and the Arts: Agreements and the Law*, Clark Boardman Co., Ltd., New York, 1977, $85. (Two-volume reporter with many useful forms, for lawyers.)

GENERAL BOOKS—CRAFTS

Scott, Michael: *The Craft Business Encyclopedia*, Harcourt Brace Jovanovich, New York, 1977, $10. (Covers legal, management, marketing, and accounting aspects of the craft business in an encyclopedic style.)

GENERAL BOOKS—WRITINGS

Applebaum, Judith and Evans, Nancy: *How to Get Happily Published*, Harper and Row, New York, 1978, $9.95.

Crawford, Tad: *The Writer's Legal Guide*, Hawthorn Books, New York, 1978, $10.95. (Basic book in this area.)

Balkin, Richard: *A Writer's Guide to Book Publishing*, Hawthorn Books, New York, 1977, $9.95. (Practical, useful guide by a long-time insider in publishing.)

GENERAL BOOKS—PHOTOGRAPHY

Chernoff, George, and Hershel Sarbin: *Photography and the Law*, 5th ed., Amphoto, New York, 1977, $7.95.

LEGAL REQUIREMENTS OF STARTING A BUSINESS

Kamoroff, Bernard: *Small Time Operator: How to Start Your Own Small Business, Keep Your Books, Pay Your Taxes and Stay Out of Trouble*, Bell Springs Publishing, Laytonville, Calif., 1977, $6.95. (A must for every small business.)

Wettlaufer, George and Mary: *The Craftsman's Survival Manual: Making a Full or Part-Time Living from Your Crafts*, Prentice-Hall, Englewood Cliffs, New Jersey, 1974, $2.95.

McQuown, Judith H.: *Incorporate Yourself: How to Profit by Setting Up Your Own Corporation*, Macmillan, New York, 1977, $12.95.

Porter, Sylvia: *Money Book*, Avon Books, New York, 1976, $5.95.

COPYING

U.S. Copyright Office: *Circulars.* (Simple brief explanations of various copyright subjects prepared for the general public. Available free of charge from the Copyright Office, Washington, D.C. 20559)

TAXES

Holcomb, Bill, and Ted Striggles: *Fear of Filing,* Volunteer Lawyers for the Arts, 1977, $3. (Pamphlet available from VLA, 36 West Forty-fourth Street, Suite 1110, New York, NY 10036. Regularly updated.)

Lasser Tax Institute, *Your Income Tax,* 1978 ed., Simon and Schuster, New York, 1978, $3.95. (Clear, thorough treatment of the current income tax laws.)

U.S. Department of the Treasury, Internal Revenue Service: *Tax Guide for Small Business.* (Published each year and available free from your local Internal Revenue Service Office.)

U.S. Department of the Treasury, Internal Revenue Service: *Your Federal Income Tax.* (Published each year and available free from your local Internal Revenue Service Office.)

LAW FOR THE LAYPERSON

Matthews, Douglas: *Sue the B*st*rds,* Dell Publishing Co., New York, 1975, $1.50. (Useful guide to small claims court.)

Reader's Digest: *You and the Law,* The Reader's Digest Association, 1977.

Siegel, Edward: *How to Avoid Lawyers,* Fawcett Publications, Greenwich, Connecticut, 1971, $1.75.

PERIODICALS

Art and the Law, a publication of Volunteer Lawyers for the Arts. (Published four times a year at $12 a year. Contains discussions of current legal issues in the field of art law.)

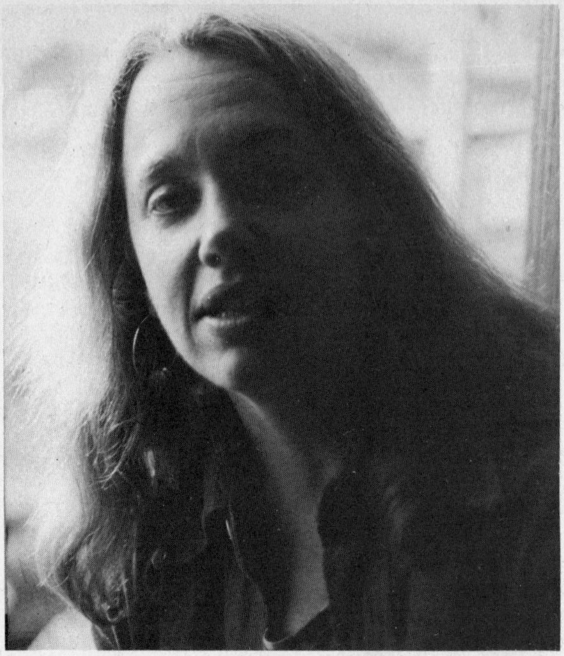

ABOUT THE AUTHORS

Marion Davidson is currently practicing law, teaching and writing near Albuquerque, N.M. A graduate of New York University School of Law, she has worked with the Legal Aid Society, the United Welfare League, the Mississippi Freedom Democratic party and DNA, People's Legal Services in Window Rock, Arizona.

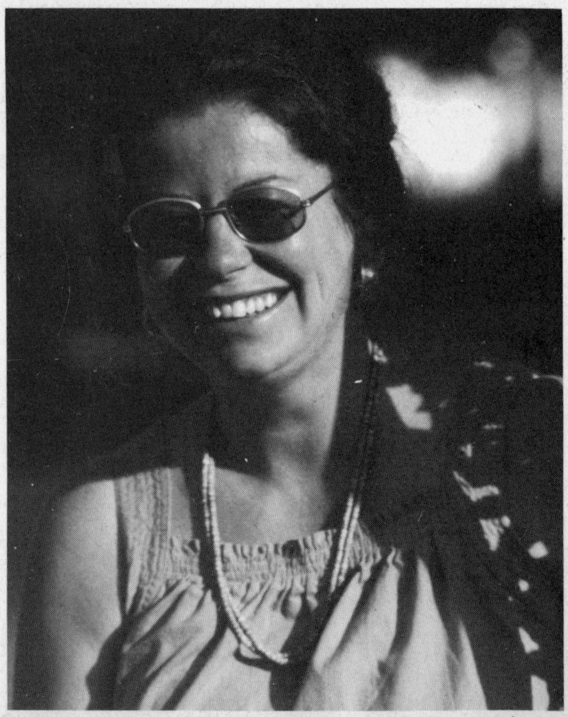

Martha Blue is an attorney in private practice in Arizona as well as a weaver. She worked on a Navaho Reservation for a number of years and also with Micronesian Legal Services. She received her law degree from the University of Arizona.

Index